ELLEN PHILLIPS

SHOCKED,

APPALLED,

AND

DISMAYED!

D0356119

Ellen Phillips is a twenty-seven-year veteran in education and an oral communications specialist. Also a noted storyteller in northern Virginia, she is the author of *The Tale-Teller Tells All*. Phillips is the founder of Ellen's Poison Pen, Inc.®, and a reader's advisory board member of Tax-Wise Money, a consumer publication. Her articles have appeared in *Kiplinger's Personal Finance Magazine*. She resides with her husband, Bruce, who is the recipient of most of her complaints.

SHOCKED, APPALLED, AND DISMAYED!

How to Write Letters of Complaint That Get Results

ELLEN PHILLIPS

VINTAGE BOOKS
A Division of Random House, Inc.
New York

A VINTAGE ORIGINAL, JANUARY 1999

Copyright © 1998 by Ellen Haygood Phillips

Library of Congress Cataloging-in-Publication Data
Phillips, Ellen Haygood, 1947–
    Shocked, appalled, and dismayed! : How to write letters
of complaint that get results / by Ellen Phillips.
        p.   cm.
    "Vintage original."
    ISBN 0-375-70120-6
    1. Consumer complaints.   2. Commercial correspondence.
    I. Title.
    HF5415.52.P48   1998
    381.3—dc21   98-13819
                        CIP

www.randomhouse.com

Manufactured in the United States of America
10   9   8   7

To my husband, Bruce,
whose support is unfailing
and whose love is constant
in spite of my
complaining nature

and also to my grandchildren,
Ellie and Tyler,
for whom I dream
beautiful dreams

A kingdom founded on injustice cannot last.
　　　　　　　　—SENECA

ACKNOWLEDGMENTS

I finally understand why Academy Award winners feel compelled to thank everyone from their producer to the nursemaids they had as infants. I'll try to keep my list shorter than that, but I must express a big thank-you to some pretty terrific folks.

First and foremost, without my immediate family and especially my parents, Eddie and Lucy Haygood, I wouldn't be the "Ellen" that I am. They instilled two basic values in me: my mother taught me to believe in the humanity of others and to lend a helping hand whenever possible; my father's example was one of personal integrity and the will to fight for my beliefs. My brother and sister-in-law, Joe and Jean, nursed Mama and Daddy through serious illnesses while I remained in Virginia to write this book. My little sister, Nan, who grew up to be my best friend, tore up the interstate going back and forth to tend to our parents. Not only is she our mainstay and often the cord that holds our fragile lives together; she's the only person who can always make me laugh. My daughter, Beth, whom I found enormously inspiring while writing this book, gave me my beautiful grandchildren. Thank God for family!

Thanks to Michael Guiles, artist extraordinaire, whose pen-and-ink skull and crossbones became the symbol for my business, Ellen's Poison Pen, and to his wife, Carol—my friend, my compatriot, and my sounding board. Thank God for friends!

Phil McCombs, *Washington Post* correspondent, placed me in the right place at the right time, which resulted in a big nod of gratitude to Paul Bogaards, Division Vice-President of Alfred A. Knopf, Inc., the book publisher, who personally knocked down the transom door for my entrance into his world. Acknowledgments go to my editor, Dawn Davis, and to the copy editor, Maggie Carr, as well. Thank God for publicity!

My "lawyering" advice wouldn't have been possible without some special people. My cousin, Paul Haygood, started the ball rolling immediately and worked long (and nonbillable!) hours to make my *poison pen* a protected trademark. Paul's trust in my abilities also placed me in contact with Bob Barnett, the best contracts attorney around, who decided to count a hick from the sticks among his famous clients; his associate, Jackie Davies, became one of my lifelines too. John Morrison, family friend and attorney, also rushed to the rescue with a lot of (nonbillable!) footwork on my behalf. Thank God for attorneys who have faith in me!

Carol McGuirk, my other set of typing fingers, put up with my moans, groans, and expletives deleted. Thank God for helpers!

This book wouldn't be complete without the statements from corporate and company officials who stand behind their own products and are fair in their dealings with customers (sorry the other 135 I contacted didn't wish to appear in print). Thank God for professionalism!

All the rest of my family, my friends, my colleagues, and my students both believed in me and enjoyed the ride. And certainly I can't forget two final groups: consumers everywhere who called or wrote simply to express their appreciation for my attempts on the behalf of others; and my own clients, who have had enough faith in me and in my abilities to trust me with their secrets and who have become my friends along the way. Thank God for people!

As an English teacher with a master's degree in that subject, I apologize to those language purists who are "shocked, appalled, and dismayed" at my unorthodox departure from *proper* grammar and usage.

CONTENTS

Why did I write this book?

Well, first of all, in this stressful age in which we live, we seem to be bombarded on all sides by inferior products and second-rate services. On top of these we often must deal with a multitude of obnoxious, rude, and cold-hearted people who could not care less—and don't care who knows it. Somebody had to respond to the nonsense, and it might as well be me.

I learned very early in life to let the world know when I was dissatisfied. I found the art of effective complaining to be very cathartic, and it usually provided relief, not only for me but also for those who were forced to be within earshot. Over the years since I started my letter-writing business, Ellen's Poison Pen, Inc.®, in 1988, my pen and I have helped hundreds of people. I have gotten results from companies that refused to honor my clients and me as customers entitled to first-rate service and products and from government agencies that mistakenly believed that they could plug us into some black hole of a switchboard, leaving us at the mercy of the proverbial dentist's office music at the other end. Little did they know that my persistence is such that I will hang on till hell freezes over.

To help *you* learn to write effective complaint letters, I provide in the coming chapters samples of different kinds of "poison pens," from letters to manufacturers of shoddy products to letters to insurance companies about insufficient coverage to letters to hotels or airlines that don't honor your reservations. While most of the letters included in this book are based on actual letters I wrote on behalf of clients of Ellen's Poison Pen, Inc.®, most of the names and addresses have been changed to protect the innocent *and* the guilty, except for Susan Lust, Pamela Reid, Sheila Daniel, and Jennifer Hamilton, who gave me special permission to use their letters. But all the names and addresses of folks at government departments, regulatory agencies, and consumer advocacy organizations found in the "carbon copy" (cc) part of the letters—and in the appendices in the back of the book—are real. Consult the appendices to find the proper name and agency to use in your letter, and make sure you also cc the pertinent organization or government agency. Your letter is more likely to be taken seriously if you carbon copy important people and agencies that might have an interest in the subject of your complaint. Just remember that personnel and room and suite number changes occur quite frequently, so call first to make sure that you are copying the person currently filling the appropriate position at the correct address. Bear in mind, too, that the letters I've included are not "forms" that should be copied; they are here to give you ideas but, of course, must be tailored to the specific situation.

I believe that if you follow the advice I offer in this book, you will be able to assert your rights as a consumer, a customer—a citizen—in an effective way. You should take note, however, that I am not a lawyer and my book is not intended to give legal advice; you can only get that from a lawyer, and if you have any concerns, you should seek guidance from an attorney before putting pen to paper.

But what *Shocked, Appalled, and Dismayed!* does contain is good, old-fashioned, sometimes hard-nosed common sense, which many times is all you need in order to ensure that you are taken seriously and get the results you want.

So—read on to discover the power of the pen.

SHOCKED, APPALLED, AND DISMAYED!

How to Write Letters
of Complaint That
Get Results

CHAPTER 1

The Power of the Pen: Don't Get Mad, Get (Appropriately) Even

> I am in earnest—I will not equivocate—I will not excuse—I will not retreat a single inch *and I will be heard.*   —WILLIAM LLOYD GARRISON

What do you do when you have a problem with a product, a service, or a company? Do you just stew—or do you *do* something?

The problem could be as unnerving as buying a defective CD player at the local electronics store or as inconvenient as arriving late for an important business meeting because the airline you chose has oversold your flight and bumped you onto the next one. It would be one thing if such problems were addressed up front completely and fairly: "I'm sorry, Madame, that the CD player is defective. Per our store policy, we will gladly see that the machine is replaced, and for your inconvenience, here's a twenty-five-dollar certificate." But it's never that simple. Before the product is replaced or you're booked on another, more favorable flight, you have to deal with at least three people, and you better believe they are going to dish out some attitude. The concern, compassion, and even politeness of bygone days has often been replaced by "get ahead quick" and "in your face."

Most of us just accept this as our lot. We sit in traffic jams with half a million of our closest friends going to work each morning and returning home each night, our impatience and irritation over such incidents getting the best of us. I'd like to say that as we wait, we relax, think beautiful thoughts, and are at one with the cosmos. In reality, however, when we are cut off by that driver who swerves in and out of our lane, we usually curse him or her violently, and our blood pressure rises to the point of a stroke. Many of us even feel the tug of that middle digit as we strive to fully express our outrage. But, okay, we survive, we take a deep breath, we calm down, and we find our way home to our refuge, our castle.

Then in the middle of dinner the phone rings. "Hello. You've supported the Hairy Flea Preservation Society in the past. May we count on your support this year?" Nowhere is safe. Our castle has been assaulted by uncouth invaders, its defenses breached at the most inconvenient times. Sometimes I wonder if there is a little spy satellite orbiting above us, which flashes a signal to the caller when we sit down at the dinner table, or when we rush breathlessly from the garden to answer the ringing telephone only to hear a perky, cheery voice trying to sell us a cemetery plot.

Some of us are saints; we merely adjust our halos, turn the other cheek, and get on with our lives. That is, until we have occasion to dial out to a particular company to schedule a repairman or to book that dream vacation we've been anxiously awaiting. It should be a simple phone call, but we are met with a perfect electronic voice (which seems to be the same voice used by every company in the world—I do hope that person or mass of electrons gets a royalty) spewing out those never-ending choices: "If you have a touch-tone phone, please choose from the following options. . . ." By the time we've worked our way through three or four menus per option, our patience is wearing a little thin.

When things go wrong with a purchase or a service we have paid for, some of us say, "Oh, well, things happen. *Caveat emptor*, let the buyer beware." But most of us get angry, and, as we all know, when we're royally ticked, we say and do things that we would never say and do under normal circumstances. We shout, we whine, we spew obscenities, and for kicks we may even hang up on people. (What may be even worse, our children sometimes observe our tantrums. We aren't always the wonderful role model for our kids we hoped to be.) And if we truly feel put upon by the response (or lack thereof) to the problems we have experienced with a product or service, the fuse is relit and our anger rises once more. We grab the telephone, and the volcano erupts. We have the satisfaction of our rage, but very, very rarely do we achieve the results we seek.

Then, too, there are the multitude of times when we say to ourselves, "By golly, I swear that I'm going to write a letter!" We plan just what to write on the ride to the supermarket. While trying to decide between the cheaper store brand's ice cream and the better-tasting, more expensive gourmet stuff, our ideas arrange themselves in a bulleted list in our brains. But at the checkout counter, upon discovering the total is $24.67 more than is in our checking account, our letter-writing mission, superseded by new priorities, falls by the wayside. Inevitably, we are so busy with work and home and family—we don't want to miss that favorite TV show, that card game, that one pleasurable activity we need to squeeze into our crowded lives—that the thought of writing a complaint letter usually recedes to the back of our mind and slips away, soon to be forgotten. Unfortunately, without this "official" confrontation of our wrongs, we may have to go on suffering the same injustices, and remain implacably ticked. Such used to be my way. But not anymore. Should anybody choose to mess with me, be they a customer rep from an airline, a federal government employee, or the CEO of an electronics store, he or she will soon realize that I'm the Scarlett O'Hara type. You know, the loudmouth Southern wench who is determined to do things *her* way. I can just see myself ripping the rotten draperies down from the wide windows of Tara to make a new gown to impress Rhett Butler. This same O'Hara tenacity embodies the spirit behind Ellen's Poison Pen, Inc.®, a letter-writing business I began in 1988. Here's how I got my start.

If your household is like mine, you get loads of advertisements for discount goods and services. As all of us do at one time or another, one day I decided to use a special coupon for a $39.95 expert carpet cleaning service. Well, they came, they cleaned (sort of), and they went. They also left a big splotch that wasn't there before their arrival. An honest mistake, I assumed, so I called the company to politely request a new cleaning, just on that one spot. The man who answered the call began screaming at me, literally, and then he had the audacity to say that I had spilled something deliberately after the service left just so that I could get a free pick-me-up cleaning!

All thoughts of being a nice person voicing a simple concern lay dashed by the wayside. I sprinted to my typewriter and banged out a missive to the owner of the business. (For more on always addressing complaints to the *top* store, company, or corporate officer, see Chapter 3.)

Dear Mr. Cleaner Owner:

I am absolutely appalled at the rudeness and hostility exhibited today by one of your employees, and I am certain that you will be as shocked as I was when you learn of what has transpired.

After your personnel from Corrupting Cleaners, Inc., left my home this afternoon, I noticed quite a large spot on my living room carpet that had not been there previously. I assumed that perhaps some of the cleaning solution had been accidentally spilled; therefore I called your company to set up an appointment for someone to come and remove the spot. Imagine my dismay when my request was met with abusive hostility on the part of Mr. Michael Meany. After literally screaming at me that I was simply a dishonest customer who had deliberately spilled something on the carpet after the personnel left in order to

receive a free cleaning, he then abruptly
hung up on me!

I cannot believe that you have knowledge
of or condone this type of abrasive and
unprofessional behavior on the part of your
employees. I expect an immediate investigation, a personal apology from Mr. Meany,
and the removal of the spot on my carpet.

Thank you, and I look forward to hearing
from you within five business days.

Sincerely,

Ellen H. Phillips

Mr. Cleaner Owner called me two days later and did a lot of groveling. The only reason Mr. Meany wasn't offering his own apology was that he had been *fired*. By the way, not only was that spot immediately removed, but my entire house was steam-cleaned—for free! Oh, what sweet satisfaction.

Although I had written numerous personal letters of complaint, I realized that it was necessary to rethink certain strategies if I was going to actually charge others for the privilege of writing on their behalf. My naturally volatile nature (which I had already toned down immensely) was forced to be further moderated. After all, one of my key precepts is detachment from the problem at hand.

While researching corporate heads and helpful agencies, it became evident just what a daunting task I was undertaking. Was I truly prepared to become "The Poison Lady"? Stacks of files accumulated on my desk and in the little three-drawer file cabinet I had bought for my venture. Lists of names and addresses, clippings from newspapers and magazines, and government documents soon outstripped my meager surroundings. Scam busters, hotlines for health care problems, airline laws, and every heavy hitter in between answered my question for me. There were too many folks just *like* me—consumers who buy in good faith but all too often receive a swift kick in the pants if their purchase doesn't meet their standards or expectations and who deserve someone to speak out and stand up for them, even if in a ghost-writing position. Once we have learned the tricks of the trade, all of us can complain effectively and increase the pressure by informing state and federal agencies and overseers.

After writing that initial letter to Corrupting Cleaners, Inc., I became so effective at writing letters that achieve results that word quickly spread, for it seemed as if everyone had a gripe and wished for me to help solve it. The next thing I knew, requests were coming in from friends, from friends of friends, from my colleagues at the middle school where I taught, and even from strangers on the street (all right, I do admit to thrusting business cards into their unsuspecting hands). As a result, I discovered very quickly that there were many people who needed someone with the tact and courtesy of a "sweet Southern lady," but one who was not afraid to deliver a stinging slap. It was only a matter of time before first-time customers came back for another jolt of empowerment, and then word of mouth became the best source of advertisement for my fledgling business.

At first, the problems ran the gamut of the typical irritations of everyday life that we all sometimes experience: airlines losing luggage, car repair rip-offs, and dissatisfaction in dealing with local businesses. Letters flowed from my pen, venom dripped, results flooded in. Within no time I was writing letters that were more personal in nature. Sometimes they were petitions for child custody or child support issues; sometimes they were delicate letters to employers or HMOs. I must admit that most of the first years were lean ones (the Internal Revenue Service can certainly attest to that), but as my business expanded and I realized the vicarious pleasure of helping others resolve their problems, I decided that surely many more people could benefit from my trade secrets of effective, result-oriented complaining. What better method to help the masses than by writing a book and using my three favorite complaint adjectives in the title—*Shocked, Appalled,* and *Dismayed.* My idea was to inform consumers how they could go about pressing forward with their own professional letters of complaint. With a little groundwork (and, in some cases, *a lot*) such as previously mentioned, anyone can make his or her complaints known. The chapters in this book contain checklists of somewhat similar steps, but each pertains to the set of circumstances addressed in that chapter. By the time you've finished reading this book, you'll find yourself a much more coherent complainer, and your results may be nothing shy of astonishing. Just think of what Scarlett O'Hara could have pulled off if she had taken pen to paper instead of relying on that Southern drawl and those big eyelashes of hers.

Dear President Lincoln:

I am shocked, appalled, and dismayed at the atrocious manner in which General Sherman marched through Atlanta. He left my beloved city in flames as he and his troops trampled their way through Georgia. The beautiful homes, at which I was always the belle of the ball, fell prey to the fires of hell. To add further insult to injury, my poor Aunt Pittypat had the most horrendous case of the vapors afterward. It was all I could do to revive her with her smelling salts without slapping her first.

I expect you to conduct a thorough and immediate investigation, and I demand that you officially reprimand General Sherman,

strip him of all rank, and parole him to me
so that I may teach him better manners.

I look forward to hearing from you within
the next two weeks.

Thank you.

Sincerely,

Scarlett O'Hara

CHAPTER 2

The Verbal Approach

> Although no one likes to get complaints from a customer, at least the complaints provide the immediate opportunity to *discuss* possible solutions before the problem escalates, resulting in an unhappy client.
> —RICK SORBER, OWNER, MT. VERNON BUILDERS

We sit down excitedly to open that beautifully wrapped birthday gift only to find, to our utter shock and dismay, a shirt that even Jim Carrey wouldn't wear on his back. We finally purchase the big-screen TV for which we've scraped and saved, yet when we plug it in to the den outlet, we're blinded by bright sparks instead of the stadium lights of that highly anticipated football game. How often have we returned to a store with a purchase that is defective or one that we simply didn't like once we got it home? If we're lucky enough, that place of business is one offering a no-holds-barred policy of "Satisfaction Guaranteed," but unfortunately this isn't always the case. The key to achieving satisfaction is to *discuss* your concerns. That's right: I'm suggesting that you first try to talk your way into an exchange of a product or service or a refund.

While the intent of this book is to outline and demonstrate how to write effective complaint letters, à la Ellen's Poison Pen, Inc.,® many problems may be reconciled far more quickly and painlessly with a "face-to-face" (as opposed to an in-your-face) meeting with an owner or a manager. Small business owners, in particular, often prefer to talk directly with customers who are having problems, and usually they will bend over backward to satisfy a good client. After all, you can always fall back on the pen if the verbal approach doesn't work to your satisfaction.

I've conducted a local poll with a cross section of merchants in my city, and their replies are certainly engaging ones. Robert St. Clair, who along with his father owns St. Clair Distributors, a kitchen and bathroom design and sales company in Alexandria, Virginia, feels strongly that a personal call to first attempt to solve a problem is always the better recourse:

> As a business owner, I like to feel that we develop a long-term relationship with our clients. I hope that each client is comfortable enough to call when a problem arises, because we want to correct it as much as our client does. In the event of what a client considers to be a serious problem, I would suggest a call to request a meeting before writing a letter. The customer should be prepared to discuss both the items that need correction and a fair and reasonable solution to problems. In most cases, a business owner and a reasonable client can agree on a plan of action and solve problems fairly quickly. A follow-up letter the next day should be well received and will also serve as a confirmation of the agreement between both parties.

I am in total agreement with St. Clair, for as they say, "What goes around comes around." If we are fair and reasonable to the company executive, then chances are he will act the same way with us. This especially holds true when we are dealing with merchants who both live and work within the same community. But we should still remember that if this verbal dialogue doesn't work, the pen is still waiting backstage, ready to make its grand entrance.

St. Clair goes on to advise, as I do in Chapter 10, that good behavior is usually rewarded.

> Most companies live on referrals, and in many cases the best referrals are from clients who saw their problems corrected in a timely and efficient manner. If a business responds in the manner in which you hoped, this response also deserves a letter. This positive

feedback will probably help to resolve future problems that others may face.

Once the new kitchen is built and our beautiful designs are complete, we know that problems don't just vanish along with the drywall dust. Another local merchant, George Callaghan, who owns Callaghan's Exterminating Company (oh, yes, we've all had our own experiences with pesky critters), thrives on customer satisfaction. He states that he will do everything possible to resolve an uncomfortable situation *"as long as the customer remains calm and realistic."* Because he is in a service industry, he certainly realizes that occasional problems and complaints will occur. Mr. Callaghan lives by the adage, *"If I won't give the customer what he wants, my competitor will. It's our name out there, and we take our business personally."*

So now that we all know that the verbal method is often preferred as the first step, how do we guarantee that our grievances will be heard by the appropriate person? Generally, a sales clerk or receptionist doesn't have the authority to trade or to reimburse if that's not the store's policy, so there's no rhyme or reason for even considering for one moment getting into an insult-swapping exchange with this person. If the person you are dealing with lacks the authority to *fix* your problem (that is, exchange the shirt or the television set), then politely ask to see the manager or the owner.

Let's assume, just for a minute, that the sales clerk either refuses to call the head honcho or that that person is out to lunch (I mean this literally, of course). If he or she truly isn't there, then you can always make a return trip, and you can even solidify your chances for a meeting by making an appointment for a mutually convenient time. If, on the other hand, the employee you are speaking with proves to be uncooperative or, even worse, the manager refuses to speak with you, your grievances have now multiplied like jackrabbits. What do you do? Trust me, your fingers will tingle with anticipation as you reach for your *pen* for there's always someone (or some agency) who has jurisdiction or influence over this business. Chapter 3 discusses these instrumental parties in greater detail.

If your request for the meeting with the Big Boss is met, briefly explain your problem and indicate how you would like it to be resolved. It helps if you've been a patron of that business in the past; right now is the time to emphasize this point: your hard-earned cash has flowed into those gulping pockets and will continue to do so—if your request is granted.

On the off chance that this approach doesn't work, you should start to seriously consider writing a letter. But first seek out as many senior people in the chain of command who will listen to you. Make sure you *record* the name of everyone with whom you speak—the helpful as well as the worthless ones. It's important to note that occasionally your appeal will be granted simply because the person in charge wishes to get rid of you. Who cares as long as you exit the store with your claim fulfilled? There is a right way and a wrong way to stand your ground. For example, although I don't advocate screaming and jabbing your finger in that person's face, I do promote standing your ground and making your wishes known.

Out of the mouths of owners themselves you've learned that many if not most owners and managers do want to hear from us. As we go along we'll learn more about how to get to the person in charge. For now, let's go over some sensible tips on how to be effective in voicing your complaint. These hints will also be useful when you are talking to clerks and nonmanagerial staff.

1 Calm down. Lower your voice. You have a better chance of being heard if you keep your head together and proceed methodically.

2 Tone down the rhetoric, don't accuse, don't curse, and don't threaten. Even when you're talking to the decision maker, the "junkyard dog" approach won't solve your problems. I was always taught that one can "catch more flies with honey than with vinegar." When threatened, we all throw up our defenses. You may have the best argument in the world, but if you precede it with verbal abuse and you direct unnecessary anger at the person to whom you are speaking, you've already lost both the battle and the war.

3 Be polite but assertive. Being polite will not only help you convey your point to the Top Dog; it will also help you get through to him or her. Who do you think has a better chance of swapping that new television, the person who calls the clerk a bumbling idiot or the deferentially assertive dear Mr. Brown? Whether to the salesperson or to his boss, you also need to explain your concerns and problems as well as what you wish done to restore your faith in the company's or store's products or services. This is not the time for recriminations. Think back on what Mr. Callaghan said: *"As long as the customer remains calm and is realistic . . ."*

Some people are natural orators, but others quickly get sweaty palms at the thought of a personal confrontation. If this is the case, then take notes on what your specific complaint is and what you wish done. You might even wish to write out a script. It's certainly better to have *read* your complaint than never to have complained at all.

4 Line up your facts. Have dates, names, invoice numbers, receipts, and so forth, at your fingertips. Remember, today's world runs on data, whether you're dealing with a small company or a Fortune 500 one. (Note: In the event that you simply don't like a product and wish to attempt to return it, some of these points are not necessarily applicable. Use the data to serve your own particular circumstances.) Also, if you later need to unsheathe the infamous *pen*, you will once more need to produce all of this documentation.

5 Tell them what you want. Clearly state what needs to happen to make it all better: replacement, repair, reimbursement, the owner's firstborn . . . But be fair and reasonable.

A couple of years ago, one of my colleagues renovated her kitchen, and in the process she bought an expensive gas stove. Her husband, the gourmet cook of the household, really wanted this particular model, and she wasn't going to argue with the man who cooked her dinners. Now, this woman did whip up an occasional meal, but she was having a devil of a time adapting to that new stove. After almost a year of wishing that she hadn't been so accommodating of her husband, she wanted to trade the stove for an electric model. She followed the tips I've suggested, and, after all was said and done, she obtained a more than fair trade. The gas stove was a year old, and she and her husband received a brand-new stove. The owner of the store offered the exchange if the two of them agreed to simply pay the labor costs for installation. See, being "fair and reasonable" does work.

Not so long ago, I had an experience with a NYNEX cellular phone that I couldn't get to work for the life of me. Even though the phone I bought was fully charged, the calls would not go out. I returned the product to the local store, spoke with the assistant manager, and he immediately exchanged the phone with no problem. But the second phone acted in the same manner as the first. By now I was beginning to believe that specialty phones and I weren't cut out to be best buddies, but I decided to give it one more chance as I do so dearly love those instant teacher-student-parent interventions.

Once again, less than a month later, I returned to the store in question with the phone, but this time I spoke with the manager himself. Politely and assertively, I explained that this phone was also giving me a great deal of difficulty, and I gave him specific details about how it wasn't working properly. Without question, I received a third phone and an apology. All this in less than a two-month period! To quote Judith R. Haberkorn, Vice President of Consumer Marketing for NYNEX, Inc.:

We view customer complaints and other interactions as an opportunity to listen to our customers, learn more about their needs and reaffirm our commitment to meet and exceed their expectations. Our first priority is to address our customers' complaints and assure them that we stand behind our brand. Secondly, we monitor prob-lems and complaints for trends that can be used to improve our products and services through root cause analysis. Finally, such interactions are an opportunity to establish a better relationship with our sophisticated customer base.

Whether or not you consider yourself to be "sophisticated" is beside the point. What does matter is that you contact that head honcho so that your concerns can be directly addressed. Judging from the responses of my merchant poll, it's clear that company leaders really *do* want to hear you voice your concerns. Apply this same rationale to the most trivial of complaints, too. Are the French fries cold and greasy at the local fast-food joint? Stroll on up to the counter and *calmly* and nicely ask for a fresh batch. Does the neighbor's barking dog interrupt your leisure time in your backyard? Before you call the police, call your neighbor or walk over and *politely* ask what can be done to solve the prob-lem. And, yes, it does matter that the house-cleaning service left the bedspread crooked. *Firmly* let them know that you are pay-ing them to satisfy your standards. As always, be calm, be polite, but be consistently firm in communicating your expectations. Most people would far rather settle a dispute, no matter how minor, if they know you mean business and are prepared to take the disagreement to a higher authority.

When all your calmness, fairness, and reason fail, then it's time to adjust the pressure up a notch. Buckle yourself into your computer chair, hang on for dear life, and produce the heavy artillery—the pen!

CHAPTER 3

How to Write an Effective Complaint Letter

> Anger is a momentary madness, so control your passion or it will control you. —HORACE

Let's assume that for whatever reason the verbal approach didn't work for you. Maybe you just couldn't quite get up the nerve to confront Mr. or Ms. Authority in person. Maybe he or she quit/retired/died or just simply wasn't interested in talking to you. Perhaps his or her successor wasn't either. Not to worry. Regardless of the problem, your next plan of attack is to *write* your first poison pen letter.

The key here is to type or to word process your letter and mail it. Electronic poison pen letters are unacceptable because e-mail is not really confidential. If your e-mail is directed to the CEOs, new problems may arise. Let's say that you've included personal information, such as your store account number or your bank card number (as you would in an official complaint letter), and a disgruntled or unscrupulous individual sees this information on the e-mail message. What's to stop this person from going on a shopping spree at your expense? Other legal problems may arise if you use e-mail, particularly if you've made comments that libel someone or a company. You're on extremely shaky ground when you circulate damaging or false information about a company or its employees via the Internet. For more facts on when and how you might violate libel laws with statements you make in complaint letters, see Chapter 4.

There are two camps of people: those who are already comfortable expressing themselves verbally and in writing and those who utter pitifully, "I can't do that. I don't have the necessary skills to write what needs to be said." So what if you've only dabbled with writing letters before now? Even an inexperienced rookie can easily become a professional-sounding complaint writer. Just think how awesome it will be for you, your family, and your friends to read a response letter that includes an apology, a promise of a new product, or even a check. *You must have faith in your own abilities.*

No matter what kind of writer you think you are, it's important to know that many other people share complaints similar to yours. Indeed, there are certain industries or companies that receive more than their fair share of correspondence in the complaints department. Let's take a peek at the biggest bugaboos:

- 🖎 apartment rental agencies
- 🖎 appliance repair shops
- 🖎 architects
- 🖎 auto repair shops
- 🖎 cable television providers
- 🖎 computer dating services
- 🖎 doctors and nurses in hospitals
- 🖎 employment agencies (the top of the list)
- 🖎 furniture and appliance rental companies
- 🖎 mail-order companies
- 🖎 moving and storage companies
- 🖎 nursing homes
- 🖎 the postal service
- 🖎 plumbing and home repair services
- 🖎 remodeling, decorating, and landscaping firms
- 🖎 roofing, siding, and painting firms
- 🖎 taxis

✍ television, radio, and computer repair shops
✍ trains

Regardless of what's throwing a wrench into your life, you can effect change and better service by writing a letter that is free of bitter and angry invective. Anger may have its place, but we must acknowledge that there are indisputable times when it must be set aside, or at least channeled in such a way that it benefits us. Writing a complaint letter is one of these instances.

You will want to write a thoughtful and organized letter. No matter the merits of your situation, you're less likely to get a satisfactory response if you write a long and incoherent letter that circles around the topic at hand. If your letter isn't clear and compelling, you're wasting your valuable time and energy. A letter riddled with repetition and unclear thinking obscures the way for creating understanding and getting your message across.

Just recently a lady mailed me a hand-written letter (a real no-no) that typifies this type of correspondence. This woman had owned a condominium, but upon vacating it, the property manager had refused to return part of her equity, stating that she owed money for cosmetic repairs. She was furious at being forced to pay for these nonexistent repairs. She had already paid for other repairs herself out of pocket, since she couldn't get the condo association to cover them. The letter she wrote started out nicely, but then the effect was ruined because she began repeating herself over and over. She was justifiably irate when she sat down to write, and the result was a lot of rambling. She numbered each point (which is good practice in and of itself), but instead of concluding each separate point before going on to the next, she continued to weave in and out with information she had already stated. Even after the letter's conclusion and her signature, she continued to write. She closed and signed the letter twice, yet she continued to write after each signature. The more she wrote, the angrier she became, and even her handwriting began to disintegrate, until finally at the *real* end of the letter her handwriting was almost illegible. The letter was so confusing that *I* was having trouble making heads or tails of its contents.

And she had mailed this letter. It should come as no surprise that her letter elicited zero response. Most likely it went to that big dead-letter box in the sky.

How, you may ask, could anyone be so disorganized, so blinded by angry passion, so inarticulate, so inexperienced as to have written such an incoherent letter? Most people do not set out to write a bad letter. Even the most educated and articulate people may simply have no time to spare to write a well-thought-out letter, or maybe they cannot remain detached enough to express themselves coherently. It is possible to avoid this pitfall if you follow certain key guidelines for letter writing, which I've set forth later in the chapter.

The following actual poison letter I wrote for a client to a major beer distributor (and its response) is not only one of my favorites; it also contains all the elements of an effective poison pen letter. "99 Bottles of Beer on the Wall" could very easily be its theme song.

```
                        101 Redbud Lane
                        South Bend, IN 33445
                        October 12, 1998


John K. Brewski, President/CEO
Suds Beer Corporation
123 Brewery Street
Seattle, WA 17860


Dear Mr. Brewski:


This past Saturday evening, my husband
and I were entertaining guests and served
Suds, which is the favored beer among our
circle of friends. Imagine my shock and
embarrassment when one of the guests
opened one of the bottles and half of its
rim came off with the cap! This occurred
not once, but twice. At that point, fearful
```

that the tops of the remaining bottles might break off in the same way, my husband traveled to the supermarket to buy more beer (not Suds!).

I do not know if this was simply a defective case of beer or if certain bottles were prepared improperly at the factory; however, I do know that it certainly inconvenienced our guests and my husband, and it became a topic of negative conversation throughout the evening. Even worse, however, it could have led to physical danger if the glass portion had exploded rather than imploded, making both your company and us liable for damages.

I am appalled, as are my (formerly) Suds-drinking friends, and I wish to have this matter investigated immediately. Enclosed you will find the cap and the glass remnants of one of the two bottles. I can assure you that neither my husband and I nor any of our fifteen guests who were present that evening will purchase this product again until I hear from you to my satisfaction.

Thank you.

Sincerely,

Emma Embarrassed

cc: Mala Nagarajan, Supervisor
    Consumer Protection Division
    Office of the Attorney General

```
103 East Holly Street, Suite 308
Bellingham, WA 98225

Lisa Hays, Chief Counsel and Director
Consumer Protection Division
Office of the Attorney General
Indiana Government Center South, 5th Floor
402 West Washington Street
Indianapolis, IN 46204

Consumer Product Safety Commission
4330 East West Highway
Bethesda, MD 20207

Federal Trade Commission
Sixth Street and Pennsylvania Avenue, NW
Room 240
Washington, DC 20580
```

The results "Emma Embarrassed" got were even better than she expected; all she wanted was an acknowledgment of the beer maker's error. Mr. Brewski's response wasn't a letter—it was a phone call and the offer of a free case of Suds beer as well as a six-pack of a new beer soon to appear on the market (he was smart enough to realize that a little direct promotion never hurts). The company lost no real revenue, my client was happy, and the Poison Pen could once again rest on its laurels . . . until the next time.

If you want to write an effective letter like this one, follow this series of steps:

1 Calm down. The very first pledge we must make to ourselves is to remain calm, cool, and as detached as possible from the situation. Try to stand back and view the problem as an outsider would. Take a cold shower, try deep breathing, repeating mantras, or any other method to slow your elevated blood pressure. Allowing the anger to die down may take a few hours or even a few days. Once you feel calm enough to begin sorting through your information (without forgetting the incident), you are ready to begin. Don't wait too long, however. As the days spin out of control, you'd be amazed at how quickly you can forget events and particulars.

2 Keep receipts. These are your proof of purchase/service. Remember to mail only *copies* and not the originals with your correspondence; otherwise your only firsthand documentation of service or payment will be gone forever. Include not only receipts for purchased products but also other types of verification, such as airline boarding passes. As time goes by, your stack of ammunition should grow as quickly as Jack's beanstalk; after all, remember the giant residing at the very top will gobble up all your precious arguments if your evidence is not complete.

It is imperative to place any and all data in proper chronological order to include within the final packet. Once you have compiled everything from your list (or as much of it as you can find), you are ready for the next step.

3 Document and organize. Gather *all* the information that is on hand; include every scrap, no matter how insignificant you may think it might be. You have probably spoken with people personally about your problem. It may have been a secretary, a supervisor, or it could have been someone as high as the manager. As I suggested in Chapter 2, you should keep some sort of record of the event and your attempts at a resolution so that you have the dates and the times of the conversations, as well as the names of the persons with whom you have spoken, either on the telephone or in person. Is there any correspondence that you yourself have already written? Send along a copy. It is a pay-better-attention heads up to the recipient that you have already addressed this problem in writing, and it sends the message that you don't intend to give up and go away.

4 Discover the name of the person at the highest level. Sadly enough, all too often we do not take the time to do our research and find out the name of the appropriate person or persons to whom we should address our complaint letter. It is critical to unearth the name of the company's CEO and/or president, if your complaint is with a product, service, or place of business. This is the person at the top, the one who will prove of invaluable assistance because the higher the rank, the quicker the response. If you cannot discover this person's name by calling the company's corporate headquarters or main office, then check the reference section of your local library. Books such as *Standard and Poor's Register of Corporations, Trade Names Dictionary,* and *Dun and Bradstreet Directory* are valuable resources to elicit that one certain name and title. Check the appendices of this book for much of this same information. The names of local management may be easily obtained simply by calling the main office and asking. Your local Chamber of Commerce or city/county offices may also be of help.

If you write directly to the Big Chief, himself (or herself), even if your letter is passed to a subordinate, that subordinate is usually someone in a position of authority who can react immediately. It's far better to address your letter to a CEO/president and have it passed on to a vice president than it is to direct it to a manager and have the task delegated to his secretary for response. There are many times when a CEO is so taken aback with the information he or she sees in a letter that he or she sets the ball rolling, and you, the complainant, will hear directly from him or her. One of my clients had a CEO who took great pleasure in being personally involved in an intervention and used the opportunity to "shake up" his organization. Because you are addressing a person of importance, your letter must look professional and possess certain characteristics, which are discussed in the following paragraphs.

5 Use polite language. It's not to your advantage to come across as a rude or hostile person, even if you feel like vilely cursing over this problem. No one reacts well to being attacked. It's important to be as objective and detached as possible, even to the extent of pretending that you're writing the letter for someone else.

6 **Use the standard business letter format.** Type or word process all letters; do not handwrite; do not send e-mail. As you can see in the preceding letters, the body of the letter is always single-spaced. The only abbreviations allowed are for the names of the states in the heading and the inside address, as well as some titles, such as Mr., Ms., Dr., and so forth. Review the Suds beer letter to see where the heading (your address and the date) and the inside address (the same as will appear on the envelope) are situated. Make sure your signature is written *above* your typed name; it's surprising how many people make this tiny error, which throws off the entire *professional* format.

7 **Grab the reader's attention at the beginning of the letter.** After the salutation, an immediate attention getter is a *must*. It may only be one sentence, but it must catch the recipient's eye. My favorites are "I am shocked and appalled at the unprofessional treatment to which I have been subjected by [company name] personnel" or "I am sure that you will be as shocked and appalled as I am over the recent incident I have experienced with company X." This method will pique the curiosity of your reader, and it is a not-so-subtle encouragement to continue reading the rest of the letter.

8 **Be concise.** When presenting your problem, be as succinct as possible. No one, particularly someone who has less time than most to read correspondence, is going to want to wade through reams of paper. If your reader snoozes off, you're the loser. Your letter should be no more than one to one and a half pages long unless your situation is extremely involved.

9 **Review the history.** Introduce your problem and the ways in which you have tried to solve it. After all, you want the person reading your letter to understand you are not whining; you have a legitimate problem, you have exhausted all other avenues, and he or she is, indeed, your last possible recourse. Compile a listing, in chronological order, of pertinent dates, costs, prior conversations and correspondence, the persons with whom you have been in contact, and any other relevant information.

10 Suggest that the company could lose your business. Hint that you may decline to have future dealings with the company in question. This particular part of the letter is also an implied "threat" that the company or corporation will lose income (more on the importance of an *implied* threat in Chapter 4), because you will tell family, friends, and strangers on the street, who will also be "appalled" at your problem and the manner in which you have been treated. The CEO who receives your letter will surely realize that a lot of people will think twice before they, too, take a gamble on losing money on a product or service offered by his or her company.

11 State your expectations. Do you want a product repaired or replaced, do you want a refund, or will a simple apology make you feel all warm and fuzzy? If you don't specify exactly what it is you want, then the recipient of your letter can only guess. Note that the writer of the letter to "Mr. Brewski," the Suds beer manufacturer, explained what she wished him to do to solve the problem to her satisfaction. She didn't even request more beer, which would have been justified. What she did declare, however, was that none of the people who had been present at her party would purchase this product until she got a satisfactory response from the CEO. It's always a grand idea to write that you "have been a loyal customer" (just as this beer drinker did) or even better, when you're dealing with a large store or credit card company, a "faithful credit card holder for years" if such is the case. It is indeed rare that one of my Poison Pen customers doesn't get something back in response to a letter.

12 Close firmly and politely. The last paragraph is where you should not only thank the reader but also let him or her know that you expect a quick answer. You can specify the need for a response "immediately," or give a fixed period of time; for instance, "I expect to hear from you within two weeks [or one month] regarding this situation." Although it has been my experience that most people rarely get a response quite as quickly as "within two weeks," making such a request does place the brass on alert that you are not twiddling your thumbs and waiting around for the mail carrier. You want quick action to be taken, and the inference, of course, is that if quick action is not forthcoming, more poison will flow. In closing, be sure to say "thank you." After all, this is a *polite* letter. The thanks is both for the recipient's reading your letter as well as for the assistance you anticipate.

⓭ Proofread for errors. Even if you need someone else to check it for you, your letter must be grammatically correct and comprehensible. There are any number of inexpensive books available to use as a tool for foolproof editing. If you have access to a computer, use the grammar and spell-check function, though you should be aware that the final copy will still need a thorough examination. The more professionally written your letter is, the more likely the chances you will receive a prompt and thoughtful response. Eyeball what you think is your final copy. Even the best of us make mistakes.

⓮ Copy key people. The last dose of power—and often the most effective of all—now appears. Whenever appropriate, include a listing of people to whom you will mail copies of your letter, including officials at local, state, and/or national regulatory agencies, as well as professional organizations. These names are listed after "cc:" (for "carbon copy") at the bottom of the letter. Some people prefer not to do this the first time around; they would rather wait and see what type of response they receive; they may resort to using cc's if they don't receive a response or the problem isn't solved to their satisfaction. I believe otherwise. Why do something twice when you can win the first time? Once you notify watchdog agencies of your problem by sending them copies of your letter, and they step in—and believe me, many of them do—very often you will receive prompt action. There are very many organizations out there in Consumer Land (you'll find them in the appendices and in the cc's of the sample letters throughout) that have been created to represent us and to "help" corporate America live up to its responsibilities. If there is someone who upon initially reading your complaint letter doesn't become interested, we'd all like to be that fly on the wall when he or she flips through to the closing and discovers the carbon copy section of your letter.

Trade organizations can be important, too, such as the **American Society of Travel Agents**, (703) 739-2782, if your complaint has to do with contracted travel arrangements. No matter the agency, even the sleaziest of persons hates to be held up to the spotlight for his or her peers to see. A vital telephone number to memorize is that of the **Tele-Consumer Hotline** (800) 332-1124; this outfit often has information on certain products and services and the names and addresses of the corporate leaders, if you're unable to find this information elsewhere.

One particular Maryland complainant had a beef with a roofing company. The shingles on her home were disintegrating faster than you could say "slipshod shingles" three times quickly. The cc's for that complaint letter, minus the names of the people and the companies that were directly involved, follow.

```
cc: William Leibovici, Chief
    Consumer Protection Division
    Maryland Office of the Attorney General
    200 St. Paul Place, 16th Floor
    Baltimore, MD 21202-2021

    H. Russell Frisby, Chairman
    Public Service Commission
    6 St. Paul Street, 16th Floor
    Baltimore, MD 21202

    Office of Public Affairs
    United States Department of Labor
    Washington, DC 20210

    Office of Public Liaison
    Environmental Protection Agency
    Washington, DC 20460
```

```
Consumer Affairs
Small Business Administration
409 Third Street, SW
Washington, DC 20416

United States Federal Trade Commission
Sixth Street and Pennsylvania Avenue, NW
Room 240
Washington, DC 20580

Toxic Substances Control Act Assistance
Environmental Protection Agency
Washington, DC 20024

Joseph T. Giloley, Acting Director
Montgomery Office of Consumer Affairs
100 Maryland Avenue, 3rd Floor
Rockville, MD 20850

Dwight K. Bartlett, III, Commissioner
Maryland Insurance Administration
501 St. Paul Place, 7th Floor
Baltimore, MD 21202
```

Trust me, prospective poisoners, copying key people will *definitely* be the signal for your addressee to wake up and smell the coffee. To obtain current names and addresses of companies and agencies for yourself, request a free copy of the *Consumer's Resource Handbook* from the U.S. Consumer Information Center, a publication that lists a huge number of agency and corporate contacts. Each year, I call the Consumer Information Center at (719) 948-4000 and look forward to receiving my updated version. I always anticipate reading the foreword because it, too, changes every year. In the 1997 edition, former Congresswoman Leslie L. Byrne, Special Assistant to the President and Director, writes: *"The information presented is based on the premise that consumers need to know their rights and how to*

*make the right choices. . . . This handbook offers information and
advice to help you gain knowledge about your rights and how to
make the right choices—and, yes, how to protect yourself."* The
Consumer's Resource Handbook is my bible and my right hand.
In addition, an extensive listing of agencies is at your fingertips
via the Internet (www.consumer.gov). But don't forget that
much of the same information is provided for you in the appendices of *Shocked, Appalled, and Dismayed!*, where you can also
find a great deal of data the government publication and the
Internet don't provide.

⑮ Never give up! I'm not going to lie and tell you that each
and every letter you write will provide instant relief, or even that
you will receive results 100 percent of the time. And sometimes
the clock ticks away, and your two weeks become four, or your
one month becomes three. I always tell my clients that if a month
passes with no satisfactory response—or certainly if they receive
no response at all—to fire off another missive, along with a copy
of the first letter to anyone and everyone on your carbon copy
list. Personally, I have had to write several times over a period of
months to get action from some resistant authorities, as have several of my clients. But the secret is that you hang on, you harangue, you harass, you document your efforts, you build a
paper trail. You may get discouraged, but you must not forfeit
the fight. This is your *cause*, and you must see it through until
the end.

One recent letter exemplifying all the suggestions I have just
set forth concerns the exasperation experienced by an elderly
woman who had purchased a defective light fixture from a
major hardware chain. Even though we didn't use cc's because
this woman didn't want copies of her letter to be mailed to regulatory organizations, the complaint letter we wrote to the CEO
resulted in a new fixture, a $100 credit to her account at the
hardware store ("faithful credit card holder"), as well as reimbursement for the electrician's services as described in her letter.
Here's the letter that brought her these results.

699 Robin Road
Newport News, VA 23606
June 14, 1997

H. C. Handyman, CEO
Hardluck Hardwares
990 Hardware Circle, Suite 402
Washington, DC 22229

Dear Mr. Handyman:

I am appalled at my recent experience with
Hardluck Hardwares. On May 18 I purchased
a light fixture from your store in Newport
News, Virginia (receipt enclosed). On June
20, the lightbulb popped, and I returned to
the store to obtain another (free) bulb. The
clerk in that department claimed that it
was not their bulb and that I had switched
it in order to receive a new one. I stood
there, aghast, as this woman continued to
directly imply that I was a liar. She continued to harangue me, until she finally
seemed to realize that an eighty-four-year-
old woman was not out to cheat your company
of a single light bulb! Finally, she gave
me another one, but as soon as I installed
it in the fixture, it, too, promptly popped.

This bulb also was replaced, but the same
thing occurred once again. I then called an
electrician to remove the fixture; so that
I could avoid further insults from your
personnel, he returned the fixture but was
unable to obtain a refund. He purchased another bulb and fixture from a different
manufacturer, and then successfully installed the fixture.

Even though I am on a limited income, the money I spent on the fixture (or even the continually blown bulbs) is not the issue. What is so shocking is the atrocious manner in which I was treated, the number of trips I had to make to Hardluck, and the eventual need to pay for the services of an electrician. It is obvious that I along with every other customer cannot depend upon your guaranteed satisfaction policy. It is even worse to think that one can be a loyal credit card customer for years and be treated so horribly.

I am certain that you will resolve this matter to my satisfaction immediately by providing me with a credit for the second, <u>working</u> light fixture.

Thank you, and I look forward to hearing from you within the next ten business days.

Sincerely,

Samantha J. Senior

In his written response to her—and, I might add, he got back to her in a far shorter period of time than her prescribed time limit—the Big Guy said that he appreciated that she had let him know of the problems she had experienced, not only with the fixture but also with the attitude of some of his employees. He promised to investigate the matter and to send someone in to work on customer service so that no further fault would be found with his store.

Just as the CEOs of the beer company and the hardware

ON COMMUNICATING WITH CUSTOMERS

At NABISCO, we value our consumers and realize that every time a consumer contacts us, we have an opportunity to build, cement, or repair a very important relationship. NABISCO's Consumer Affairs Department serves as the vital link between our consumers and our Company.*

chain found it difficult to ignore my poison pen, your letters can produce similar results. Maybe you will only get a letter of apology, but more than likely you will receive some or all of the recompense you desire. The company is the beneficiary if it satisfies that one customer who took the time to write, since there may be thousands of others who don't do so and instead just stop purchasing the company's service or product. "Mr. Big Boss" knows that word of mouth is sometimes the best form of advertisement. If he has done something to your mutual satisfaction, then you are going to talk about it. You are going to tell your friends and your neighbors, and they, too, will tell others who will trust this company and continue to do business with it. Because competition in today's business world is so feverish, almost all enterprises wish to assure further patronage through old and new customers.

Most heads of companies really are appreciative of a complaint letter as long as that letter is set forth in the manner I have described. Many, many of my clients have been greatly amazed at the steps that company leaders have been willing to take to correct a problem. Evidence of this attitude comes straight from the mouths of certain corporate executives.

Upon reflection, what can we really learn from these state-

*Karen J. Elam, Ph.D., and Senior Director of Consumer and Scientific Affairs.

ON CUSTOMER LOYALTY

We at Heineken USA are very interested in obtaining input from consumers. It helps us monitor the perception of our products relative to quality and image, the maintenance of which is critical to our continued success. In addition, learning about a negative experience helps us correct it, which will normally result in establishing strong loyalty from the affected consumer.*

ments? The philosophy of building, cementing, or repairing the relationship with the customer certainly holds at many responsible corporations. Also, one single person, the one "affected consumer," who complains for the hundreds and perhaps even thousands who don't may obtain results for all of us.

ON THE IMPORTANCE OF CUSTOMERS

Perhaps the Pepsi-Cola Company's reaction says it best:

We not only consider consumer letters (or phone calls) important—we've established an entire department to respond to them. And by "respond," I mean we thoroughly investigate any issue raised, gather the relevant facts and data, and report back to the consumer as quickly as possible. Consumers to us are anything but an interruption of our business. They are our business.†

---

*T. Daniel Tearno, Vice President of Corporate Affairs.
†Rebecca Madeira, Vice President of Public Affairs, Pepsi-Cola Company.

As you can see, whether you're complaining to a corporate giant like Pepsi-Cola or to a local pest exterminator, letter writing is an effective way to reduce the anxiety and stress that results in the course of modern-day trade. And as an added bonus, you may reap benefits, whether it's apologies or money, replaced merchandise, or just plain old peace of mind.

HELPFUL SERVICES AND AGENCIES

The American Society of Travel Agents handles disputes between consumers and its members, and may be reached at (703) 739-2782.

The *Consumer's Resource Handbook* lists consumer agencies and corporate contacts and may be obtained by writing the Consumer Information Center, Pueblo, CO 81009. Call (719) 948-4000 or by ordering from their website: www.pueblo.gsa.gov.

The Tele-Consumer Hotline provides information on special products and services, especially with regard to consumers with disabilities and on low income. Contact the Hotline at (800) 332-1124.

CHAPTER 4

Advice from the Legal Experts

> Never throw mud. You may miss your mark; but you must have dirty hands. —JOSEPH PARKER

N ow that you've decided to sit down and write the perfect poison pen letter, you must be careful that the "ink" doesn't splatter back in your face in the process. Yes, you may have gotten my instructions down to the nth degree, but maybe you decide that a little threatening language is in order to scare the Head Honcho into agreeing to your wishes. Don't do it. Tort laws concerning libel and defamation of character make it legally very tricky to say something about people and corporations that the *courts* may interpret as defamation or an attack on their good reputation. Words such as *unprofessional, lies,* and *misrepresentation* are ones we should use with care. There are other legalities you should consider whenever you're about to dash off a letter.

Tort laws have an enormous impact in our court systems. A tort action is loosely defined as any private or civil injustice, not including breach of contract, for which damages may be claimed by the wronged person. What it all boils down to is this: if someone is in the wrong and thus does an injury to you, that person or company must pay you any damages. Tort law covers any number of disputes, but for our purposes, of course, we'll narrow it down to what might occur when we write a letter of complaint.

Anyone who publishes a defamatory statement that he (A) knows is false, (B) cannot prove is true, or (C) states as fact rather than opinion is guilty of an indictable offense. The penalty can be up to five years in prison and big bucks in fines. Of course, if you have "proof positive" of your statements, then you're home free. Unfortunately, today many of us don't really think about these repercussions because we find ourselves all too often in a confrontational mode. We're angry about perceived or very real injustices, and we want to reassert our power. "Sue the Bastards" becomes our battle cry. Before we know it we have written something that may bring on *dismaying* consequence, tort.

We hear the terms *slander* and *libel* all the time, and often it's hard to tell the difference. *Defamation* is an attack on someone else's reputation, and both slander and libel are forms of defamation. Strictly defined, *slander* is a false statement maliciously spoken that damages a person's reputation. In the context of this book we're more interested in *libel*, which is defined as a *published*, that is, written, false statement that damages the good reputation of someone or something (for example, a company). Libel involves the *written* word. Read this chapter very thoughtfully because you probably do not want to write your next complaint letter from behind bars. I should know; I almost landed there myself.

Several years ago, after my daughter's wedding, I took her wedding dress to be cleaned at our local dry cleaners, a little neighborhood business that I had been patronizing for many years. When I returned to pick up the gown after it had been cleaned, I examined it carefully before I left the store. Immediately I noticed that there were spots on the dress that were not there when I first brought it in to be cleaned. When I asked to speak with the manager—let's call him "Mr. Obnoxious"—whom I knew on a first-name basis, he informed me that the spots *had* indeed been on the gown when it was brought in to be cleaned, that they were obviously some strange substance that had been spilled on the dress, and that the dry cleaner could not remove them. His tone intimated that I was trying to gouge money out of him to have the dress recleaned.

I must admit that I became a *little* upset at this point. After all, this was a man with whom I had done business for a long time.

I tried to tell him that all I wanted was for the dress to be recleaned, but he became louder and angrier and began shouting at me at the top of his lungs. Mind you, this was in front of a whole shop full of customers.

Swearing that it would be a waste of time to clean the dress again since the flaws couldn't be removed the first go-round, he continued ranting, "I'll never touch this dress again!" Furious and biting my tongue, which doesn't come naturally to a great many of us, I grabbed the wedding gown and left in a huff. At another nearby cleaners I was immediately informed not only that the dress could be restored perfectly but also that the spots were soft drink stains that had recently been spilled on the material. Because by now it had been several days since the wedding, I concluded that probably an employee at the first cleaners had accidentally spilled soda on the dress and was afraid to tell the owner (and with his temper, I surely didn't blame her!).

Dashing home, I immediately wrote a most venomous letter to the owner of the cleaners, with copies to all the other store owners in that small merchant association. I stated the facts as I've previously suggested you do, but I also did a little lambasting while I was on a roll. I felt this man was rude, hostile, hateful, and very unprofessional in his dealings with patrons, and I stated this in the letter as well. Less than a week later, I received a letter from the cleaner owner's attorney, stating that I had libeled his client and that the dry cleaner was suing me for $350,000 in damages. If I hadn't been so terribly frightened at that moment, it would have been laughable; yet at the same time I knew I was innocent because I had written only what I believed to be true.

I found a "mean as a junkyard dog" attorney and showed him my letter. Laughing, he explained that the wording of my letter didn't justify any libel claim from the dry cleaner. I had simply written my own opinions and, more important, I had stated them as such—as my opinions: *"In my opinion, Mr. Obnoxious behaved highly unprofessionally. . . . It is my belief that his rude and hostile conduct is detrimental to your Merchant Association."* Here was a lawyer after my own heart, for his next words to me were "Let's get him!"

He immediately wrote to Mr. Obnoxious's attorney bemoaning the fact that I had been caused most grievous mental and emotional anguish by both the verbal attack in the store and the threat of this lawsuit, and unless it was withdrawn immediately, I would countersue to the tune of $750,000. Neither my lawyer nor I heard a word from the other side ever again. Needless to say, I do not patronize that dry cleaner anymore, and I learned to be extra careful in phrasing any future accusations. From that time on, I made sure that in my poison pen letters and subsequently those I wrote for my clients I never, ever made any accusation without stating it as *personal opinion*.

Although I never again encountered a lawyer from the "other side," when I started Ellen's Poison Pen, Inc.®, I decided to consult with a few attorneys so that I'd know my legal limits when writing complaint letters. I myself surely didn't want to experience an unsettling situation like the one with the dry cleaner ever again, and by no means did I intend for my clients to do so. The lawyers I consulted had this to say:

❶ Don't embellish. *In most jurisdictions, the elements of defamation and libel are that you make an untrue statement about a person that diminishes that person in the eyes of a third party.*

❷ Stick to the facts. *This is the best way to avoid liability. Don't complain about a bald bartender by calling him a "skinhead" merely because you are angry. In fact, avoid any unnecessary language altogether. Recite the facts and separate them from the opinions: "I came into your establishment. I requested service. I was told to wait. Ten minutes later no one had waited on me, so I left." Then you can add your spin: "I believe this treatment to be rude and unprofessional, and I do not intend to frequent your establishment again." Avoid name-calling by pairing nouns with adjectives, such as "the rude salesclerk." Refer to the "clerk" and then state that in your opinion the treatment you received was "rude." Depersonalize the offending parties as much as possible, and concentrate on the effect their conduct had. More probably than not, it's the effect that will get you results anyway, and the* *cause will either be forgotten or only serve to impact someone else's livelihood.* [*]

3 Avoid claims for extortion. *While there is some risk of libel claims with complaint letters in general (particularly if you circulate copies), a greater risk may come from what, at first blush, may seem a much less likely source, a claim for extortion: "If you don't do x* [fire the waiter], *then I'm going to do y* [report your establishment to the authorities]*." Such a threat can be very risky. As the old expression goes: "He who represents himself has a fool for a client."* [†]

4 Less is more. *The initial impression you make may be the key to the ultimate resolution of your problem. A long, rambling complaint may give the impression that the writer is unfocused and the complaint is without merit.* [††]

5 Be careful of defamatory statements, which tend to expose a person to public scorn, hatred, contempt, or ridicule. *Publication communicates to a third party* [the recipient of a complaint letter that spews venom about a specific employee, for example] *who reasonably recognizes the statement as being defamatory to another.*

6 People shouldn't confuse what is considered permissible by voicing their thoughts or opinions in a written form during the heat of the situation. *Their own anger, innuendo, and belief that they have merely voiced their "opinion" when done in such a way for publication of that opinion to third parties may place them in a defensive posture to a defamation action.*

7 It is true that the pen is mightier than the sword. [But] *one must know that when one attacks with the pen, and*

---

[*]Arnold Wayne Jones, Esquire, The Law Office of Armando De Diego, PC, Dallas, Texas.
[†]Paul M. Haygood, Esquire, Correro Fishman Haygood Phelps Weiss Walmsley and Casteix LLP, New Orleans, Louisiana.
[††]John C. Morrison, Esquire, Morrison and Reynolds, Alexandria, Virginia.

*when the sword is swung, he must remember to duck or be pre-
pared to become a "client."**

Just be glad we live in a somewhat civilized society today. In
earlier times, some of the repercussions of making libelous statements make our present punishments look like a birthday party.
In Barbara Dill's book, *The Journalist's Handbook on Libel and
Privacy: The Most Comprehensive and Up-to-Date Guide to
Avoiding Lawsuits*, some *very* unusual punishments are brought
to light.† For example, if a person accused another of being a
coward in the primitive era of Iceland, the libel victim could
legally *kill* his accuser. One of the more humorous anecdotes
comes from the Norman period. If one person falsely accused
someone else of thievery, he had to publicly confess his remorse
by standing in the middle of town, holding his nose, and loudly
crying, "I'm a liar! I'm a liar!"

Dill also tells us that libel in early England was a serious matter indeed; those found guilty could have their tongues or ears
lopped off. She identifies three types of insults as leading to our
present idea of libel. Accusing someone of having bad manners
was tantamount to accusing that person of being a criminal. And
for heaven's sake, you never talked openly about someone's bad
health since that meant you were probably accusing him or her
of having the plague, leprosy, or syphilis. (So much for sympa-
thizing with friends about a mutual friend's migraines.) The
third form of libel occurred when a person "fingered" bad work-
manship, which was interpreted as calling a tradesman incompetent. So although today we do not suffer such awful consequences
for written slips, we still need to pay strict attention to what we
write, about whom we write, and to whom we write it.

You may think to yourself, "Hey, wait a minute. I'm not out to
extort or to libel anybody here." But there's a very fine line in the
unpredictable world of libel law, and without knowing what
you're doing, you might just cross it if you make a definite threat

---

*Robert H. Hillman, Esquire, Magazine & Hillman, PC, Rockville, Maryland.
†(New York: The Free Press, a division of Simon and Schuster, 1986).

in your complaint. As we learned earlier, it's imperative to avoid making extortion claims. Statements such as "If I do not receive the $499.65 that you owe me within the next two weeks, my attorney and I will see you in court" may see *you* there first, handcuffed to a deputy sheriff.

Also be careful of the rule concerning the "third party." It's important to remember Attorney Jones's definition of the elements of defamation. When you specifically attack by name and in writing a company's employee, for instance, and as a result that person loses his or her job or, perhaps, a salary increase, or something else, you've opened a can of worms, since you risk being named in a libel suit brought by that individual for "publishing" a statement that damaged that person's reputation.

Along these same lines, also beware of going to your local newspaper and paying for a big space on the front page where you proclaim that a company or person is unprofessional. It's always better to err on the side of prudence when you're complaining. As the French philosopher Jean-Paul Sartre once remarked, "Words are loaded pistols."

Let's say, for example, that a used car salesman (you know, the stereotypical one who is always showing up on *60 Minutes*) sells you a hot red convertible with a 25,000-mile odometer reading. Because it's that car of a lifetime you've always dreamed of owning, and the price is right, you buy it on the spot—many of us have given in to impulse at one time or another. Only after signing the next three years of your life away at the bank and forking over a couple of thousand dollars for a down payment do you realize that maybe, just maybe, you should have had the car checked out with your friend the local mechanic first. After racing to his shop with your *new* car, you're horrified when he tells you that the odometer has been rolled back and your dream car actually has been driven 125,000 miles!

Furiously you race back to "Mr. Smarmy," the salesman, only to discover to your indignant surprise that he refuses to refund your money. If you decide to proceed to writing a letter of complaint rather than taking legal action and you have "paper proof," such as an affidavit from your mechanic verifying that the odometer has been tampered with, you may certainly state that the salesman was a *"liar who misrepresented the facts surrounding the sale of this automobile."* On the other hand, if the matter of the mileage is just the salesman's word against yours, and you have nothing to back up your argument, the letter you send must be written very differently and very carefully. You can write *"I believe that Mr. Smarmy deliberately misrepresented the facts. I feel he is unprofessional. It is my view that his manner of doing business reflects negatively on your company"*—all statements that avoid defamation of character or libel and protect you from legal action. All citizens have the right to express their own thoughts *if* those thoughts are phrased appropriately.

Yes, we do have freedom of speech as defined by the First Amendment, but this isn't an absolute freedom. It doesn't preclude our responsibility not to libel someone else. Following are two sample letters—one I wouldn't recommend sending, and another one that gets my stamp of approval.

Not Recommended

Dear Mr. Used Car Dealer:

I find myself in an appalling and shocking situation due to flagrant misrepresentation on the part of one of your employees.

On November 8, 1998, I purchased a used convertible from Red Hot Cars in Salem, Massachusetts. I was assured by Steve Smarmy, that toupee-wearing liar, that this vehicle had been driven only 25,000 miles. Because I trusted the word of this totally unprofessional fast talker, I paid $2,000 down in cash and financed the other $18,000.

Only when I took the car to my own mechanic did I understand that your organization is in the business of swindling people.

As it turns out, the odometer had been rolled back, and the car's actual mileage is 125,000!

If I do not immediately receive my money back along with a verification that that lout Mr. Smarmy has been fired, I will hire a lawyer and sue both Red Hot and the Used-Car Corporation for $3 million.

Thank you.

Sincerely,

Thomas J. Trustin

Recommended

231 Outraged Avenue
Ireville, NC 36037
January 2, 1999

Bruce Used-Car, President/CEO
Used-Car Corporation
555 Service Circle
Anywhere, GA 99990

Dear Mr. Used-Car:

I recently purchased a used car from your dealership in Charlotte, North Carolina, and now I find myself in a shocking and appalling situation brought on by the actions of one of your employees.

On November 8, 1998, I purchased a used convertible from Red Hot Cars. The salesman, Steve Smarmy, assured me that this vehicle had been driven only 25,000 miles. Because I trusted his word, I paid $2,000 down in cash and financed the other $18,000 (documentation enclosed).

Only when I took my new car to my own mechanic, Enrico Earnest, did I understand what must have transpired. As it turns out, my mechanic confirms that the odometer had been rolled back, and the car's actual mileage is 125,000 (statement enclosed).

It is my personal belief that Mr. Smarmy had knowledge of this fact and deliberately misrepresented the truth in order to sell me this automobile. Because, in my opinion, he acted most unprofessionally, it places your dealership at risk for being thought of as cognizant of this action.

I am sure that you will wish to investigate this situation immediately and thoroughly. I look forward to both a reply and a check in the amount of the $2,000, which I paid to Red Hot, plus reimbursement of the $65 I paid the mechanic (receipt enclosed), within the next thirty days.

Thank you.

Sincerely,

Thomas J. Trustin

```
cc: Barry Reid, Administrator
    Governor's Office of Consumer Affairs
    2 Martin Luther King, Jr. Drive, SE
    Atlanta, GA 30334

    Alan S. Hirsch, Special Deputy Attorney General
    Consumer Protection Section
    Office of the Attorney General
    Raney Building
    P.O. Box 629
    Raleigh, NC 27602

    United States Department of Justice
    950 Pennsylvania Avenue, NW
    Washington, DC 20530
```

Since it contains only the facts, avoids claims for extortion, and is cautious about diminishing "Mr. Smarmy" in the "Eyes of the Third Party," the second letter is likely to get results and would not land you anywhere near a courtroom.

As a wise lady once told me, "Don't ever put in writing what you don't wish someone else to read." And caution is critical when phrasing complaint letters so as to avoid libel charges.

LAWYERLY ADVICE

Attorney John C. Morrison lends us some words of advice in conclusion:

Well-written letters of complaint that obtain results will benefit commercial efficiency and may help us as a society to return to a fundamental precept that "self-help" should be the first level of recourse for problem solving.

CHAPTER 5

Common Complaints I: Airlines, Automobiles, Restaurants, and Hotels

> Nothing succeeds so well as success.
> —TALLEYRAND

Once upon a time there lived a very odd family: a daddy, a mama, and a child. Everyone complained about their behavior, but the family didn't always know why. Perhaps it was their curious last name, they thought. It wasn't Smith or Jones or even McGillicuddy like their next-door neighbors, but what in the world could possibly be wrong with the name Corporation? All they really knew for certain was that they had no friends.

Early one afternoon, the dad, Victor Vehicle, told his wife, Annie Airline, to call their little boy. It was a fine day for a stroll through the woods.

"Henry Hospitality," shouted his mother, "let's hurry. Daddy wants to take a walk." Henry came a-running, and the Corporation family set out.

Now, they hadn't been gone too terribly long when a little girl appeared at the edge of the forest beside their home. She had long golden hair, but one pigtail was loose, and her bright pink dress was all dirty and torn. "Why, I declare," she thought to herself, "there's got to be someone living in that house to help me find my way home or my name isn't Carol Consumer!"

You see, Carol had wandered away from home, even after her mother told her that it was dangerous to go beyond the back gate.

Mrs. Consumer knew stories about the big, bad Corporation family who lived on the other side of the woods, and she didn't intend for Carol ever to have to face them.

Normally a very quiet child who never disobeyed or complained, this day Carol had decided to be a brave girl and set out on her great adventure. She had heard that all sorts of outlandish people lived on the other side (like the Corporations), but she was determined to judge for herself whether they were truly as rotten as her own family and friends proclaimed them to be.

Carol Consumer knocked on the big iron door (she was a very polite child), and when no one answered, she gently pushed open the door and peered in. "Is anyone home?" she called. But only silence greeted her. Hesitantly, she walked in only to gasp in surprise at the disarray inside the house!

Boxes and boxes and more boxes—little ones, larger ones, and even great humongous ones were piled up on top of each other. Why, Carol couldn't even see one single chair on which to rest her weary little legs. Taking a deep breath, she decided to investigate further, so she climbed up on top of one of the smaller boxes. All she could read was the word COMPLAINTS written on the ones she could reach. She couldn't understand why this family had hundreds of boxes labeled with this single word, until all of a sudden, it hit her. "Oh, no! This must be the Corporations' home!"

Scrambling down as fast as she could, Carol raced to the door only to be met by the unsmiling trio who lived there.

"Who's the unauthorized trespasser in my realm?" thundered Victor Vehicle.

"Who's been rude enough to walk into my domain?" screamed Annie Airline.

"I don't care about any of that," cried Henry Hospitality. "All I want to know is how this person is brave enough to come to visit. Did you come to play with me? I get awful lonesome."

Carol just froze right there in heart-pounding terror. The only thing scrambling around in her brain was the realization that she was face-to-face with the dreaded Corporation family, the very same *ones that all of her Consumer relatives talked about in hushed whispers after they believed the children were safe in bed at night.*

"I . . . I . . ." she could barely gasp. As the family looked searchingly at her, Carol, afraid to make a run for it, stared back. As she carefully looked at them, she realized something truly amazing, something her parents had never once mentioned. The Corporations were people, just like her! And the family suddenly knew, too, that this Consumer wasn't out to treat them with hostility or to serve them with a summons, or even to cuss at them. She was a person, too!

From that time on, Corporations and Consumers treated each other with respect and dignity, and they all lived happily ever after.

Now I know this tongue-in-cheek fairy tale is really pretty silly, but there's a point we consumers can take away. All of us need to realize that all of us—corporations and consumers, alike—are just people. When we appeal to those with whom we have a problem as individuals, politely and respectfully, chances are they will respond in kind.

I have handled very specialized needs for many of my clients, but there are certainly enough of what I term "common complaints" to go around. The majority of the complaint letters I write for folks concern "vehicles, airlines, and hospitality" (along with other common areas covered in the next chapter). All too many of us encounter one or more of these problems and wish to lodge some complaint about a product or a service. As you read through the information and the letters in this chapter, I expect you'll find at least one that suits your needs (but remember, the folks to whom we're complaining are all just *people!*).

● AIRLINES AND TRAVEL COMPANIES

Airlines

You're late. Late for the meeting you *must* attend in order to get the promotion and the 25 percent pay raise. Late for your best friend's wedding for which you're to act as maid of honor. Late, God forbid, for the funeral of a member of your own family. It's not your fault. You got to the airport. No, it's a shortcoming of the airline. Many of us have been foiled by an airline at one time or another. Strains of the lines "My bags are packed, I'm ready to go . . ." drift through the airport, but you don't leave. You sit, you wait, you look at the departure and arrival times, you get more and more steamed—all to no avail. The ticket agents are all performing a soft-shoe song and dance, and by this point you don't even care that you're grounded because your plane's engine is hanging on by a wing and a prayer; you just want to get the hell out of that airport and in the air to your destination. What do you do now?

No, it's not time to whip out your poison pen or the laptop, even if you desperately want to do so. Calmly find a customer service representative and ask to see **Airline Rule 250**. Although most airlines should have the rule handy at their desks, this little-known magical solution isn't well advertised. I keep a tiny copy in my billfold to remind me that even if you must travel on a different airline, your own Appalling Airlines *must* get you to your destination sooner than the one it chose for you. **Rule 95** is equally satisfying for delayed passengers because it guarantees a hotel room for one night. (Unfortunately, an airline may park you at *The Roach Motel from Hell*; so don't think that the Ritz Carlton or even a Holiday Inn necessarily awaits you.) Depending on the airline—and your attitude—the usual practice is to also provide both meals and transportation to and from the airport.

Also deserving of your attention is your means of rescue if you're bumped from a flight. So what if they overbooked by 110 percent, maybe your cab to O'Hare got a flat tire in the midst of downtown Chicago, and you check in a scarce five seconds later than the required one hour. Because the airline overbooked (and you're just a nanosecond tardy because of that flat), they may try to justify having sold your ticket to someone else or bumping you off the oversold flight. Take note, friends; also because of **Rule 250** and according to *Fly-Rights: A Consumer Guide to Air Travel*, (202) 366-1111, published by the U.S. Department of Transportation, if the next plane you're booked on lands between one and two hours later than your original arrival time, the carrier is to pay you the lesser of $200 or the cost of the fare. This rule also applies if you missed a connecting flight because of the delayed arrival of a prior flight. Even better, the sum rises to $400 or double the cost of your fare if you're delayed for more than two hours (four hours internationally). And, to make the pie a little sweeter, you can keep your original ticket to use for another flight. Caution, though: none of these rules applies if the delay is caused by unavoidable circumstances, such as lightning bolts striking the runway . . . or the engine hanging by a thread, and certainly not if your own "nanosecond" of lateness for check-in turns into minutes.

For domestic flights most carriers require that you arrive twenty minutes before the scheduled time of departure, but these days some may require that you arrive as much as an hour before departure. For overseas flights your required time of arrival for check-in can be up to three hours before departure because of security measures. Even if you hold advance boarding passes/seat assignments, arriving thirty minutes in advance of departure is usually the minimum. Be sure to check out the requirements of the airline you're travelling with, because if you fail to observe the airline's regulations (and the "unavoidable circumstances" are in play), the airline owes you nothing, although there are a few that still provide some sort of compensation, especially if you're dealing with someone with a sympathetic ear and your temper remains cool.

Federal regulations are clear, and by simply opening your mouth, perhaps a letter won't be *as* necessary. Don't allow the customer service representative to use his or her own talking talents to persuade you to accept a voucher as a replacement gesture unless that is what you want. You have the right to demand cash, and if you don't get it, you can actually sue. The Supreme Court has ruled that a suit for compensatory damages is allowed if you need to recover any losses caused by the delay. I don't know how many of us really want to take that route, though. The legal fees might quickly surpass any money we feel the airline owes us (or the amount we may potentially receive from the airline, since we can sue for damages only, not for lawyers' fees).

Another element to remember is that *timing* is the key to everything when you're dealing with airline complaints (or really any other kind, for that matter). Whether you voice your concerns directly to that gate agent or in a letter you write to the airline management as soon as you reach your destination, don't put off your huffin' and puffin'. Make your complaint known in a timely manner.

If for some reason the verbal approach doesn't work for you, perhaps because the agent refuses to comply with your request for the service you feel is due you, remember to

- ✎ take notes on what happens, what is said and done;
- ✎ document the fiasco, with receipts, boarding passes, credit card slips, and so forth; and
- ✎ prepare to write a poison pen letter the moment you get home or to your destination, while the events are still fresh in your mind (even better, begin a draft while you're waiting at the airport).

Take the following illustration of one poor woman who experienced not only delays, but also nasty personnel attitudes *and* lost and damaged luggage. Travelers everywhere can probably empathize with her problems.

571 Camden Street
Jackson, MS 53944
April 6, 1998

Frederick First-Class, President/CEO
Unfeeling Airlines, Inc.
111 Airline Avenue
Chicago, IL 60606

Dear Mr. First Class:

I have just been through an exasperating
and unbearable fiasco with Unfeeling Airlines, involving travel delays, lost and
damaged luggage, and rude treatment from
Unfeeling personnel. First, I want you to
be aware that this episode was preceded by
another one, which I will briefly relate.

In December 1997 I had a terrible experience flying with Unfeeling Airlines. My
luggage was placed on the wrong flight,
and as a result I had to wait twenty-four
hours while the airline tracked it down.
The lady with whom I originally spoke made
no effort to excuse the airline's ineptness
and issued me a $75 voucher. I also wrote to
you, and ultimately (several months later) I
received a very nice follow-up call from
Customer Service. I decided to use that $75
voucher to travel this past week. I decided
I would try travelling with Unfeeling one
more time.

Before I give you the scenario of what
has just transpired, let me emphasize that
there have been two wonderfully nice peo-

ple about whom I am writing commendations. On the other hand, you have a number of personnel working for you, primarily in your baggage claim office, whom I believe to be unprofessional. They are rude and hateful and take great happiness at the power they perceive themselves to have at the expense of _your_ customers, in my opinion.

1. 4/4/98: My plane was due to depart Washington's National Airport (DCA) at 4:15 P.M. for Nashville, Tennessee. Because of the weather in Florida, Alabama, and Tennessee, I called the 800 information agent to _make sure_ that no flights would be cancelled. I emphasized that I would pay to change my travel to Thursday rather than take a chance of being stranded in Atlanta. The woman I spoke with _assured_ me that there would be _no_ cancellations, and that even though the flights on the smaller planes had been cancelled to Nashville, my jet's flight would not be. Since I trusted she had checked out the situation, I went on to the airport and departed.

Of course, the weather was atrocious, and upon my arrival at Hartsfield Airport in Atlanta, I found that all flights to Nashville had been cancelled. Luckily, my father had had the foresight to contact someone from Customer Service for assistance, and one of the persons about whom I will write a commendation had already arranged to get me to Columbus, where my sister lives. The gate agent in Atlanta _assured_ me that I had over an hour until this departure and that there would be absolutely no problem getting my luggage on that plane. Three hours later we finally departed, but when I arrived in Columbus, I had no luggage. I filled out a claim and was told that my luggage would arrive on the 10:00 flight the next morning; otherwise, it would go on to Nashville.

2. 4/5/98: At my sister's in Columbus, I spent the entire morning on the telephone—to Nashville's airport to your 800 baggage claim number. Not only was my suitcase not in a logical place, but no one had any idea whatsoever of its whereabouts! I might add that both the claims agent in Nashville and one person with whom I spoke at Customer Service stated that there was no excuse for the luggage not to have been placed on the plane headed to Columbus given the three-hour delay! My last attempt to speak with someone at the 800 claims number was met with no helpful response; a woman informed me that there was no way she could tell me anything. When I tried to explain to her that I had to leave Columbus in one hour to get to my original destination, Nashville, she very bluntly told me that this was my problem. When I asked about the airline paying for some clothes for me (remember, I had nothing), she said, "That's not my problem. If we don't find your luggage in five days, then maybe we can talk about some reimbursement." At that moment, I asked to speak with her supervisor. Not only did she say she had none; she then refused to identify herself. When I threatened to call any- and everyone I could think of, newspapers included, she

admitted she did have a "floor manager"--
Mr. Doofus. I asked to speak to him. After
being placed on hold for almost ten minutes (deliberately, I am sure), she said
that he was on another call. I told her
that I was leaving at 12:30 and insisted
that he call me before that time, as I
needed to know what to do. Even though I
waited until almost 1:00 to leave, he never
returned my call--again, I am positive that
this was deliberate on his part. My biggest
regret is that I was unable to obtain the
name of this woman.

When it became evident that Mr. Doofus was
not going to return my call, I called Customer Service and finally got through to a
Ms. Sweetie in Los Angeles--the only other
person who tried to be of any assistance
and consolation. She was appalled at the
manner in which I had been treated and
assured me that Unfeeling would reimburse
me for up to $150 for clothing, etc.

3. 4/6/98: My luggage was finally located
(even though I still have been unable to
discover where it had been all this time)
and was delivered to my parents' home at
approximately 3:00 P.M.

I understand completely that the terrible
weather was a factor in this nightmare,
and I would far rather have been delayed
than have been exposed to any possible danger. But I am concerned about the horrific
way that I was treated, the lies that I was
told, and the general lack of concern
demonstrated by most of your personnel.

To add insult to injury, when I returned to Washington today, my suitcase was damaged!

I have travelled with Unfeeling for years, but I would not dream of flying with your airline again given my last two experiences. I am sending my replacement clothing and essentials receipt to Los Angeles, but I also insist that my suitcase be replaced.

I have enclosed copies of my tickets, my receipts, and my baggage claims forms. I certainly expect you to investigate this matter and to respond to my letter within the next two weeks.

Thank you.

Sincerely,

Elizabeth Enraged

cc: The Honorable Rodney Slater, Secretary
    United States Department of Transportation
    400 Seventh Street, SW
    Washington, DC 20590

    Office of Intergovernmental and Consumer
    Affairs
    United States Department of Transportation
    400 Seventh Street, SW
    Washington, DC 20590

    Federal Aviation Administration
    Aviation Consumer Protection Division
    800 Independence Avenue, SW
    Washington, DC 20591

Leyser Q. Morris
Special Assistant Attorney General
Director, Office of Consumer Protection
P.O. Box 22947
Jackson, MS 39225-2947

This beleaguered traveler may have initially lost both her flight and her luggage, but the result of her complaint letter was a brand-new suitcase.

The naval officer who found himself in the situation outlined in the following letter should have rowed, rowed, rowed his boat instead of depending on this one particular airline.

1467 View Terrace Drive
Newark, NJ 33300
May 1, 1997

Horace Hangar, President/CEO
Atrocious Airlines
777 Pilot Street
Los Angeles, CA 99999

Dear Mr. Hangar:

As a loyal customer and frequent flier of Atrocious Airlines, I am appalled by my most recent experience with your airline. Although some attempt has been made to respond to my concerns, I strongly feel that Atrocious Airlines must take full responsibility for the expenses I incurred and the hardship I suffered as a result of the airline's malfunctioning equipment.

I am a Navy officer. On April 3, 1997, I boarded Flight 3503 from Newark, New Jersey, to Ft. Lauderdale, Florida. The flight was scheduled to depart at 0600. I purposely booked myself on the first available flight that day to ensure ample time for joining my vessel at 1:00 P.M. After we had boarded, the attendant informed us that the plane had engine trouble, and we would have to deplane and wait for the next available flight. I still had time to make my vessel's departure, even though I lost approximately one and a half hours.

After we had boarded the second plane (Flight 1901, to depart at 0730), we were once again notified that this plane, too, had problems--brake malfunction. Once more I deplaned to await another flight. Unfortunately, the next scheduled departure on any airline would arrive in Florida too late for me to connect with my vessel; I ended up being one and a half hours late.

Because of the mechanical malfunctions of two Atrocious airplanes, one a turbo prop, the other a jet, I lost four days of work on my vessel, which meant four days of pay equaling $1016. In addition, the chief mate, whom I was scheduled to replace, had no choice but to remain on board and fill in for me. This absence did not endear me to my superiors or to my coworker, nor did it instill confidence in my dependability as a seaman.

I realize that nothing can be done to change what happened, yet I strongly feel that refunding the cost of my flight hardly begins to address my loss of pay and the damage my professional reputation has suffered. It is my belief that Atrocious Airlines should reimburse me for my lost wages ($1016), write a letter to my superior officer taking full responsibility for my absence on the vessel, and, in addition, offer me a free round-trip ticket to anywhere in the United States.

I have patronized your airline for many years, both in my professional and in my personal life. I am certain that your expectations of employee and airplane performance should reflect reliability and teamwork at a minimum. The United States Navy expects no less. I can assure you that back-to-back malfunctioning airplanes do not inspire consumer confidence in your airline.

I am sure that you will address this matter promptly, and I look forward to your reply within the next ten business days.

Thank you.

Sincerely,

Alvin Aggravated (Lieutenant, USN)

cc: [The same people and organizations were copied here as in the previous letter, with the addition of Lieutenant Aggravated's commanding officer and the Secretary of the Navy.]

The lieutenant did not receive the $1016 or his round-trip ticket to anywhere in the United States, but his superior officer did get the requested letter of justification.

Travel Companies

Sometimes your airline performs just fine, and it's the travel company with which you have problems.

Sheila Daniel of Huntsville, Alabama, dreamed of basking in the Hawaiian sun with her own personal male hula dancer swaying at her side. To her delight, one day she saw a travel agency ad in the newspaper that seemed too good to be true. It turns out it was.

```
                        190 Western College Road
                        Huntsville, AL 19022
                        May 15, 1998


Mr. U. R. Flawed, President
Unethical Travel Services, Inc.
971 Palm Avenue
Miami Springs, FL 55309

Dear Mr. Flawed:


I am appalled at the misrepresentation that
took place concerning four round-trip air-
line tickets that I purchased from Frank-
lin Fibber of Unethical Travel Services
of Miami, Florida. Instead of receiving
the four round-trip airline tickets from
Unethical Travel Services as promised, I
received vouchers from the company Liars,
Liars, Pants on Fire. Not only had the com-
pany Liars, Liars not been mentioned by
your travel agency, but the vouchers con-
tained stipulations about which I knew
absolutely nothing.
```

On February 23, 1993, there was an ad in the
Huntsville Times newspaper in Huntsville,
Alabama. A copy of the ad is enclosed. As
you can see, it refers only to airline tickets. I called the number listed, which was
Unethical Travel, and spoke with Ms. Prissy
and Mr. Feeble on several occasions within
a twenty-four-hour period to ask questions
and to verify the information presented in
the ad. I explained to both agents that I
was interested in tickets only as I already
had a place to stay in Hawaii. I was assured
by both Prissy and Feeble that the entire
deal was only for airline tickets, that I
could transfer two of the tickets over to
my sister and her husband, who would leave
from Chicago to go to Hawaii, and a friend
and I could use the other two tickets to
leave from Huntsville. Several times I
asked whether there were any other costs
involved or any other stipulations. I was
repeatedly assured that what I was purchasing was only airline tickets and that
there were absolutely no other strings attached.

On February 25, a Federal Express service
person came to my home and picked up a check
for $599. After I did not receive any cor-
respondence from Unethical Travel, I called
the firm on March 5 and was told that the
airline tickets were being mailed to me
that day. On March 12, I received a pam-
phlet containing five vouchers from Liars,
Liars. The vouchers stipulated that in
order to use our airline tickets we had to
stay a minimum of seven nights at a resort
or hotel of their choice, at an estimated
cost of $99 per person per night. On March

13, I called Liars, Liars and spoke with a representative who confirmed that in order to use the airline tickets, we would have to purchase hotel/resort accommodations. I tried to explain to the representative that I was not aware of any requirements being attached to the airline ticket offer. I was then told again that I could not use the airline tickets unless I purchased hotel/resort accommodations. I was also informed that any complaints I had should be directed to Unethical Travel Services.

I immediately called your agency and was informed that no one was in who could help me and that my call would be returned later that same day. The call has never been returned. I have repeatedly tried to reach Unethical Travel Services; finally on March 13 I reached a real person and asked to speak to the manager. She very rudely stated that Liars, Liars was no longer affiliated with Unethical and that I needed to contact the detective in charge of the Economic Crime Unit [the actual investigator].

I did as advised, and the detective told me that the deal was a scam; she had received numerous reports of the same nature, and she was investigating the matter. At this point I notified the legal department of the bank where I hold my checking account. The check had cleared on March 3 with a Terry Thief's endorsement on the back with the number 11111 under his name. I notified the <u>Huntsville Times</u> newspaper about the ad they had run. I also notified Federal Express, and they documented the matter. I am presently still trying to reach Liars, Liars, but no one answers the phone there.

I believe that Unethical Travel should be held responsible for this misrepresentation, which is criminal fraud, whether the company originated the misrepresentation or not. Your company was associated with Liars, Liars in this matter when I purchased the tickets, and since the vouchers were issued in the course of this association, I feel that Unethical should take back the vouchers and refund the $599 immediately.

I expect to hear from you within five business days concerning an immediate and full refund of the $599.

Thank you.

Sincerely,

Sheila Daniel

cc: United States Department of Justice
    Federal Bureau of Investigation
    Fraud Division
    Washington, DC 20535

    Direct Marketing Association
    1111 Nineteenth Street, NW, Suite 1100
    Washington, DC 20036

    Dennis Wright, Chief Director
    Consumer Affairs Division
    Office of the Attorney General
    11 South Union Street
    Montgomery, AL 36130

Although she never saw hide nor hair of her money, Ms. Daniel felt more than vindicated. The letter we wrote prompted an investigation by the FBI! The scam artists were chased the length and breadth of Florida, arrested, prosecuted, and now languish not on the silver sands, but behind bars.

Unfortunately, this wasn't an isolated event. There are too many unethical individuals—aka scam artists—searching for victims, and each of us must become an informed consumer. If we become familiar with agencies like state and federal con-

CUSTOMER LETTERS

As is evidenced in the following quotes by corporate leaders in the airline business, some people do listen to and "address the matter promptly." Herbert D. Kelleher, CEO, president, and chairman of the board of Southwest Airlines offers his thoughts:

Customer letters, whether disapproving or complimentary, are a gauge by which Customer Satisfaction and product effectiveness are measured. At Southwest Airlines, we read and respond to all of our mail, and we use it to track trends, adjust our procedures, and train our Employees.

In essence, an influential letter delivers a handshake, suggests eye contact, and makes a favorable impression on the reader. Powerful letters are also concise, factual (offering dates, city-pairs, and flight numbers), and attractively packaged.

People who read and respond to consumer mail, no matter the company, are taxed and frustrated when they must struggle to decipher scribbles on Big Chief paper, or search for pertinent information. Likewise, they are demeaned by (and often less sensitive to) customers whose letters are hateful, profane, derisive, or unattractive.

SATISFYING CUSTOMERS

Delta Air Lines, Inc. also believes in consumer satisfaction. In the words of Mr. Ronald W. Allen, chairman, president, and CEO:

Delta intends to become the leader in customer satisfaction among U.S. air carriers. To do that, we put customers first. We listen to what they say about their needs and wants and how we are meeting them so that we can create products and services that meet their expectation—every day on every flight. No customer request is too small.

sumer protection offices and the National Fraud Information Center, we can avoid being sucked into the net of the corrupt and becoming victimized ourselves. Advice on protecting yourself can be found throughout *Shocked, Appalled, and Dismayed!*

Always watch out for any travel offer that you don't seek out for yourself (that is, they call you). There are just too many unscrupulous travel companies out there waiting in line to steal your money and run with it. Also if you're told to make out a check to a certain "company" you are unfamiliar with, or to Joe Blow, the manager, hang up quick. If an outfit wants money in advance, you can just about bet your bottom dollar that it's a scam. If you absolutely positively cannot help yourself and you fall into the Scam Swamp, at least make sure you've allowed yourself a safety net or two. One way to protect yourself in the event of a bad deal is to use your credit card. If you don't get what you paid for, you can get your account credited (see Chapter 5). Use lots of caution, though; when you use your credit card you always run the risk that the crooks will use your card number to make unauthorized charges. If you write a check, you could face similar difficulties. Unscrupulous people have been known to find a way to withdraw money from your bank account. Never give out your mother's maiden name to such people.

It's always a good idea to request copies of the agent's brochure or a contract before you shell out any money or give somone your credit card number. You can't rely on good-faith promises if the guy is felonious.

If you sense you have been scammed, act right away. Call your credit card company or your bank and inform them of the situation. Then contact your state consumer protection office to check out the business or write and/or call the **National Fraud Information Center,** 815 Fifteenth Street NW, Suite 928-N, Washington, DC 20005, (800) 876-7060.

According to Jodie Bernstein, director of the FTC's Bureau of Consumer Protection, in an article that appeared in *Leisure Living,* "*Consumer complaints about travel consistently rank among the top five categories in an FTC* [Federal Trade Commission]– *Attorney General complaint system, and annual losses to travel-related fraud are estimated to exceed $12 billion.*"* We are further reminded in this article that unscrupulous persons, just like the ones Ms. Daniel encountered, offer an inexpensive and enticing travel package and then reel in unsuspecting consumers, just like their biggest catch of the day. Bernstein asks us to follow some valuable counsel: "*Buy vacation travel only from a business you know, get the details of your vacation and any refund policy in writing before you pay.*"

If you think you've been defrauded or simply want to be extra vigilant in the future, *Leisure Living* recommends ordering the following guides: **Travelers' Advisory: Get What You Pay For; Telemarketing Travel Fraud;** and **Timeshare Resales.** These publications may be acquired by calling (202) 326-2222 or by writing the **Federal Trade Commission, Public Reference**

---

*"FTC Launches Campaign Against Vacation Frauds," *Leisure Living,* June 1997, p. 19.

Branch, Room 130, Sixth Street and Pennsylvania Avenue, NW, Washington, DC 20580. (I'm telling you, there's just no end to the many uses of this tool!) This branch of the FTC is also useful if you're lost in the arms of disreputable dating services, as we'll see later on.

● AUTOMOBILES

"A car, a car, my kingdom for a car!" I'm having a little fun with the "horse" quote from Shakespeare's *Richard III*, but I'm not too far off the mark, since most people over the age of eighteen own or drive a car. We may long for the good old days when we could walk to the post office or the park, but the truth is that hardly any of us could survive without a car. Today an automobile is no longer a frivolous purchase; it's a necessity, and an expensive one at that.

As our dependency on automobiles grows, so too does our need to be ever vigilant about defective vehicles—both new and used—and shoddy repairs. There are defective automobiles slipping past the quality controllers more often than we like to think. When the vehicle of our dreams transforms into our worst nightmare, sometimes returning to the place of purchase just doesn't work. It has been my experience that out of the gobs of complaint letters I write, the most frustrating for both the clients and for me are those having to do with automobiles. These are usually the ones that take more than one letter and *lots* of follow-ups.

Consumer Smarts for Automobile Buyers

The affliction I call "lemonitis" is unfortunately more and more prevalent these days. Most states now provide automobile purchasers with a lemon law consumer guide. The *Virginia Lemon Law's Consumer Guide*, written by Attorney Stephen L. Swann, defines *lemonitis* as a

> *serious, stress-induced disorder, sometimes debilitating, and accom-*
> *panied by financial, emotional, and occasionally life-threatening*
> *symptoms. Known to attack nervous systems of some purchasers of*
> *new automobiles with significant impairments to use, or market*
> *value, or safety. Complications frequently caused by disgusting*
> *attitudes of dealer service managers and manufacturer representa-*
> *tives. Prognosis generally favorable with early diagnosis, good doc-*
> *umentation, toughness of character, and aggressive advocacy.*

The definition may be humorous, but the reality is not.

Given what's at stake with automobile safety, a defective car poses a much more serious problem than does a defective CD player. The best bet is to do extensive research on a car before you buy it. In the long run, this may save you not only money but a lot of headaches to boot. By heeding the following advice you should be able to minimize the chances that you will become saddled with a lemon:

1 Read consumer magazines. Any library in any town or city has a load of consumer magazines on hand that you can study before you start shopping for a car or anything else. One good source is the *Consumer Information Catalog,* which you can order via e-mail at www.pueblo.gsa.gov on the General Services Administration's Web site or by writing to the Consumer Information Center, Pueblo, CO 81009.

2 Contact the **Public Reference Section of the Federal Trade Commission,** (202) 326-2222 (see page 110), and the **Center for Auto Safety** (see page 72) for new-car–buying hints, such as negotiating a price, trading in your old car, and entering into service contracts.

3 Shop around for the vehicle of your choice and for the best finance institution.

4 Get quotes from several dealers and ask whether the price listed reflects any available rebates. If you can find the car of your dreams with a manufacturer's rebate, then more power to you (and more jingle in your own pockets). Get the dealer's invoice price for the car and for any options you're interested in. That electric sunroof could end up costing you an arm and a leg if you don't know what it costs before you begin negotiations. Go to your local library and find consumer publications, such as *Car and Driver* and the FTC's *Best Sellers*, that will provide you with the kind of information you need to make a wise decision.

5 Carefully inspect the car, new or used.

6 Get your local mechanic to inspect the vehicle as well.

7 Don't be pressured into signing a contract too quickly. Before signing a contract, make sure your decision is final. Make sure you read and understand the contract before signing your life away, and never sign before you've made your final decision. It's sometimes awfully easy to succumb to high-pressure tactics, and car salespeople are notorious for being the best there is with such measures. One rule of thumb to remember is if you're surrounded by the salesperson, his manager, and *his* manager and they're all putting the screws to you, just get up and walk out. That'll teach 'em! Seriously, the same car and the same people will still await you with open arms if and when you decide to return. Even better, the mass coercion will probably have eased somewhat, because you've demonstrated that you won't be pushed.

Let's say that after careful research, you've decided to buy a certain car, sunroof and all. You drive it home, never dreaming that this brand-new, top-quality *high-priced* automobile, van, or truck suffers from that miserable condition—lemonitis. It stands to reason that it should be easy for you to return or exchange this dud for a good one, right? Not necessarily. Despite what the lemon laws generally state—that if a vehicle can't be "repaired to standard" (that is, the car cannot be put into acceptable condition) in a reasonable amount of time and after a reasonable number of attempts, the owner is entitled to either a replacement or his or her money back—the consumer product that is the hardest for which to receive action, regardless of the problem, is the automobile, even when lives are literally at stake. But if you have made numerous complaints about the car and have made repeated trips to the dealership or to the mechanic in an effort to fix even one problem (for example, the brakes), you're more likely to have the law work in your favor. It will certainly help, however, if you document each and every occurrence, no matter how insignificant you feel it is. It's the accumulation of numerous complaints that may truly transform your problem from an ordinary one to one that is actually redressed.

But before writing a poison pen, you need to be aware of what you may and may not reasonably expect from manufacturers and automobile dealerships. A summary of this information can be obtained by sending a self-addressed envelope, with a fifty-five-cent stamp, to **Lemon Law Summary, Center for Auto Safety,** 2001 S Street, NW, Suite 410, Washington, DC 20009. The Center for Auto Safety is also a great resource because it monitors auto deficiencies. Even when the law is on your side, don't expect that getting your exchange or refund will be a piece of cake.

If it's a used car like that "hot red convertible" mentioned in Chapter 4 that beckons to you, first call the **Auto Safety Hotline** at (800) 424-9393 to get any relevant recall information. If the car dealer is legitimate, he must perform any necessary recall work for free regardless of the age of the car. Another tip is to inspect the car in broad daylight when you can eyeball any and all deficiencies. Test-driving during the day is also preferable. Your mechanic should be the only one to give the "Good Housekeeping Seal of Approval" to your prospective purchase, so get the vehicle checked out before you sign anything. Also, before money changes hands, ask questions about the previous owner and mechanical problems he or she might have had. Don't stop there, either; personally contact the former owner to find out about any problem or accident that might have occurred. Be a smart consumer. Get everything in writing in case a poison pen letter becomes necessary. This includes records of recent repairs, replaced parts, accident reports, and so forth. To be extra cautious, examine the car yourself using an inspection checklist. Checklists can be obtained from magazine articles, books, and Internet sites that deal with buying a used automobile.

Repairs

Whether they're purchased new or used, cars will inevitably need repairs, and repair shops certainly receive a large portion of automotive-related complaints. Sometimes your car just breaks down owing to regular wear and tear. But what about problems that arise when some idiot runs a red light and slams into your back door? The least awful scenario is that you aren't injured or killed but your car needs emergency medical assistance. What should you do in matters like this? Make sure you *check out* the auto body repair shop before you take *Old Injured* in for surgery, and even if you like the first estimate, get more than one—in writing. Be extra thorough, because if the mechanic doesn't know his business well enough, you could be worse off afterward than before you placed our vehicle in the "hospital."

Or perhaps you're facing a routine repair. Here's a familiar scenario: *Old Injured's* starter has just been replaced to the tune of $299.99. You drive it home, and the next morning when you jump into the driver's seat, switch on the ignition, and pump the pedal, absolutely nothing happens—zero, zip, nada! Your car is once again as dead as a doorknob, and you're out $300. You frantically call the mechanic who not so gently advises you to get lost. Your poisonous juices begin to flow, and a letter similar to the following goes flying through the mail.

729 Maddened Lane
Burlington, VT 05679
October 24, 1998

Melvin Mutilate, Owner
Mechanics-R-Us
1117 Pea Brain Parkway
Burlington, VT 05680

Dear Mr. Mutilate:

On October 19, 1998, I took my 1996 Plymouth Neon into your shop for repairs. Your
mechanic, Ubee Mistaken, assured me that
the starter needed to be replaced. Unfortunately, I believed this diagnosis, and
Mr. Mistaken performed the replacement for
$299.99 (copy of receipt enclosed).

On October 22, I picked up my automobile
from Mechanics-R-Us and drove it home with
the full assurance that I would have no
further problems with the starter. But the
following morning the engine only made a
grinding sound and would not turn over.
After ascertaining that the problem was
not with the battery, I immediately called
Mr. Mistaken, and I was subjected to total
rudeness and, in my opinion, utter unpro-
fessionalism. His remark to me when I questioned the nonworking starter was, "I did
the repair that was necessary. If you call
me again, I'll report you to the police." He
then called me a vulgar name and abruptly
hung up on me.

I may have neglected to investigate Mechanics-R-Us's credentials, but I did speak with

Mr. Mistaken prior to taking in my car. I mistakenly believed that his (and, there-fore, the management's) integrity was not in question. I was obviously in error.

I expect an immediate refund of the $299.99 and a letter of apology from Ubee Mistaken, as well as one from you as the owner of this business.

Thank you, and I expect to hear from you within the next five business days.

Sincerely,

Fred Furious

Enclosure

cc: John Hasen, Assistant Attorney General and Chief
    Public Protection Division
    Office of the Attorney General
    109 State Street
    Montpelier, VT 05609-1001

    Bruce Martell, Supervisor
    Consumer Assurance Section
    Office of the Attorney General
    120 State Street
    Montpelier, VT 05620-2901

    Federal Trade Commission
    Sixth Street and Pennsylvania Avenue, NW
    Room 240
    Washington, DC 20580

Mr. Furious didn't check out this repair shop before bringing in his ailing car. But you should know better. There are certainly some steps you can take so that you will have better success with automobile repair services. Contacting AAA or your local Chamber of Commerce, or asking your neighbors for their recommendations will help in your search.

Should a letter not do the trick, further action may be necessary. Some states, cities, and counties have particular laws dealing with specific aspects of car maintenance and repair, such as mandatory arbitration panels (more on this in Chapter 8). Find out what is applicable to your situation by contacting your state or consumer protection office, which is part of the attorney general's office. See the appendices for further information about these agencies.

If something does go wrong with your new or used car and a dispute arises, first try to resolve the issue with the owner of the dealership. But if the dealer disagrees with you (see Mr. Livid's letter and the dealership's response in the following section) or the service or coverage under your warranty doesn't cover the existing problem, contact the local representative of the manufacturer. This zone representative has the authority to adjust your coverage under the warranty and make decisions about repairs. As a matter of fact, even if your car is still covered under warranty but the specific problem is not, the zone representative may be able to assist you in obtaining repairs free of charge.

If you bought your car from a franchised dealer, you may be able to seek mediation (see Chapter 8, "Sue or Arbitrate?") through the Automobile Consumer Action Program (**AUTO-CAP**) at (703) 821-7144. It is a dispute resolution program that is nationally coordinated by the National Automobile Dealers' Association and handles the automakers listed in the appendices. Check with the dealer association in your locale to see if a mediation program is offered. You should also know about **AUTOLINE,** an arbitration program sponsored by the Council of Better Business Bureaus, at (800) 955-5100, that covers other automakers (see the appendices).

DEALING WITH CUSTOMERS

Certainly, your first step in launching a complaint having to do with your car should be to contact not only the dealer but the manufacturer. Toyota Motor Sales, U.S.A., Inc., supports this advice. Mamie Warrick, Corporate Customer Relations Manager, shares Toyota's commitment statement as well as some ideas of her own.

Our dedication to product satisfaction is only surpassed by our dedication to customer satisfaction. She adds, *Toyota makes every effort to manufacture a quality product. Both consumer opinion and perception play an active role in our ongoing efforts to lead the automobile industry in quality, innovation, styling, and reliability. It is through communications from the customer that we become aware of their reactions and expectations.*

And, of course, there's always small claims court, where you can resolve disputes involving small amounts of money for a low cost to you and often without an attorney. Check with the clerk of your local small claims court to find out how to file a suit and what the dollar limitation is in your state.

Car Dealerships and Repairs

If you've tried communicating verbally with the manufacturer and it hasn't worked, once again it's time to resort to the power of the pen. The following example illustrates a case wherein Lawrence Livid needed to administer a dose of poison to get some action on his defective "exfoliating" vehicle.

1367 Pinewood Drive
Waldorf, MD 22456
May 30, 1997

Peter Peeler, President/CEO
Rusto Automobile Company
1012 Peeling Parkway South
Detroit, MI 77777

Dear Mr. President Peeler:

Having purchased Rusto automobiles for
all of my adult life, I now find myself in
a shocking situation for which no one seems
to desire to help.

In 1991, I purchased a used 1990 Zoomer in
Miami, Florida, made by Hard-Body Motors
Corporation; the vehicle currently has
130,000 miles on the odometer. The problem
is that the paint has begun to peel off in
large patches over the last year. (Please
find enclosed photo.) I have spoken to a
representative from Rusto's corporate office as well as to the local dealer, Sam
Slimy, with no success. The only excuse I
was given was that those "clear coat paints
need a lot of wax." Mr. Slimy did offer to
paint the vehicle for a reduced rate; however, the reduced rate was well over $500.

Five hundred dollars is a great deal of
money to me. After only seven years, I find
it totally inexcusable that a product from
such a giant name as Rusto, famous for
its customer loyalty, is experiencing such
drastic problems. Although I appreciate the
offer from the local dealer, it is simply unacceptable. I feel that as one who has pur-

chased your company's automobiles for many,
many years, I am owed at least a paint job,
cash toward a paint job, or even perhaps a
voucher toward my next Rusto purchase. It
was my intent, now that the odometer has
reached the mileage that it has, to buy
another Rusto car in the very near future;
yet I certainly cannot see this as a feasi-
ble solution unless I receive some satisfactory resolution to this problem.

Let me reiterate that I have been faithful
to your company. I have always been satisfied with my purchases, and I have sent
many of my friends over the past years to
purchase your vehicles. I do expect that
this loyalty be reciprocated and that you
will relieve me of my burden with this
problem. I am sure that you, too, find
it unreasonable that a properly applied
paint job at the factory would peel off
after only seven years of normal wear and
tear. I have performed extensive research
and have found that a number of vehicles
in this same age, class, and type are
exhibiting the same problem, so it is not
just my own automobile. Perhaps this may
be something of a recall issue. At any rate,
I am sure that after prompt investigation
of this matter, you will see fit to send me
money for a new paint job.

Thank you, and I look forward to hearing
from you by June 20.

Sincerely,

Lawrence Livid

cc: Customer Relations Manager
    Washington, DC Zone Office
    Hard-Body Motors Corporation
    P.O. Box 773
    Baltimore, MD 21205

    Manager, Consumer Affairs
    Automotive Consumer Action Program
    8400 West Park Drive
    McLean, VA 22102

    William Leibovici, Chief
    Consumer Protection Division
    Office of the Maryland Attorney General
    200 St. Paul Place
    Baltimore, MD 21202-2021

CUSTOMER INQUIRIES

American Honda Motor Company, Inc.'s company philosophy is, *"Maintaining an international viewpoint, we are dedicated to producing products at the highest efficiency, yet at a reasonable price for worldwide customer satisfaction."*—Sharon Mann Garrett, Coordinator for Corporate Public Relations at Honda, assures us,

Since the founding of American Honda, we have been a customer-driven company, and we consider consumer letters to be instrumental in maintaining our product and service quality. American Honda's Customer Relations department handles a large volume of inquiries from our consumers, many of which are letters. Every letter received is answered by a professional Honda Customer Relations Representative. Once a customer issue is resolved, the consumer receives a survey where he may rate Customer Relations' handling of his inquiry.

Perhaps one of the more absurd responses ever received in the history of complaints came from the service manager of the dealership where Mr. Livid purchased his minivan: *"The car was manufactured in North Dakota where you know the weather is brutal and 'they' use rock salt and all that."* After I wrote a couple of follow-up letters for Mr. Livid, an investigation was eventually launched. The Federal Trade Commission sank its teeth into the complaint, and, with any luck, the case of the scaly minivan will be shaved—I mean solved.

Though it may take several letters and though you may hear far too many excuses, don't give up. Your efforts may be rewarded, especially if you can persuade a car manufacturer to put its money where its mouth is.

Here is another example of how a letter-writing campaign was useful for the owner of a car that had much more wrong with it than just a bad paint job. Jennifer Hamilton's car problems were about the most serious I've ever seen. Given the seriousness of the problems, neither Hamilton nor I ever dreamed that the initial letter, which follows, wouldn't receive the swiftest of results.

```
                        890 Anxious Avenue
                        Ramsey, NJ 10963
                        March 27, 1997


William Wanna-Injure, President/CEO
Lemon Automobile Corporation
1335 Car Avenue, Suite 587
San Diego, CA 88999


Dear Mr. Wanna-Injure:


As a long-time Lemon customer I have al-
ways been satisfied with my vehicles and
impressed with the help, service, and
courtesy of all Lemon personnel. My latest
```

Lemon vehicle, however, has recently caused me the greatest of emotional, physical, and mental anguish and <u>almost caused the death of my son.</u>

I leased a Danger V.I.D. #0000 at the Cruel Crook dealership in Ramsey, New Jersey, in February 1996. It had problems from the beginning, all of which are documented, including faulty security and electronic systems, untimely interior disintegration, and an ongoing problem with the power steering. In early December 1996 I again requested service at Cruel Crook because the airbag light began flashing on the dashboard, and I was still having problems with the power steering. I stated at that time that I did not wish the car returned to me unless all the problems had been rectified. The dealership arranged a rental car for one day, and then my car was released to me. The airbag light no longer flashed, but I was informed that the parts had been ordered and that I should return at a later date to the service department. Once again I questioned the safety of the car and was assured that everything was satisfactory.

On December 20 my son was returning home at 11:15 P.M. following a car that stopped abruptly without signaling. He had problems steering to avoid collision and was unable to avoid impact. He was wearing his seatbelt, which was indeed fortunate, for although both airbags deployed, the driver's side airbag did not inflate. Because the airbag did not inflate (please remember that the airbag light had been checked

only two weeks before, and I was assured of
the safety of the airbags), he was thrown
to the windshield on which he hit his
head, causing the windshield to crack. He
is still currently under the care of Dr.
Kindman, and everyone agrees that he is
indeed lucky to be alive.

Officer Helpful of the Ramsey Police Department and I. B. Trucking at Truckin'
Towing, who are familiar with accidents of
this nature and who were both present at
the scene of the accident, can verify each
fact that I have specified. As they pulled
my son from the wreckage, they, too, were
appalled that the driver's side airbag had
not inflated.

I contacted my insurance company, Major
Insurance, and my attorney, Lawrence Lawyer, who advised me to secure adequate compensation for the loss of my car. I contacted
the Cruel Crook dealership shortly thereafter to arrange for an adequate replacement vehicle. It has now been three months
that I have had this rental car, and as of
yet I have not been reimbursed one penny or
been offered a replacement vehicle. I have
placed my case before the New Jersey State
Attorney General's Board of Consumer Affairs for arbitration, and I am prepared to
go further with this matter. I am assured
that legal action can be sought and that the
law would most certainly be on my side; however, I wish to avoid this if at all possible.

I have spoken with many persons at Lemon,
not only about how the dealership could

let a vehicle as dangerous as this slip by
its notice but also about the expenditures
that I have had to carry, because I have
not been reimbursed for the rental car.
Provided that there are no further compli-
cations with the health of my son, that I
am provided with an adequate vehicle to
replace the defective one under lease to
me, and that I will be reimbursed for the
expenses incurred for the rental car from
December 21, 1996, to the present, this matter will then be resolved and I will take
no further legal action.

I cannot believe that you would be aware of
the enormous dangers that exist with your
dealership's quality control services. I am
sure that you are as shocked and appalled
as I at what has transpired. I am positive,
too, that you will wish to investigate this
matter thoroughly and promptly--since this
problem almost cost the life of my son and
now is costing me great distress, as mentioned earlier in this letter. I also feel
that you will wish to look into your representative, the Cruel Crook Auto Company, so
that perhaps you can get answers from them,
because I have been unable to get even
simple, common, professional courtesy from
this outfit.

Thank you, and I look forward to hearing
from you within the next two weeks.

Sincerely,

Jennifer Hamilton

```
cc:  Deputy Attorney General
     New Jersey Division of Law
     P.O. Box 45029
     124 Halfey Street, 5th Floor
     Newark, NJ 07101


     Auto Safety Hotline
     National Highway Traffic Safety Administration
     United States Department of Transportation
     Washington, DC 20590


     Mark S. Herr, Director
     New Jersey Division of Consumer Affairs
     P.O. Box 45027
     Newark, NJ 07101


     Perry Payback, President
     Major Insurance Company
     5513 Windshield Lane
     New York, NY 10022
```

Mr. Wanna-Injure turned out to be the personification of his pseudonym. The only response Mrs. Hamilton received from Lemon Automobile was a letter stating that the corporation believed Cruel Crook's report. After several more appeals to Mr. Wanna-Injure, Hamilton and I stepped up our campaign and began writing to the New Jersey state government and Attorney General Janet Reno. Our letter to the U.S. attorney general's office concluded:

> Never did I dream that the office of the New Jersey Attorney General would blatantly ignore my requests for assistance. This office is ostensibly the ultimate protector for people like me. Although this may not be a federal affair, it is appalling and saddening to discover that those in the highest positions of the Justice Department cannot be depended upon.

That got people moving.

The New Jersey Division of Consumer Affairs called Mrs.

Hamilton and informed her that a *directive* from the Justice
Department had just arrived at the New Jersey office. The pow-
ers that be in Washington had decided that the car easily fell
within the lemon law category, and they wanted something to be
done about her problem. The National Highway Traffic Safety
Administration and the National Center for Auto Safety also
received copies of the mandate for possible action on their parts.
Finally, someone called from the carmaker's corporate office,
and, in addition, a computer printout has been discovered, providing evidence that the vehicle had a faulty frame. After further
investigation, New Jersey's Division of Consumer Affairs has
decided that rather than falling under the lemon laws, Hamilton's problems involve fraud. All paperwork is being expedited to
the New Jersey Consumer Fraud Division. Even though the fur
is thoroughly flying now, you can bet your bottom dollar that my
client will never give up until her original request for a new and
safe automobile is granted.

I hope your problems with a defective automobile won't be as
excessive or as serious. In the event that you, too, are not being
heard, remember, you have a host of resources from the attorney
general to the National Center for Auto Safety at your disposal.
You only need to write.

It sometimes seems as if automobile horror stories are never end-
ing, whether the cars are new, leased, or have been a member of
the family for a while. Sandra Snoggled bought a used car that
she *thought* had power steering. The window sticker indicated
that the car had this feature, and, just to be totally positive, Sandra asked two salesmen and the manager. They both assured her
absolutely, "Yes." Believing the sticker and both men, Sandra
drove home in her newly purchased pride and joy.

Less than three months went by, and then the problem
started: the steering became progressively stiffer and harder to
maneuver. Sandra took the car to two mechanics who verified
that there was no power steering in the car—the steering was

manual all the way. Her letters and calls to the general manager of the dealership got her nowhere. In fact, all her requests—for a refund of the value of power steering; for exchanging the car for one equal or better; or for just installing power steering in her present model—were turned down by the manager, Mr. Misrepresent." He went on to further inform her that *she* had made the error in communication, and the dealership was under no obligation to honor its word.

After a great deal of back-and-forth conversations, Sandra and Mr. Misrepresent agreed he would start looking for another car, and she could use her current one for a trade-in, although this deal meant that Sandra would have to shell out more money. Two months passed and still no word from Mr. Misrepresent. Because she was experiencing some severe physical problems owing to the manual steering, Sandra came calling on me. The following is an abbreviated version of a poison pen letter we devised in which we made our displeasure very obvious to the president of this chain of dealerships. (Note the difference in Big Bosses; a copy of her letter also went to the head of the car manufacturer to alert the corporation that the manual steering in this make of car deteriorated over time.)

```
                        8903 Denny Lane
                        Falls Church, VA 44588
                        June 28, 1998

I. B. Hindrance, President
Fast-Talking Autos
Virginia Beach, VA 17076

Dear Mr. Hindrance:

I am sure you will be as shocked and ap-
palled as I was when you learn of my expe-
riences with the Fast-Talking dealership
in Alexandria, Virginia.
```

Nine months ago, my husband and I decided to replace our 1990 Racer with a newer, upgraded model. We particularly wanted power steering, since our 1990 model had manual steering, which was regularly causing me considerable shoulder pain.

We test-drove a Speeder, and I noticed that the steering was far looser and easier to handle than that of our old car. Because I had no trouble at all turning or parking and because the sticker stated "power steering," I assumed that the ease of steering was owing to the power steering. I asked the manager, Freddy Fibber, just to be absolutely sure, "Does this car have power steering?" With his absolute assurance that it did have power steering we purchased the car.

In December 1996, I began to notice that the steering was becoming progressively stiffer. When I took the car to the mechanics Jim Smith and John Jones at the Royal Amoco, 1756 Fairfield Drive, Fairfax, Virginia, they verified that there was no power steering whatsoever on this vehicle. At that point, I consulted a Speeder mechanic who informed me that manual steering on Speeders tends to get tighter and harder to handle as a function of age, and that the steering would not get loose again; he went on to state that this is normal for Speeders.

I wrote Michael Misrepresent, the general manager at the Fast-Talking dealership (copy enclosed). I reminded Mr. Misrepresent that not only did the window sticker indicate that this automobile had power steering, but also I had been assured by the two salesmen and the manager that the car did have this feature. His response was to offer to have the mechanics see if they could loosen this manual steering at no charge (please remember that a <u>Speeder</u> mechanic had told me this was impossible). He also offered to make me a deal on another car using mine as a trade-in, even though the second option involved my paying additional money. I did tell him, however, that I would discuss the matter with him if he found a comparable car. He assured me he would search for one and call me. Two months have gone by, and I have yet to hear from Mr. Misrepresent.

By now I realized I had made a horrendous error ever purchasing a car from the Fast-Talking dealership because I believe its employees, <u>including its management</u>, were unprofessional, and misrepresented this car so that I would buy it.

I am a certified trigger point myotherapist. I have completed highly specialized training and am one of only a few dozen practitioners in the United States to have passed board certification. I am qualified to recognize why I experience pain and muscle weakness in my arms and shoulders when parallel parking a car that has no power steering. Because I use my body, specifically my arms and my shoulders, in my profession, I am unable to work on days following spasms caused by what should be normal instances of parallel parking. This is particularly difficult because I am self-employed; if I am unable to work, I have no income.

This entire ordeal has been a travesty of justice, beginning with the car having false information on its sticker and my bringing up the necessity of having power steering and being lied to by the dealership. I might add, too, that I spent a great deal of time prior to the sale in trying to lower the price, which is entirely too high for this model. I met with little success because I continued to be assured that the car had many options. Power steering was specifically stated as a reason for the price not being lowered to the extent I wished.

I cannot believe you are aware of or that you would condone this type of mismanagement and misrepresentation on the part of one of your dealerships. I have been assured I can take legal action on this matter, but I do not wish to do so. All I wish is to be fairly reimbursed in one of the following manners: a trade-in for a comparable car with power steering or a refund of the original money I paid for the power steering function. I expect a thorough and immediate investigation, and I look forward to hearing from you within ten business days.

Thank you.

Sincerely,

Sandra Snoggled

```
cc: William Whippersnapper, President/CEO
    Wheelin Motor Corporation
    P.O. Box 777
    Los Angeles, CA 34555


    Frank Seales, Jr., Chief
    Antitrust and Consumer Litigation Section
    Office of the Attorney General
    900 East Main Street
    Richmond, VA 23219


    Ronald B. Mallard, Director
    Fairfax County Department of Consumer Affairs
    12000 Government Center Parkway, Suite 433
    Fairfax, VA 22035


    Automotive Consumer Action Program
    8400 West Park Drive
    McLean, VA 22102


    Robert E. Colvin, Project Manager
    Office of Consumer Affairs
    Washington Building, Suite 100
    P.O. Box 1163
    Richmond, VA 23219
```

Did Sandra hear from either Mr. Hindrance or Mr. Whippersnapper right away? No. Has she since received one single line from them? No. They both must be located so far up in those corporate offices that the clouds have obscured not only their vision but also their sense of responsibility. As I stated in Chapter 3, you must never give up. Accordingly, we began some "wheelin'" of our own. Sandra began to harass the folks at the regulatory agencies. Mr. Misrepresent, the sales manager, in his infinite compassion, finally offered Sandra the grand amount of $250 and a trade for her car. But by now a smart consumer, Sandra did some research and found out that there is a substantial difference between what a dealer gives on a trade-in and the amount for which he can sell a comparable car. This amount could easily exceed $2000. There was no way she could obtain an equal or better car with the necessary power steering through a trade-in plus $250.

Letters kept a' going, and finally one found a sympathetic ear. The Federal Trade Commission, one of the most active and cooperative of the big regulatory agencies, investigated Sandra's problem *and* the fact that no one else had presented her with a window of opportunity into which to peek. As a result of her perseverance, she finally received a refund check to cover what she had originally spent for the power steering feature on her car.

Auto Insurance

Getting a new paint job or ensuring that a truly dangerous car is taken off the road might sometimes be less complicated than getting a deadbeat driver (or in this case, the driver's employer's insurance company) to live up to certain responsibilities. Take the example of one of my clients who experienced just such a hit-and-lie, involving the driver of a truck owned by a moving company. After Ted Truthful had made many attempts to get the cooperation of the moving company and its insurer by first using the verbal approach and then corresponding with the various parties concerned, he enlisted my help. In addressing the need for the other party to take responsibility for the damages his car sustained in the accident, Mr. Truthful faced the challenge of doing battle with two adversaries: the other driver's employer's insurance company and the moving business that employed the driver who had hit him. Here is the letter he sent to the president of that insurance company.

1000 Remington Place
Philadelphia, PA 66880
March 16, 1998

James Jeopardy, President
Insurance of America
198 Policy Drive
West Chester, PA 33346

Dear Mr. Jeopardy:

It is appalling and unjust that I am being
held responsible for repairs made to my
automobile because of the carelessness of
your insured driver, Mr. Blind Bat.

On October 11, 1997, I was pulling into a
local convenience store for gas when my
vehicle was struck on the right front
fender by an AAZ Trucking Company vehicle
driven by Mr. Bat. He was obviously at
fault, and he admitted as much in testimony he gave at the time of the accident.
Here is what occurred: He pulled up by the
first gas tank with me behind him and
abruptly began backing up in order to turn
to the right and to get to the other side.
At this point, his vehicle struck mine on
the right fender side. Not only did Mr. Bat
state that he was simply backing up for
gas; he also said that he did not see me. I
do not understand how this is possible
when my vehicle was right behind his.

I immediately called the local police department, and Officer Fanelli arrived.
He made us aware of Pennsylvania State
law, which states that when one vehicle is

struck on the right side in a situation
such as we were in at that time, it is the
fault of the other vehicle (Mr. Bat). The
ticket that was issued by the officers at
the scene of the accident names Mr. Bat as
being at fault in this accident.

Because of inaccurate statements made by
Mr. Bat to the insurance company, Addled
Adjustment Service, Inc., which represents
AAZ and its drivers and which is a subsidiary company managed by Insurance of
America, Addled subsequently denied any
liability on the part of its insured driver;
the company also denied any claims that I
have relating to this loss. Mr. Bat said we
were both trying to pull into the same space
at the same time and only because I acceler-
ated to get in front of him was he unable to
avoid hitting me. This is blatantly untrue.
After receiving this letter, it was suggested to me by my car insurance company,
Good Guys, that I write directly to you. I
might add that before doing so I did try to
follow up immediately, but no one would
take my calls at your local office, specifically Randy Rude and Heather Hateful.

Even though the AAZ driver was 100 percent
at fault in this accident, I know that accidents do happen. There is no doubt in my
mind that he did not intentionally back
into me; but nonetheless, the situation occurred, and someone needs to be held responsible.

I have enclosed a copy of the estimated
repair bill for my car for $313.66 from Fix-

It-Up Auto Body, Inc., in Podunk, Pennsylvania. I am not even asking for remuneration for the work time I have lost in trying to resolve this matter, which includes several visits to the police department and talking with investigators, paying for copies of the ticket, researching the laws, etc. All I ask is what I am fairly owed: the money to repair my vehicle.

I am sure that you will investigate this matter promptly and thoroughly, and I look forward to hearing from you within the next two weeks.

Sincerely,

Ted Truthful

cc: Andrew Anthony Zooey, President
    AAZ Trucking Company
    111 Batson Lane
    Philadelphia, PA 19104

    Linda Kaiser, Commissioner
    Insurance Department
    1326 Strawberry Square, 13th Floor
    Harrisburg, PA 17120

    Joseph Goldberg, Director
    Bureau of Consumer Protection
    Office of Attorney General
    1326 Strawberry Square, 14th Floor
    Harrisburg, PA 17120

    John E. Kelley, Deputy Attorney General
    Bureau of Consumer Protection
    Office of the Attorney General
    21 South Twelfth Street, 2nd Floor
    Philadelphia, PA 19107

KEEPING IN TOUCH WITH POLICYHOLDERS

The State Farm Insurance Companies believe in delivering top-quality service for claims. The president and CEO, Edward B. Rust, Jr., explains:

At a National Association of Life Underwriters Convention 24 years ago, my predecessor told the gathering that the day he stops paying attention to communications from our policyholders "is the day I should resign as head of (State Farm) because that is the day I will have begun to lose contact with the real world in which we operate."

It's a philosophy our company and I personally adhere to. We are the world's largest property and casualty insurance company. But our policyholders measure us, not by our size, but by the personal, quality, one-on-one service we provide. Superior service is what sets us apart. But we also sometimes hear from policyholders whose expectations were not met. We pay special attention to those letters and work hard to make sure we've responded properly to our customers' needs.

We don't even know if the cc'ed authorities had time to act, because less than two weeks after he sent this letter, Mr. Truthful pocketed his $313.66.

● RESTAURANTS AND HOTELS

Restaurants

We've all heard variations on that long-standing joke about the hungry customer sitting down and ordering a delectable and expensive meal. When the soup course arrives, the diner picks

HANDLING COMPLAINTS

Two industry experts tell us that their own expectations of customer satisfaction run as high as our own. Ralph LaPorta of LaPorta's Restaurant in Olde Town Alexandria, Virginia, says:

The nature of the restaurant business is such that we receive very few letters of complaint; most often a guest will complain immediately if something is truly wrong. However, some guests may feel uncomfortable complaining in person and prefer to write a letter instead.

On the rare occasion that we receive such complaints, we first attempt to establish the validity of the complaint. Discussions are held with all members of the staff who worked that shift. . . . [O]ften staff members not directly involved in the incident have valuable insight. We will generally provide gift certificates to guests anytime they complain, no matter how minor the incident, assuming we establish that there was in fact a problem. Upon establishing the merit of the complaint, we generally contact the individual and ask him or her to return to the restaurant as our guest, rather than crediting his or her (bank card) account. This gives us opportunities both to provide a goodwill gesture and to attempt to cultivate return business. Restaurants rely heavily on word of mouth advertising, so it is important for us to correct any negative impression a guest may have formed.

up his soup spoon, holds it aloft ready to plunge in when, to his horror, he sees a live fly swimming merrily throughout the sautéed mushrooms.

"Waiter! Waiter! What's this fly doing swimming in my soup?" he cries.

Peering into the bowl, the waiter calmly replies, "Why, monsieur, it is performing a superb backstroke."

Although most of us haven't undergone something of this disgusting nature, we have experienced times when we have been equally *appalled* because of the nature of the service or the quality of the food at a restaurant. We can make demands, many of which aren't perceived as unreasonable by most restaurants or hotels. If we're served poor food, we can send it back. Perhaps the food is cold when it should be hot, the meat is tough, or an item just doesn't taste good. Make sure you say something immediately after the food is served. Don't wait until the check is delivered. Remember the advice about the one person who complains? No reputable restaurant owner or manager wants you to leave unhappy with your dining experience—especially if he or she is concerned you'll tell the world about the restaurant's inadequacies.

According to the **National Restaurant Association,** 1200 Seventeenth Street, NW, Washington, DC 20036, (202) 331-5900, customer satisfaction in "dining" establishments, as opposed to your local fast-food joint, has soared during recent years and now stands at 69 percent. The other 31 percent may be dismayed with the service they receive, and they're probably the patrons who don't complain but should.

If the verbal approach seems to be getting you nowhere, then you should always take further written action, because corporate officers such as Mr. Bollenbach of Hilton Hotels *do* listen.

LETTERS ARE TAKEN SERIOUSLY

And as we hear from Stephen F. Bollenbach, president and CEO of Hilton Hotels Corporation:

Anyone who takes the time to write obviously has strong opinions to convey. In any service-oriented business, meeting (and, ideally, exceeding) customer expectations is key to success. Therefore, it is prudent to review and carefully consider thoughts committed to paper by one's customers.

The Frigid family and I had to take further action to handle offensive and totally unacceptable behavior on the part of some employees of a well-known restaurant.

344 Apple Lane
Severna Park, MD 11222
December 27, 1997

P. U. Odor, Owner
The Fishy Odor Restaurant
909 Water Wharf Circle
Baltimore, MD 33557

Dear Mr. Odor:

On Christmas Day my family and I (a total of nine people) had reservations for brunch at your establishment, The Fishy Odor, at 1:00 P.M. At 12:50 we arrived on what was a bitterly cold and windy day, only to stand at a locked door with two small children and the rest of us in frigid discomfort. Each time I got the waitress's attention, I frantically motioned for her to just allow us into the foyer; each time she pointedly ignored me.

Finally, my grandfather tried the other door by the bar and discovered that it was open, and we walked into the foyer--again just to escape the cold. Your hostess, Natalie Nasty, ran over and began berating us in a very rude and abrasive manner. At that point, I demanded to see the manager. This young man arrived and was most apologetic, stating that he had known nothing of the "closed door" policy; I must admit that I find this hard to believe.

To add insult to injury, upon receiving the bill for $215, we produced a coupon for your restaurant, which <u>stated</u> that one Christmas brunch was half price when accompanying one full-price meal, but the coupon was denied! I realize that $10 deleted from a $215 meal is a pittance, but on top of the rudeness to which we had already been subjected, your staff's unwillingness to honor that coupon was the last straw. The one exception was our waitress. She was very nice and obviously humiliated by the conduct of her unfriendly and, in my opinion, unprofessional peers.

I expect an immediate response from you upon receipt of this letter. I cannot imagine that you condone this type of behavior from your employees.

Thank you.

Sincerely,

Frances Frigid

Frances Frigid received her "immediate response" even though she hadn't used cc's on her letter. Although she hadn't actually stated her desire for a free meal, she received a coupon for Sunday brunch for four people, and an apology from the owner. And as a result of Frances Frigid's letter the restaurant eliminated its "closed door" policy.

The following letter involves a smoldering cigarette that happened to land on a diner's coat. If a cigarette, a glass of red wine, or a touch of sauce that's been too swiftly handled damages one of your garments, you may need to write a similar letter.

916 Robin Hood Court
Woodbridge, VA 34967
May 14, 1998

Mortimer Munchy, Owner
The Delectable Dungeon Restaurant
400 Madison Avenue
New York, NY 10273

Dear Mr. Munchy:

I am sure you will be as shocked and appalled as I was about a problem I experienced with your restaurant for well over a year.

On December 2, 1996, a friend and I ate lunch in your establishment, the Delectable Dungeon. Our coats were checked at the front of the restaurant. After our meal, we retrieved our coats, left, and almost immediately noticed heat at our necks. Upon further examination, we saw that the coats were burned and literally smoldering at certain spots. Immediately returning to the Dungeon, we spoke with your service person, Ms. Upset Tummy. We brought to her attention that when the waiter removed our coats from the checkroom, he laid them on the table in front. I had noted that this waiter had been smoking, and therefore I surmised that the coats had been laying over the ashtray that he was using. Ms. Upset Tummy offered to reweave my friend's coat since he lives in New York. I was advised to get mine repaired upon my return home and then mail the receipt to her.

I had my coat repaired and mailed the receipt to your restaurant. There was no response. Once it became apparent that the $100 reimbursement for my own reweaving bill was not forthcoming, I began to make the first of many calls to Ms. Tummy. The first call was in March. At that time she stated she would mail the check by the end of the week. This call was followed by others in April and May, and each time her response was the same: "It had fallen by the wayside. It was lost at the bottom of the heap," and so forth, but she would forward it on immediately.

On April 26, 1997, I spoke with Saul Snippy, Dungeon's manager, who advised me that he had spoken with Ms. Tummy and would remind her again to send the check on the following Monday when she returned from vacation. Since I still had not received the $100 on May 30, I emphatically informed Ms. Tummy that if the reimbursement plus an additional $20 for telephone calls did not arrive immediately, I would no longer be in contact with Dungeon's personnel but would proceed to my next step.

As the owner of Delectable Dungeon, you are ultimately responsible for this matter. Regardless of whether it was simply ineptness on the part of your employees, or, a worse scenario—they were deliberately delaying payment and trying to avoid paying the cost of the repair—I do not know. Certainly, after all this time I could ask for full reimbursement of the coat itself, but I am an honest person and only wish for Dungeon to reimburse me for the charge of repairing my coat and for my phone calls.

I expect that you will investigate this matter promptly and thoroughly, and I look forward to hearing from you within ten business days.

Thank you.

Sincerely,

Bella Burned-Up

cc: Susan Somers, Deputy Chief
    Bureau of Consumer Frauds and Protection
    Office of the Attorney General
    State Capitol
    Albany, NY 12224

    Shirley Sarna
    Assistant Attorney General in Charge
    Bureau of Consumer Frauds and Protection
    Office of the Attorney General
    120 Broadway
    New York, NY 10271

    Timothy S. Carey
    Chairman and Executive Director
    New York Consumer Protection Board
    5 Empire State Plaza, Suite 2101
    Albany, NY 12223-1556

It was only a few days after the stated deadline that Ms. Burned-Up received the full $120, an apology, and a dinner gift certificate for two.

Hotels

Restaurants are usually extra careful not to make more reservations than the number of tables they have available, but hotels, like airlines, overbook. If you're met at the desk with, "Oh, I'm so sorry, but . . . ," firmly demand to see the manager. Tell this person that you have a confirmation (and all the better if you're clutching said affirmation in your hot little hand), and that you *will* have a room that is comparable or better. Unfortunately, there may literally be no room at the inn, and you'll have no choice but to go elsewhere. Before your haughty departure, make sure you've noted the names of the desk clerk, the manager, and whomever else you've come in contact with so that when you whip out your poison pen, you can name names in the complaint.

A few hotel chains such as Embassy Suites promise a refund if you've experienced a problem like this. Holiday Inn advertises that if a complaint isn't handled to the customer's satisfaction by checkout, a portion of the stay is on the house. If all your cries of criticism remain unheard and unanswered, then when you're back in the confines of your own home (where you *know* the sheets are clean), write a complaint letter to the hotel president, manager, and so forth, *and* cc the **American Hotel and Motel Association** at 1201 New York Avenue, NW, Suite 600, Washington, DC 20005-3931. Once you have registered a complaint in writing, even reputable local hotels will run the extra mile to make you a happy overnighter, as one of my repeat clients found to her delight.

13 Morgan Avenue
New York, NY 11111
July 1, 1997

Arnold Aloof, Owner
Aloof Inns
356 Fifth Avenue, Suite 909
New York, NY 10271

Dear Mr. Aloof:

As owner of the Aloof Inn on Seventh Avenue in New York City, I feel that you should
be made aware of the appalling and slipshod treatment I was subjected to by the
management of your hotel.

My husband and I had a reservation for a
double suite with a jacuzzi, for which we
had made arrangements a month before our
arrival. We had informed the reservations
desk in advance that we had a free gift
certificate to cover the cost of our stay
at the hotel. Upon our arrival on February
24, we were informed that the suite was
no longer available because the hotel had
overbooked. We requested to speak with the
manager, Mr. Beastly, three times, and
each time he refused to speak with us. My
husband became very angry and demanded
to see Mr. Beastly, and finally, the fourth
time we asked, your manager decided to
address the issue with us.

We then requested the same suite at a
future date, since our gift certificate was
to expire on February 24; alternately we
even said we would settle for a discount

price. Not only did he deny both requests, but Mr. Beastly then had the temerity to suggest that he dispossess the couple who was arriving for that evening and return the suite to us. This infuriated us even more, especially my husband, who travels extensively and depends on <u>honest</u> hotel bookings.

After we had spent two hours at the desk, we felt that it was too late to obtain a decent room elsewhere. Therefore, we had no choice but to accept the standard double room that was available. Your hotel certainly cleared some profits for that particular evening, considering that you did not honor our free reservation for the suite and got another couple to pay full price.

We have always thought of Aloof Inns as a chain of reputable hotels that treats its guests well. Obviously we were wrong on both counts. If this type of what we believe to be unprofessional conduct is the norm, then I strongly recommend that you promptly and thoroughly investigate your services and your employees.

I look forward to hearing from you about this matter within ten business days.

Thank you.

Sincerely,

Suzanne Sleepless

cc: Susan Somers, Deputy Chief
Bureau of Consumer Frauds and Protection
Office of the Attorney General
State Capitol
Albany, NY 12224

Timothy S. Carey
Chairman and Executive Director
New York State Consumer Protection Board
5 Empire State Plaza, Suite 2101
Albany, NY 12223-1556

Shirley Sarna
Assistant Attorney General in Charge
Bureau of Consumer Frauds and Protection
Office of the Attorney General
120 Broadway
New York, NY 10271

The American Hotel and Motel Association
1201 New York Avenue, NW, Suite 600
Washington, DC 20005-3931

Two weeks and three days passed before a fancy $175 gift certificate arrived, along with a letter asking this couple to please give the Aloof Inn one more try. Wow, if that jacuzzi could only talk!

Use what's at your fingertips, the resources I give you, and your own common sense. When you confront a commonplace problem, such as the ones discussed in this chapter, you can most assuredly be successful if you apply your knowledge of what to say and how to say it and concoct your own special brand of poison. But what about the other "common" issues that all too many of us experience from day to day? We'll address problems with credit, bank deposits, and retail purchases in the next chapter.

BETTER BUSINESS BUREAUS

You'll find the names and addresses of many, many helpful and important persons and regulatory agencies scattered throughout this book and an even more complete list in the appendices, but what you *won't* find are **Better Business Bureaus** (BBBs). Without pinning the tail on this particular donkey, suffice it to say that I haven't been real thrilled with the assistance of these organizations. They are simply nonprofit groups that promote good relations between buyers and sellers; they have no authority to force their business members to resolve complaints. The key word here is *members*—that's right, the very same companies about which you're complaining in many instances are on the roster of your local Better Business Bureau. Also each of the more than one hundred Better Business Bureaus across the United States is a separate entity with the right to operate as such. Even though they all "belong" to the national **Council of Better Business Bureaus,** 4200 Wilson Boulevard, Arlington, VA 22203, which supposedly oversees the individual offices, we should keep in mind that all of them have a pro-industry position.

If you report a problem to your local Better Business Bureau, that office will generally contact the company for you and will even sometimes attempt to negotiate a settlement. But unfortunately, the buck often stops there. To their credit, BBBs publish a whole lot of material to help consumers if they find themselves needing to issue a complaint, and you can order these and other publications online at http://bbb.org/bbb or from your local or state office. Here's a sampling:

BETTER BUSINESS BUREAUS

Automobiles
Filing an Auto Insurance Claim
Don't Get Soaked Buying a Flood-Damaged Car
Black Market Freon Could Damage Your Car
Auto Repair

Health
Home Health Care
Weight Loss Promotions
Ordering Medications from Abroad Is Risky

Home
Buying an Unbuilt Home
Hiring a Home Improvement Contractor
Tips on Hiring a Snow Removal Contractor
Childcare Services

Scams
Yellow Page Invoice Scams Proliferate
How the Faithful Can Avoid Investment Scams
How to Avoid Check Cashing Fraud
Boiler Room Scams
Foreign Lottery Scams

HELPFUL RULES, AGENCIES, PUBLICATIONS, AND SERVICES

Airline Rules 240 and 380 explain consumer rights concerning overbooking, delays, and compensation.

The **American Hotel and Motel Association,** 1201 New York Avenue, NW, Suite 600, Washington, DC 20005-3931 is a watchdog organization for hotels/motels across the country.

AUTOCAP, at (703) 821-7144, is an arbitration organization that handles automobile disputes between the consumer and the manufacturer. See the appendices for a listing of those manufacturers that participate.

AUTOLINE can provide assistance if you're dealing with one of the companies not participating in AUTOCAP. Call (800) 955-5100. See the appendices for a listing of these manufacturers.

The **Auto Safety Hotline,** at (800) 424-9393, provides immediate assistance concerning recall information.

The *Consumer Information Catalog* is a valuable source for ordering consumer publications. Write to the Consumer Information Center, Pueblo, CO 81009 or access it on the Web at www.pueblo.gsa.gov.

The **Council of Better Business Bureaus,** 4200 Wilson Boulevard, Arlington, VA 22203, publishes materials to help the consumer make decisions about purchasing products and services.

Federal Trade Commission, Public Reference, at Room 130, Sixth Street and Pennsylvania Avenue, NW, Washington, DC 20580, or call (202) 326-2222, provides consumers with many helpful brochures and pamphlets.

HELPFUL RULES, AGENCIES, PUBLICATIONS, AND SERVICES

Fly-Rights: A Consumer Guide to Air Travel, which can be obtained from the Department of Transportation, at (202) 366-1111. This publication thoroughly explains consumers' rights and responsibilities with regard to air travel.

Ask for *The Lemon Law Summary* at the **Center for Auto Safety,** 2001 S Street, NW, Suite 410, Washington, DC 20009. It provides information about consumer expectations and available recourse if you have purchased a defective automobile.

The **National Fraud Information Center,** at (800) 876-7060, assists consumers in avoiding scams and fraudulent practices.

The **Public Reference Section** of the FTC can provide you with hints for purchasing a car. Call (202) 326-2222.

The **National Restaurant Association,** 1200 Seventeenth Street, NW, Washington, DC 20036, (202) 331-5900, assists consumers with complaints about restaurants.

Travelers' Advisory: Get What You Pay For, Telemarketing Travel Fraud, and *Timeshare Resales,* (202) 326-2222, are informative brochures to help the consumer to avoid the common pitfalls you may encounter when making travel arrangements. Contact the **Federal Trade Commission,** Public Reference Branch, Room 130, Sixth Street and Pennsylvania Avenue, NW, Washington, DC 20580, (202) 326-2222. The FTC also issues advisories regarding scams, automobile purchases, and so forth.

CHAPTER 6

Common Complaints II: Credit, Bank Deposits, Retail, and Services

> We pride ourselves on being a consumer driven retailer. We listen and learn a great deal from our customers. Every consumer letter we receive, whether a complaint or a compliment, is a wonderful window of opportunity for us to learn more, . . . and we do.
> —LEONARD H. ROBERTS, PRESIDENT, RADIO SHACK AND THE TANDY CORPORATION

Problems with credit, bank deposits, retail, and services are major sources of concern to consumers, especially since if these issues are not addressed promptly and thoroughly, the result may be further troubles in the future.

O CREDIT PROBLEMS

The idea of credit has been around forever. How could our ancestors ever have existed much less thrived if the general store or other merchants hadn't issued credit for food and supplies? Unfortunately credit problems have also been a part of life since the idea of monthly payments replaced trading in cold, hard cash. Whether you need credit to buy a house, furniture to place in it, or clothing, if you get into trouble with your current creditors—maybe some idiot types in incorrect data on your account, or there is an unauthorized charge on your account, or you get behind on your payments—the end results may be the same—

your creditworthiness is in the Dumpster, you can't qualify for a mortgage, a car loan, or a new credit card, and you passionately need to complain to anyone who might listen.

How do you help yourself if you become embroiled in a mess with a creditor and phone calls get you nowhere?

1 Document everything. You should check off and document expenditures, receipts, and records.

2 Know your rights under the law. If there's a question on your credit card statement, then you can file a dispute. The **Federal Fair Credit Billing Act,** which applies to credit card and charge accounts, has saved many a cardholder's bank account and his or her sanity. This act helps to protect the consumer against billing errors, unauthorized use of his or her account, goods or services charged but not received, and against paying charges until an explanation or written proof of purchase is produced. Some of us are prone to buying via mail-order and other such non-store methods, such as shopping parties or the Internet, and if we pay by credit card, the protection afforded by the Federal Fair Credit Billing Act also extends to those kinds of purchases.

If an error did occur, you're no longer responsible for that charge. If, on the other hand, it's *your* mistake or the merchant or credit card company sees it as your mistake, then the merchant or credit card company must inform you in writing of what you owe and why.

3 Write the issuing company within sixty days. You'll have a little breathing space once you have made your position clear, because you're not obligated to pay the amount while it's in dispute. Again, keep a record of any phone conversations and keep copies of correspondence and any receipts or charge slips.

Assume this is the case: You've complained about what you perceive to be a bad debt, but you still must pay it—all else has failed. You send out a barrage of letters to everyone from the manager to the CEO of the company whose charge you're questioning. In the unlikely event that your cries are still ignored and the Big Bad Bill Collector comes a-knocking at your front door, you do have a safety net of sorts to at least protect you from being harassed while you continue your search for salvation. The federal government offers such help through the **Fair Debt Collection Practices Act,** or what I call the "Resistant Rules for the Righteous." According to this law, debt collectors and collection agencies are *not* allowed to

✎ harass you with repetitious, anonymous, or collect calls;
✎ threaten violence, use abusive language, or intimidate you into believing that your property can be snatched without appropriate court action;
✎ lie and say that they are someone other than who they actually are (for example, have someone call and tell you he represents a company's legal department);
✎ call you before eight A.M., at work, or after nine P.M. at home;
✎ misconstrue the amount of money you owe (creditors can add late charges and penalties, but if you don't agree with the bottom line, dispute the charges and ask for a fuller accounting before paying); and
✎ mail you postcards, since doing so violates your protected right to privacy.

The Fair Debt Collection Practices Act *does* apply to those who collect on the behalf of others, but if you're being *harassed* you can protect yourself simply by telling these bozos not to contact you anymore. If they continue to bother you, report them to **The Bureau of Consumer Protection of the Federal Trade Commission** at (202) 326-2222. The FTC's e-mail address is http://www.ftc.gov, if you prefer to go that route.

Mortgages

Mortgages represent a particularly specialized and sensitive type of credit problem. Those of us who own our homes know that we'd better get that mortgage payment in when it's due or else we'll be assessed a hefty finance charge. But what if you *did* mail it on time, but it didn't get where it was supposed to go by the due date? The institution that holds your home and hearth is only interested in getting its payment on time. Usually the bank doesn't care why your payment is late. Sometimes, though, one might have the proverbial leg to stand on, especially when the lateness of the payment is the fault of the through-rain-and-sleet-and-snow people. If you find yourself in this spot, as always, pull out all the stops and go straight to the top—the U.S. Postal Inspector General.

112 Belvedere Drive
Alexandria, VA 22303
April 25, 1997

Maury Mortgage, President
Dreamhouse Mortgage Company
798 South Parkway
Houston, TX 33446

Dear Mr. Mortgage:

An appalling situation has occurred with Dreamhouse because of either the post office's error in delivering our house payment to you on time or your institution not crediting our account if you received the payment on or before the due date. This problem has occurred not once but three times.

In December 1995 I mailed the payment on the 11th and was assured by Clueless Clerk at the Useless Post Office in Washington, D.C., that it would be received by the 15th; it did not arrive on time, so we were billed the late charge of $141.56. In January 1996

I was advised, again by this same Mr. Clerk, to send my mortgage payment via certified mail, return receipt requested, which I did on January 10. This payment, too, was received late enough to warrant a late charge.

By this point, my husband and I realized that our creditworthiness was definitely in danger. Both of these incidences could have been the fault of either the mail service or of Dreamhouse; therefore, we hired an attorney to investigate. This, of course, meant that we had to come up with additional funds. Because there was some question as to which institution was in error, Dreamhouse decided to cancel the two months' late assessments. This occurred after much frustration on both our part and that of our attorney.

Although there may have been some dispute about who was responsible in the first two episodes, there is absolutely none with the third: the fault lies completely with the postal service. To be totally positive that the April payment was received by Dreamhouse on time, I mailed the check by Express Mail on April 14, but to my horror it did not arrive until April 20! This was a guaranteed delivery, according to Fooled-You Ferguson at the Useless branch (copies of all receipts enclosed).

Now not only am I responsible for the late charge, but because this is the third instance of a late payment on my mortgage, I am very afraid our credit rating will be bad for years to come.

Because the Chief Postal Inspector is ultimately in charge of the entire service, I
have also written a letter to request that
he investigate this matter immediately (copy
enclosed) as well as send a letter of explanation to Dreamhouse.

I look forward to hearing from you within
the next ten business days.

Thank you.

Sincerely,

Eleanor Exasperated

Other than a cc to the credit reporting agency, Mrs. Exasperated desired that no other agencies be informed about her problem, and, in this case, she got results without alerting other
agencies. She received many apologies from the top down at the
post office, notices were sent to the mortgage company, the late
fee was dropped, and the threat of a poor credit rating was eliminated.

Store Credit

Lots of us have moved, and if things go as planned, our mail
moves with us. Too bad this isn't always the case. Peggy Panicked
was one of the unlucky ones. Because her bills from a department store didn't reach her at her new address, she got behind
on her payments, her credit record was noted, and she failed to
be approved for further credit. Let's see how Peggy Panicked
tackled this problem.

127 Horseshoe Lane
San Jose, CA 95110
January 5, 1997

Sedgewick Snafu, President
Snafu Department Stores
666 Error Avenue
San Jose, CA 95111

Dear Mr. Snafu:

As a loyal and long-standing customer of
Snafu Stores, I find that you are my last
hope to resolve a major difficulty that I
have encountered with my account with your
company.

In April 1995 I moved to a new home, but my
Snafu statement did not follow me to the
new address, although I did notify your
company of my change of address. After
three months I contacted the billing department and was told the amount to send.
I was also assured at that time that there
would be no problem with my credit. But in
December 1996, when I applied for a Gasa-
holic Card account, I was denied credit
because of Snafu's credit rating. I immediately requested a Trans Union credit report, which verified that I was rejected
because I was three months late with a payment to your store in 1995.

I went to Snafu's main office on Adversary
Avenue and spoke with John Justice in the
credit department. He agreed, after study-
ing my file which clearly showed that I

had always paid my bill on or before the
due date, that this had been simply a matter of miscommunication; but he said that
he could do nothing himself to rectify the
situation. He advised that I speak with
Mr. Deadpan in the collection department.
I attempted many times to see Mr. Deadpan
but to no avail. I was also not successful in my attempts to reach him via telephone; in fact, he never even returned one
of my numerous calls. Exhausted by my
futile efforts, I simply gave up for the
time being.

I have recently married, and my husband
and I wish to purchase a new home. I am
truly afraid, however, that we will not be
approved for a mortgage because of this
one, unjustified notation on my credit rating. I realize that there was a balance due
on my Snafu account, but I did notify the
company of my change of address prior to
my move. With the distractions of the move,
I frankly did not notice that my statement
had not accompanied me. I have had a long
and happy relationship with your store,
and I trusted the customer service representative when she told me that my credit
record would not be affected by these late
payments. Certainly there must be some way
for us to resolve this misunderstanding. I
would hate to have to cancel my account
with Snafu after all these years.

Please investigate this matter for me. As
previously stated, I feel that only you
can assist me in my endeavor to clear this

credit problem, so that my future plans
will not be jeopardized.

Thank you, and I expect to hear from you
within thirty days.

Sincerely,

Peggy Panicked

cc: Trans Union
    760 Sproul Road
    P.O. Box 403
    Springfield, PA 19064-0403

    Federal Trade Commission
    Sixth Street and Pennsylvania Avenue, NW
    Room 240
    Washington, DC 20580

Ms. Panicked's credit rating was amended, and within a few
weeks she and her new husband signed the papers for their new
home.

Excessive Credit Card Debt

Letters can also be of use to those of us who get ourselves in trouble because we simply can't resist that new pair of shoes, the trip
to Mexico, or dining out twice a week. Or maybe we're going
along fine and then bad luck strikes—someone loses a job or
becomes ill or dies and we get behind on our payments.

For some of us it is too easy to charge toothpaste and a tooth-
brush because it is convenient, and maybe we're just a little short

of cash that day. Too many of us become trapped by the vicious cycle of overcharging, and then, when our monthly statement comes due, we pay only the minimum. The balance doesn't get paid down; it may even increase. The cycle continues because the finance charges keep adding up *and* we continue to buy with the credit card—that is, until we reach our credit limit for that card. The deep water gets deeper the more cards we use, because we may be struggling to hold our (financial) heads above water, and perhaps the minimum monthly payments become too much. Some people get to the point where they are in jeopardy of losing their credit altogether. Before this happens to you, try to make arrangements with your creditors to get back on track.

Fredda Frenzied was advised to incorporate her various credit cards onto a debt-consolidation card, but unfortunately because of her financial situation she couldn't afford the monthly payments. Thus she found herself having to ask her new creditor to arrange lower monthly payments. As she found out, asking for an alternative payment plan may seem straightforward, but arranging it with a creditor is not always a simple task.

```
                    12 Robinson Road, #12
                    Cleveland, OH 22312
                    April 19, 1997

Gregory M. Grinch, CEO
Greed Bank Card Corporation
1717 Grabby Circle, Suite 711
Greedyville, CA 33445

Dear Mr. Grinch:

It is with a great deal of desperation that
I turn to you for assistance because I can-
```

not get anyone from your company's 800 telephone number to offer me any solution to
my problem. In fact, I have been subjected
to rudeness and hostility from everyone
with whom I have spoken at your company,
with the exception of a representative named
Honey.

Approximately one and a half years ago, I
consolidated my credit cards into a Greed
Bank Card with a minimum monthly payment
of $189. I had no problem paying this amount
initially; however, my financial status
has recently undergone a drastic change.
Because my alimony has ceased and I still
have two children to support and a house
payment to make, one job simply is not
enough to pay all of my bills each month,
specifically the $189 to Greed. I am cur-
rently in the process of obtaining a second
job to try to make ends meet, but I certainly
do not wish my credit to be in jeopardy.

I have made many calls to your company's
800 number to attempt to arrange a lower
payment plan, just until I can get on my
feet. Each time I have called, I have been
told that there is no record of my previous
calls or pleas for assistance. I cannot
understand what could possibly be wrong
with your computers, unless your representatives are simply not logging in the information. Not only am I getting zero response
by phone, but I have also received both
telephone threats and letters from both
collection agencies and your company. One
case in point: For two months I was unable
to make the full payment, but instead of

being delinquent (as I am sure many people are), I mailed in $50 each of the two months with a letter of explanation and a request for help in lowering my monthly payment. In response to these "good faith" payments and requests I received more dunning notices and threats of collection agencies and a negative report to credit agencies. Let me state that I have <u>never</u> missed a payment, even at the expense of going without household or medical necessities.

I find it totally ludicrous that after several months and many hours on the phone, as well as my good-faith efforts, in writing, to find a solution to this problem, I find myself in this position (documentation enclosed). I cannot understand why a new payment plan cannot be arranged to our mutual satisfaction; certainly your company would be the beneficiary, too, because of the extra interest that you would receive. Surely you must have other customers with similar problems. Have you no policy and no flexibility for working with customers like me who are willing and able to pay down our debt at a lower monthly rate so that we can retain our good credit status with you?

I must reiterate that even though my finances are at a low at this time, I have <u>always</u> made some payment to Greed. I was reared to believe in the American way: if I attempt to meet my obligations as best I can, and if I do so in good faith, others will be willing to meet me half way. Obviously, this is not the philosophy of your company.

Please investigate this matter immediately. I look forward to your reply within the next twenty-one days.

Thank you.

Sincerely,

Fredda Frenzied

cc: Customer Relations, Greed Credit, Inc.
    447 Greedy Street, Suite 112
    Greedyville, CA 33445

    Helen MacMurray
    Office of the Attorney General
    30 East Broad Street
    State Office Tower, 25th Floor
    Columbus, OH 43266-0410

    Bureau of Financial Institutions
    1300 East Main Street, Suite 800
    P.O. Box 640
    Richmond, VA 23205-0640

    Federal Trade Commission
    Sixth Street and Pennsylvania Avenue, NW
    Room 240
    Washington, DC 20580

As a result of this letter, Fredda's monthly payments were lowered to an amount that she could more easily afford.

⬤ BANK DEPOSITS

Have you ever been in this position: your local bank tells you
that you haven't deposited money, but you *know* you most certainly have? I have learned the hard way, as have a number of my
Poison Pen customers, that a big wake-up call is in store for those
of us who don't save our deposit slips. If you need to confront
your bank over a deposit that hasn't been credited to your account, first try the verbal approach, bringing in any necessary
receipts, and defend yourself to a bank official. If you get nowhere with that line of attack, you will need to resort to writing
a complaint letter like the one that follows.

                                 211 Springdale Road
                                 Tempe, AZ 77665
                                 March 30, 1997

Bobbie Banker, President
BooBoo Bank, Inc.
333 Deposit Street, Suite 13
Phoenix, AZ 44987

Dear Ms. Banker:

I have recently had an appalling problem
with my account because your bank made a
record-keeping error. Unfortunately, I have
had little luck in resolving this situation
because the customer service representative
I have dealt with has been, in my opinion,
both unprofessional and discourteous, and,
what is more, she has failed to follow
through with checking on the problem.

On March 16, 1997, I learned that my savings account had been debited by BooBoo on

March 1 for $578. I immediately called and was told by Ms. Ignorant in Customer Service that this transaction had occurred because there was a zero balance in my checking account, and the bank needed to transfer the money into that account. She was not only unhelpful; she was also quite rude.

I explained that just last Tuesday I had deposited $1500.76 into my checking account, yet she emphatically stated that there were no records of such a deposit, with the strong vocal implication that I was obviously an idiot! I finally persuaded her to assure me that she would recheck BooBoo's records and call me back. After almost two weeks I still have yet to hear from her or from anyone else at your bank.

Knowing that I was correct, I went back through my records. As you can see from the enclosed copy, on March 25, 1997, I deposited $1500.76 into this account!

I wish this matter investigated and resolved immediately, and I ask that the $578 be returned to my savings account.

Thank you, and I look forward to hearing from you within the next seven business days.

Sincerely,

Ira Irate
Checking Account # 28085
Savings Account # 3091857

cc: Federal Deposit Insurance Corporation
    550 Seventeenth Street, NW
    Washington, DC 20429

    Richard C. Houseworth
    Superintendent of Banks
    Arizona State Banking Department
    2910 North Forty-fourth Street, Suite 310
    Phoenix, AZ 85018

Ira Irate immediately received a call from the bank, and the entire matter was resolved within three working days. Just to be on the safe side for future transactions, however, he did change banks soon thereafter!

● MAIL ORDER, SHOPPING PARTIES, CYBERSHOPPING, AND RETAIL POLICY

Mail Order

However you shop—by mail, the Internet, by phone, or via the shopping channel—you are not without recourse should problems with the service or the product develop. We'll talk about shopping at stores later in this section.

First, I know there are some home shopping addicts out there. If your mail is like mine, it's packed with sale catalogs that whet your appetite long enough to cause you to either race to the phone to order or dash off your credit card number on an order slip. You can protect yourself from the daily deluge of mail (and earn prayers of thanks from your exhausted mail carrier, ensuring you a place in heaven) by contacting the **Direct Marketing Association** at P.O. Box 9008, Farmingdale, NY 11735. This organization will direct its members to remove you from their lists.

Whether you prefer to shop by television or direct mail, if the product you receive doesn't match its description, what do you do then? First of all, before placing an order with a company that is new to you, make sure it is a reputable one. Determine its refund and return policies *before* ordering, and ascertain the product's availability and the total price of your order.

If the product you ordered turns out to be other than what you anticipated, you may dispute the charges if you have a problem with the company honoring the return, refunding your money, or crediting your bank card. Remember, though, you must have made the purchase in your home state or within one hundred miles of your current billing address, and the charge must be in excess of $50. Also, you must first make a "good faith" effort to resolve the dispute with the seller; there are no special procedures to follow in your attempts.

If your own efforts don't pay off, then contact your state and local consumer protection offices. Be sure to write to the Direct Marketing Association. Also call the local office of the U.S.

APPRECIATING CUSTOMER FEEDBACK

Bob Norton, President/Chief Operating Officer, FTD:

Although we enjoy reading customers' positive comments more than negative letters, FTD views all customer feedback as valuable learning tools. With our 100% freshness guarantee, quality and strong customer service are FTD's highest priorities, and we want to hear first-hand how we're doing. Although we do not take action regarding every negative comment received, FTD will respond to every customer letter with whatever feedback is requested or required. Since a customer cared enough to initiate contact with us, FTD is more than happy to build and strengthen that relationship.

Postal Inspection Service (see your local telephone book), which offers you recourse if you should hit a snag with your mail-order purchase. The **Federal Trade Commission's Mail or Telephone Order Rule** and the U.S. Postal Inspection Service protect you if your merchandise doesn't arrive within thirty days, unless the company has specified otherwise up front, or if the product you receive doesn't match the advertised description.

Gentlemen, let's say that you've ordered something *really* special for your wife after seeing it advertised on TV or in a catalog. Unfortunately, when the gift arrives, it is so out of sync with your original intention, you fear for your life (marital and otherwise). The following prototype should provide some guidance when you attempt to resolve the problem with the seller, as stated earlier. As for patching things up with your wife—there, I'm afraid, you're on your own.

```
                    1405 West Street
                    Spartenburg, SC 44554
                    December 28, 1997

Sherry Seducer, President
Seduction Nightwear, Inc.
811 Passion Parkway, Suite 214
San Francisco, CA 55432

Dear Ms. Seducer:

Because of Seduction's error in shipping,
my wife and I are experiencing an appall-
ing marital problem.

On November 15, I placed a telephone order
for item #9993, the "Sleek and Satin Seduc-
tion Promise," exorbitantly priced at $109.
```

As this gift-wrapped nightgown was to be my wife's Christmas gift, I did not care about the cost nor the $15 shipping charge (packing slip enclosed). When the package arrived on December 10, I placed it under the tree, never dreaming that your company had made a horrendous mistake.

On Christmas morning, my wife unwrapped the gift, but to her anger and to my chagrin she discovered not the size small I had ordered, but an extra, extra large! That nightie certainly didn't deliver on its promise that evening, because of my wife's fury.

I have contacted the credit card company, and I expect you to immediately credit my Discover card for the total. I also ask that you write a letter of explanation to my wife regarding what I believe to be your incompetence in this matter.

Thank you, and I look forward to hearing from you by January 10, 1998.

Sincerely,

David Doomed

cc: Kenneth Huntly, Chief Postal Inspector
    475 L'Enfant Plaza West, SW
    Washington, DC 20260

    Federal Trade Commission
    Sixth Street and Pennsylvania Avenue, NW
    Room 240
    Washington, DC 20580

```
Direct Marketing Association
P.O. Box 9008
Farmingdale, NY 11735

Discover and Company
Two World Trade Center, 66th Floor
New York, NY 10048
```

Poor "David," now he'll probably have to buy his wife something far more expensive if he wants to bring the *promise* back into her eyes.

Shopping Parties

Maybe you're one of those folks who likes to go to "shopping parties." If so, you should be aware that after you buy an item or items, you have the right to cancel your order within three days if your order total is more than $25, according to the **Federal Trade Commission Cooling-Off Rule.** It doesn't even matter if you paid by credit card, check, or cash (be wary of this practice). This rule even applies to the local elementary school selling magazine subscriptions door-to-door. If you want to cancel a subscription, make sure that when you contact the school or the subscriptions dealer, you send your cancellation by certified mail and keep the receipt. There are a number of exceptions to the Federal Trade Commission Cooling-Off Rule. For instance, you are not protected if you buy a lawn mower from your friend down the street (contracts signed outside your home are exempt)—so make sure you know where you stand regarding your right to a refund. A source to contact for further help is the **National Association of Consumer Agency Administrators** (NACAA), which enforces consumer laws. Reach them by calling (202) 347-7395. Note: when you call a pertinent agency for advice, be sure to have the name of the director and request the mailing address so you can cc the agency in your correspondence with a retailer or other business.

If you have purchased a product from a home party and later decide you don't want it but have a problem getting your money back, a letter like this one could be in order, especially to remind the seller of federal laws.

7001 Ticked Off Lane
Springfield, IL 67011
July 1, 1998

Nancy Rottenecker, President
Dishdrainer Corporation
124 Dirty Lane, 6th Floor
Dallas, TX 23091

Dear Ms. Rottenecker:

I recently experienced a shocking episode at one of your shopping parties. Before I state the problem, let me stress that I have been a faithful customer of Dishdrainer for years and have spent a great deal of money on your products.

On June 26, 1998, I attended a party at the home of Leigh Holt, one of your representatives here in Springfield. At that time I placed a large order for which I paid cash, and among the items I ordered was a set of dishware priced at $109.95 plus $12.50 for postage and handling, for a total of $122.45 (receipt enclosed). The following day I decided to cancel that portion of my order, but when I contacted Mrs. Holt, she refused to honor my request and return my money. When I attempted to explain to her that for purchases such as this there is a federally mandated three days' "cooling-off period," she simply ignored the information and continued to refuse to refund my money.

I am asking you to conduct an immediate investigation into this matter. As president, you must make your distributors aware of this law, both for their sake and for the sake of their customers. I also expect a check in the amount of $122.45. Truthfully, I do not expect to attend any more of Dishdrainer's home parties unless I receive this amount on or before July 14, 1997.

Thank you.

Sincerely,

Florence Phillips

cc: Federal Trade Commission
    Sixth Street and Pennsylvania Avenue, NW
    Room 240
    Washington, DC 20580

    National Association of
    Consumer Agency Administrators
    1010 Vermont Avenue, NW, Suite 514
    Washington, DC 20005

    Jim Ryan, Attorney General
    Governor's Office of Consumer Assistance
    222 South College
    Springfield, IL 62706

    Debra Hagen
    Assistant Attorney General and Chief
    Consumer Fraud Bureau
    Office of the Attorney General
    500 South Second Street
    Springfield, IL 62706

Cybershopping

Consumers are increasingly shopping via the Internet for everything from CDs and videos to airline tickets and gourmet food. The most spectacular feature of this device for many of us is the convenience. With a stroke of the keyboard and a click of the mouse, you can get what you want without having to worry about crowded parking lots, tired feet, or heavy shopping bags. Without even leaving your desk you can enjoy shopping for just about any item your heart desires.

But wait a minute before your fingers go flying to find the perfect product! Just as we have to be careful when shopping by mail and by phone, the same holds true for shopping from the Internet. The Federal Trade Commission advises consumers to remember the following:

❶ Unsecured information can be intercepted. Always use a secured browser, which will encrypt or scramble purchase information. The credit and charge card companies are currently working on a better level of security measures for on-line shopping. If you don't have encryption software, it is probably a good idea to call the company's 800 number or fax your order.

❷ Shop with companies you know (and trust). Always determine their return and refund policies *before* placing an order.

❸ Never give out your Internet password. Create a really original one that is impossible for a scam artist to decipher, and avoid like the plague a combination of letters and/or numbers such as house number or your birthdate. Also, do not give out your social security number. With today's horror stories of identity theft, react like a wild bull with a red kerchief waved in front of its eyes if an online company asks for this piece of private information.

4 Always print out a copy of your order and confirmation number for your records. This documentation is imperative if you need to write a complaint letter later.

The same laws that protect you when you shop by mail or phone apply when shopping through this medium. The only exception to the **Cooling-Off Rule** explained in Chapter 6 is when a company doesn't promise a shipping time and you're *applying* for credit to pay for your purchase; that business then has fifty days to ship after receiving your order.

So let's say you followed all of this advice, and you've placed a very special online order to arrive just in time for your mother's birthday—a Frank Sinatra CD. Unfortunately, she opens the package and instead of the mellow tones of "Ol' Blue Eyes," she hears the raucous screech of a heavy metal band. Determined to satisfy Mom's tastes and, at the same time, to reimburse your pocketbook, you could write a letter like the following:

```
                    899 Ringing Ears Lane
                    Tulsa, OK 73956
                    November 30, 1998


Raymond Records, CEO
CDs-to-You
1344 Digital Avenue
New York, NY 18754


Dear Mr. Record:

I am appalled at my recent experience with
CDs-to-You. On October 29, 1998, I ordered
Volumes I-V of the Frank Sinatra CD, Blue
Eyes (copy of order and confirmation num-
ber enclosed) for $49.95 plus $8.00 for ship-
ping and handling. Instead, I was shocked
to receive a CD by the band Screaming Vomit.
```

Under the Fair Credit Billing Act, I am requesting an immediate credit to my charge card (#1234567890). Please note that I returned the Vomit CD well within the required sixty-day time limit.

I have been well satisfied in the past with my online shopping, and particularly with the services offered by your company. Assuming that this $57.95 credit is applied before my next billing date, I will certainly remain a loyal customer of CDs-to-You. I also expect a letter of explanation from you regarding this mix-up.

Thank you, and I look forward to hearing from you within the next seven business days.

Sincerely,

Samuel Son

Enclosure

cc: Federal Trade Commission
    Sixth Street and Pennsylvania Avenue, NW
    Room 240
    Washington, DC 20580

    Jane Wheeler, Assistant Attorney General
    Office of the Attorney General
    Consumer Protection Unit
    4545 North Lincoln Boulevard, Suite 620
    Oklahoma City, OK 73105

    B. B. Bucks, CEO
    Big Bucks Credit Card Corporation
    909 Money Terrace, Suite 20
    New York, NY 18798

EXCEEDING CUSTOMER EXPECTATIONS

Robert Meers, President/CEO, Reebok Brands:

Customer satisfaction is a priority at Reebok. In fact, it is one of five goals that we have established for our brand. We view consumer feedback, positive or negative, as an opportunity to strengthen our relationship with our customers, as well as better understand their needs. Consumer feedback obtained via telephone, mail, e-mail, and fax is consolidated and provided to our Product Marketing, Research and Development, and Quality Control teams on a regular basis. Our goal is to exceed the expectations of consumers, which is achievable only by knowing what they expect.

Returns

There are retail businesses, both mail order and stores, in which the sky is (almost) the limit in terms of their returns policy. Certainly many smaller local companies have policies that permit consumers to return or exchange products, and so forth. But the national corporate whoppers strive to satisfy their customers as well. L. L. Bean, for one, was founded on such a premise. Its employees, whether they're dealing with customers in person or by phone, have the authority to do whatever the customer wishes (within reason), without going to a superior. The only time a manager comes into play is on those very infrequent occasions when an employee needs permission to deny the customer's request. The elite Nordstrom stores do a terrifically brisk business, not only because of the upscale quality of Nordstrom's merchandise, but also because of its don't turn the customer away refund policy. Then we have Wal-Mart—the best thing ever to come out of Arkansas. Sam Walton, the founder, once stated, *"The greatest measurement of our success is how well we please our customer, our Boss. Let's have our customers leave 100 percent satisfied every day.*" And this holds true in all the Wal-Mart stores, from the rural lands south of the Mason-Dixon line to the more metropolitan cities—100 percent.

All it takes to find out if a company has a sweet return policy is to call and ask or, even better, ask before you buy. If you didn't have the foresight to check out these policies and you find yourself stuck, try writing a letter along the lines of the following.

> 1615 Shadowbrook Lane
> Bisbee, AR 55493
> September 5, 1997
>
> Harry Hometown, Owner
> Hometown Department Store
> 129 Main Street
> Bisbee, AR 55495
>
> Dear Mr. Hometown:
>
> I am sure you wish to be made aware of the shocking problem I recently experienced at your store. On August 24, 1997, I purchased a sports coat in your men's department for $99.95 plus tax (I have enclosed a copy of the receipt). After taking the coat home, I decided I did not particularly like the fabric and attempted to return the purchase on August 30. Much to my surprise, the manager refused to accept the return.
>
> I now understand your company has a five-day return policy. I was not aware of your store's policy at the time of this purchase, nor had I had any occasion to inquire about your policy any of the other times in the past when I have purchased goods at

Hometown. Because I have been a faithful customer for several years, I believe an exception should be made in this instance, and I ask that my money in the amount of $107 be returned immediately.

Thank you, and I look forward to hearing from you within the next two weeks and receiving a check for $107.

Sincerely,

Bubba Blackwell

Perhaps because this store was one situated within a small city as opposed to a larger metropolitan area, Bubba's letter was answered with good news (although I would hope the response would be the same anyplace). Mr. Hometown apologized for not being able to refund the $107 owing to store policy, but he did offer Bubba a store credit, which more than satisfied this customer.

Damaged and Shoddy Goods

Furniture usually comes without a warranty. We know that one day we'll have to replace our old and run-down furniture when it just gives up the ghost. Replacing pieces of furniture is always much more expensive than we expect, probably because we remember what we spent to buy similar pieces ten or twenty years ago. If your new purchases are imperfect or are damaged by a moving company or the store's delivery people, you may derive some solace and ideas for your own poison pen from the following letter, written by a lady who was totally teed off about a defective dining room set.

900 Teed Terrace
Arlington, VA 10445
July 15, 1998

S. D. Censure, CEO
Erratic Furniture Stores
900 Den Parkway South
Richmond, VA 23210

Dear Mr. Censure:

A horrendous experience with one of your
stores prompts this letter. I purchased a
dining room suite on May 10, 1998, at a cost
of $3,192.95 from Store #XXX in Alexandria,
Virginia. The first suite that was delivered had to be returned because of very
inferior craftsmanship: the table did not
fit the base; the deck was chipped; and the
hutch was missing.

When the set was delivered the second time,
once again everything had to be returned
because of defects. There was no table hardware, and the hutch mirror was cracked.

The third delivery was even worse! The
hutch top was completely off, the doors were
warped, and there was a huge gap under-
neath the door. The hutch was not the same
color as the rest of the set.

Finally, on July 13, I received a new and
complete dining room suite. I must add that
Erratic Furniture Stores did, at this point,
give me the deck and table pads for free.
While I appreciate this gesture, it by no
means compensates for the time, headaches,

and inconveniences I experienced over that more than five-week period.

Please investigate this matter promptly so that I can put this ordeal behind me. As a gesture of compensation, I expect a full credit for the price of the hutch. I expect to hear from you within ten working days with a satisfactory resolution.

Thank you.

Sincerely,

Lillian Lambaste

cc: V. F. Johnson, Consumer Specialist
    County of Fairfax
    Department of Governmental Affairs
    12000 Governmental Parkway, Suite 433
    Fairfax, VA 22035-0047

    Frank Seales, Jr., Chief
    Office of the Attorney General
    900 East Main Street
    Richmond, VA 23219

    Federal Trade Commission
    Sixth Street and Pennsylvania Avenue, NW
    Room 240
    Washington, DC 20580

Not shown in the letter you just read were the paragraphs where we cited Mrs. Lambaste's telephone calls and contacts with the store.

The department store in question immediately offered my client an entire new dining room *suite*, but to her honest credit, she only accepted the hutch. I'm sure the CEO and his managers were amazed to find that greed is not the reason for most customer complaints, and they made it clear that they were more than happy to listen to her if the need arose again.

Probably everyone at one time or another has had cause to write a poison pen letter about an unpleasant experience with a hardware shop. The following complaint—almost a comedy of errors—was mailed to the president of a hardware chain.

SOLICITING CUSTOMER INPUT

Ben Cammarata, President/CEO, The TJX Companies, Inc.:

In order to succeed in today's highly competitive retail marketplace, each customer's opinion must be equally valued. By attentively listening to and addressing our customers' comments and concerns in a direct and timely basis, we foster a positive, lasting relationship built upon mutual understanding and respect.

As such, we have developed (and continue to refine) a system of constantly soliciting T. J. Maxx and Marshall customer input, both positive and negative, through a variety of feedback opportunities including Comment Cards, our 1-800 Customer Service number and Store Associates. All these vehicles are designed to provide quick customer response and, ultimately, to deliver the level of service their loyal patronage deserves.

133 Claythorne Drive
Gretna, LA 04322
February 5, 1998

Bertram Birdbrain, President
Half-Baked Hardware, Inc.
735 Company Parkway, Suite 238
Orlando, FL 32808

Dear Mr. Birdbrain:

This last week my husband and I have lived through an appalling nightmare, exclusively because of Half-Baked Hardware.

Before Christmas, I purchased wallpaper in preparation for papering a bedroom. I gave the exact measurements to an assistant at the Super Half-Baked store where I always shop. He told me precisely how many rolls to buy, and I followed his suggestion.

This week, my husband, the Half-Baked cardholder, and I began the task. Because the existing paper was very old, we realized that we needed to use something to remove it from the walls. I called the store and was quoted a price of $44 for a steamer, whereupon my husband went to purchase it. It did not cost $44, as I had been told, but was instead $71.21! Because we had no other option, my husband purchased it. After several hours of stripping the old paper, he began to hang the new paper, only to realize, after only one-third of the walls was completed, that there was not nearly enough paper to complete the task (remember, one of your personnel had told me the number of rolls to buy).

I rushed to the Super Half-Baked store, only to discover that this paper was now out of stock! I bought several rolls of a new pattern and returned home, where we stripped off all of the paper that we had just hung and threw it away. Even at $20 per roll, it soon became apparent that this new wallpaper was of a very inferior quality. The seams would not hold, and it bubbled badly in many places. At this point, however, we had no choice but to complete the job.

The next day, my husband returned and complained about the wallpaper. He was told that if he bought a product called "Paperhungyou" it would fix the seams. After working with this product, my husband realized that it, too, was shockingly inadequate, as was the "professional" knowledge offered by your assistant manager. Once more, he returned to the store.

This time he was told to buy contact cement. My husband was finally able to close the seams in the paper, but because he was now so frustrated and infuriated with all of the unnecessary problems we had encountered due to Half-Baked's incompetence, my husband lost his balance and turned over the bucket of cement--spilling it all over my new carpet, which is less than a year old! To add further insult to injury, the paper at the top of the walls, for which he had left enough to cut off a straight seam

at the top of the wall, adhered to that portion of the ceiling and refuses to come off.

After all this grief, this bedroom, which
should have cost us no more than $100 maxi-
mum to paper, has now cost us at least $1000:
this figure includes both of the paper purchases; the carpet that must be replaced;
and damages to the ceiling, now ruined.

We have been loyal customers of Half-Baked
for many, many years, and we have spent
thousands and thousands of dollars in your
stores. I am absolutely shocked and appalled about this entire disaster--from all
the misinformation to the substandard
materials. I cannot believe that you would
want any of your customers to be treated as
we have been, much less some of your most
long-standing customers. I am sure that
you will wish to investigate this matter
quickly and thoroughly and to compensate
us for the amount we have lost.

Thank you, and I look forward to hearing
from you within five business days.

Sincerely,

Janice Jerked-Around (Mrs. Jerry)
Account # 444444444

When that letter elicited no response, the following letter
(Try, try again) was dashed off to the CEO.

133 Claythorne Drive
Gretna, LA 04322
March 20, 1998

Heraldo Half-Baked, CEO
Half-Baked Stores, Inc.
735 Company Parkway, Suite 220
Orlando, FL 32808

Dear Mr. Half-Baked:

I must say that I am both dismayed and angered at Mr. Birdbrain's lack of attention and response to such a horrendous problem. It is inconceivable that someone who supposedly prizes his company's reputation and makes such an issue of "Customer Satisfaction" completely ignores the problems of one of its better customers.

Even if the earlier letter was not personally read by Mr. Birdbrain, I cannot imagine that the information was missed by someone of some consequence. If I do not hear from you immediately, I will assume that the Half-Baked Company no longer wishes our business, and we will certainly destroy our credit card and shop elsewhere in the future.

Sincerely,

Janice Jerked-Around

cc: Bertram Birdbrain, President
    Half-Baked Stores, Inc.
    735 Company Parkway, Suite 223
    Orlando, FL 32808

```
Tamara R. Velasquez, Chief
Consumer Protection Section
Office of Attorney General
1 America Place
P.O. Box 94095
Baton Rouge, LA 70804-9095

Federal Trade Commission
Sixth Street and Pennsylvania Avenue, NW
Room 240
Washington, DC 20580
```

The owner of this large chain must have really felt his hot seat burning. Less than twenty-four hours after this epistle was mailed (even the post office felt its flames), Janice Jerked-Around received a personal telephone call from both of the company's officers who apologetically extended a peace offering. They told her that she could choose any wallpaper, at any price, obtain a store credit for both sets of paper she had already purchased, as well as for all of the other connected purchases; and "Half-Baked's" own professionals would install it after taking down all of the new as well as the remaining old wallpaper, and the ceiling would be painted by a professional painter.

● WARRANTIES AND DEFECTIVE GOODS

As a result of Congress passing the Magnuson-Moss Warranty Act, when we buy something new, we always receive some kind of warranty—full, limited, or implied.* Smart shoppers need to

---

*An *extended warranty* is one we're pressured to buy, often for a good sum of money. This purchase simply extends the full warranty for a certain period of time, at which point we may opt to "extend" the warranty again.

be aware of how these "contracts" between manufacturers, dealers, and consumers work. The manufacturers are required to disclose terms and conditions of the warranty options to buyers.

✎ A *full* warranty means the defective product will be fixed
or replaced free within a specified amount of time, or, if
the product cannot be repaired, you will be given the
choice between a new product or a full refund. This type
of warranty is also good for secondary owners.

✎ A *limited* warranty may cover only parts but no labor or
handling charges, and it applies to only the original owner.

✎ An *implied* warranty offers much less protection than the
other two; this "warrant of merchantability" comes with
each sale automatically and is the seller's authentication
that the product is fit for ordinary use.

Be extra careful when purchasing merchandise labeled "as is" or
"no warranty," as this may truly prove to be a warning for the
buyer to beware.

The Magnuson-Moss Act also allows us customers to sue if
the company doesn't keep its servicing promises after we buy a
product. If you have a full or limited warranty and you have
a problem with a product, simply send the item back with a
copy of the proof of purchase. Be sure to keep the original sales
slip, the warranty itself, the owner's manual, and, if you have
more storage space than I do for large boxes, the original box
or packing. If your warranty has just expired but you think that
the problem with the item is inexcusable, consider a letter like
the following. You'll notice it's essential to specify dates, the specific problem(s), the person with whom you have spoken about
the dilemma, when the warranty expired (if it has), and the
amount you have been quoted to repair whatever is wrong.
Reminding the store or manufacturer that you've been a "loyal
customer" is very important, too. Again, review the rules in
Chapter 3. They could be your salvation.

Here is a typical example of a useful warranty letter.

454 Customer Street, # 16
Greeley, CO 80633
February 1, 1998

Samuel Shoddy, President/CEO
Slipshod, Inc.
One Appliance Avenue
Dallas, TX 76543

Dear Mr. Shoddy:

All my life I have understood that Slipshod products are the best; however recently I have found to my shock and horror
that not only is this not always the case,
but also that Slipshod does not stand behind its word or its products.

In October 1995 I purchased a new town-
house with brand-new Slipshod appliances.
One of the reasons I decided to move into
this condo was because it featured your
brand of appliances, and I have been a
loyal customer of Slipshod for many years.
In January 1997 I turned on the oven, but
it did not heat up. I called the local repair service, which sent out a service representative. He stated that the "bake/broil
glow bar" was broken, and a new "glow bar"
with labor would cost $210. The new part
and labor were not covered by my warranty,
so I paid for the repair myself.

The stove was not even two years old when
I discovered this problem. I find it appalling that somewhere along the line the
manufacturer allowed such inferior merchandise to slip past its quality control. I
have been unable to receive any assistance

from any local Slipshod representative office, and thus I am turning to you for assistance.

I cannot believe that you would knowingly
permit such products to be sold under the
Slipshod name. I also cannot believe that
you would condone my being charged $210
(half the price of a brand-new stove) for
this ridiculous repair. This may not sound
like a great deal of money--certainly not
to a giant such as Slipshod--but it is a
large sum to me since I am on a pension and
cannot afford an additional expense. But
it is also a matter of principle: having
been such a loyal customer over the years,
I find it unacceptable that I should be
held accountable for a problem that arose
through faulty manufacturing.

I am certain that you will wish to investigate this matter promptly. I do not wish to
be reimbursed for anything other than the
$210 that I paid to repair a Slipshod prod-
uct, which never should have needed repairing in the first place.

I look forward to hearing from you within
ten business days.

Thank you.

Sincerely,

Andrew Aghast

cc: Major Appliance Consumer Action Program
    20 North Wacker Drive, Suite 1500
    Chicago, IL 60606

    Colorado Consumer Protection Unit
    Office of the Attorney General
    110 Sixteenth Street, 10th Floor
    Denver, CO 80202

    Gus Sandstrom, District Attorney
    Pueblo County District Attorney's Office
    201 West Eighth Street, Suite 801
    Pueblo, CO 81003

    Rita Barreras, Director
    Aging and Adult Service
    Department of Social Services
    110 Sixteenth Street, Suite 200
    Denver, CO 80202-4147

    Horace Deets, Executive Director
    American Association of Retired Persons
    601 East Street, NW
    Washington, DC 20049

⬤ SERVICES

Some "purchases" can't be carried in a shopping bag or mailed directly to your home. That doesn't mean, however, you can't use your poison pen to address problems. When you pay someone to render you a service—a personnel office, a dating or au pair agency, for example—you're entitled to premium treatment. If you're treated like an unwanted stepchild, it's time to write a letter.

Personnel Agencies

I'm sure there are many of us who have gone to employment agencies in search of a job. Most of these organizations are great and match your qualifications with job requirements to help you obtain the position you love, but you may run into others that aren't quite as capable or even as professional. Perhaps the firm wishes to receive its fee without really taking the time necessary to place you where you would like to be. As we saw in Chapter 3, when it comes to those businesses that are the most frequent targets of complaints, employment agencies were right up at the top. The following letter clearly demonstrates why.

421 Meadow Lark Lane
St. Albans, WV 25175
June 26, 1998

Pauline Placement, President
Placement Employees, Inc.
1901 DuPont Avenue
St. Albans, WV 25178

Dear Ms. Placement:

On June 1 I interviewed with your employment counselor Vicki Vague. At that time, we discussed my hopes for a position that would incorporate my typing skills of 124 words per minute and my desire to work in a front-office capacity. She assured me there would be no problem placing me within the very near future.

On June 8 Ms. Vague called and told me to report to work the following morning at St. Albans Hospital. I must admit that as I drove to my new job I was filled with excitement. Imagine my shock when I arrived, was given a smock to put on over my new suit, and was <u>sent to the kitchen to wash dishes</u>. I immediately explained the mix-up to the supervisor and returned home to call Ms. Vague, who was unavailable to answer the telephone.

I have since made seven calls to her and returned to Placement Employees on three different occasions. As of this date, I have yet to establish any further contact with Ms. Vague whatsoever.

I would like very much to meet with you personally to discuss this matter. Not only do I wish to make my concerns known about this utter mix-up so as to avoid something of this nature happening in the future, but I also wish for <u>you</u> to act in the role of job counselor to help me obtain the position for which I am so eminently qualified.

Thank you, and I look forward to hearing from you within the next seven days.

Sincerely,

Catherine Chide

"Catherine" ended up right back at the same hospital, but this time she was working as an administrative assistant.

Dating Services

Tired of playing the ordinary dating game, for her fortieth birthday Pamela Reid of Greenbelt, Maryland, decided to treat herself to a dating service whose advertisements promised to provide her with a match made in heaven; instead she soon discovered that hell, not heaven, was to be her Promised Land.

In her own hilarious words (and in the complaint letter she herself originally wrote to this company), Reid described the *special* dates she had through the dating service as follows:

> *a workaholic, an egotistical Lurch/Addams Family lookalike, a supposedly forty-seven-year-old man who could have passed for sixty and who had only one good eye, a gentleman who had more breasts than myself, an accountant who had the personality of a slug and who could not have purchased any clothes since the turn of the century, and a gentleman who had the misfortune to have had a stroke and who had one arm and one leg completely useless.*

I couldn't beat the creativity of her descriptions, but I did work with her to formulate a letter that, we hoped, could get her her money back.

983 Bonnie Brae Road
Greenbelt, MD 33589
June 19, 1998

Stuart Scam, President
Broken Promises Dating Service
678 Fraud Street, Suite 32
Baltimore, MD 34465

Dear Mr. Scam:

I am appalled by my recent experience with Broken Promises. Your business slogan, "The Intelligent Choice," implies that yours is an organization that seriously considers the background and preferences of your clientele. Indeed, your contract states that the people one is introduced to would be "most nearly compatible to you as indicated," that is "compatible with your preferences but who may not meet all of the preferences of the profile you provided." Based on the candidates who were referred to me, and

with whom I later had contact, I cannot believe that anyone on your staff attempted
at any time to match compatibility and
preferences according to my profile.

I joined your service in November 1997. I
simply wanted to meet someone with a similar educational background, interests, and
intentions with whom I could share some
free time. I did not meet such a man through
your service. On the contrary, some of the
men with whom Broken Promises placed me in
contact had serious physical disabilities,
such as stroke paralysis or one eye. Others
were either far older than I or just simply
very physically unattractive, such as the
man who surely weighed over 300 pounds.
None of them had a similar educational
background. When I talked with members of
your staff, I did not mention these terrible problems; I had been told that negative
reports would be forwarded on. Regardless
of how I felt about these dating contacts,
I did not want to hurt anyone's feelings.

To say that I feel angered, disappointed,
and resentful about my experience with
your dating service hardly scratches the
surface. I invested a significant amount of
money to become a member of Broken Promises. I strongly suspect that this is the
only criteria your organization used when
selecting "appropriate" men for me to meet:
they paid their membership dues.

After I wrote the Better Business Bureau
about your organization, I received a letter from Diane Defame, the district man-

ager for Broken Promises. She insinuated
that I wanted my fee back because I found
fault with your matchmakers, and she offered a normal renewal package for $500.

This offer is insulting and absolutely ludicrous under the circumstances. It is an insult for Ms. Defame to imply to the Better
Business Bureau that I am only attempting
to obtain my fee back because I found fault
with your matchmakers. I find fault with
the entire management of your organization,
and I believe that the office I have dealt
with has misrepresented its services to me.
I demand a refund of my membership dues.
If, in fact, you are a legitimate business,
one that honors its legal contracts, you
will remit my fee at once; it is only fair
and just that you do so. I cannot believe
that you condone this type of performance
from your staff, and I am sure that you will
wish to investigate this matter promptly
and thoroughly. I will expect a reply from
you within the next ten working days.

Thank you.

Sincerely,

Pamela Reid

cc: William Leibovici, Chief
    Consumer Protection Division
    Maryland Office of the Attorney General
    200 St. Paul Place, 16th Floor
    Baltimore, MD 21202-2021

Stephen D. Hannan, Administrator
Howard County Office of Consumer Affairs
6751 Columbia Gateway Drive
Columbia, MD 21046

United States Department of Justice
Federal Bureau of Investigation
Fraud Division
Washington, DC 20535

Direct Marketing Association
1111 Nineteenth Street, NW, Suite 1100
Washington, DC 20036

Now, given the evidence that this was a truly fraudulent organization, it shouldn't come as a surprise that Reid didn't hear from Broken Promises. But we didn't give up the letter-writing campaign, and it is finally paying off. The U.S. Postal Inspection Service enlisted the help of the **National Fraud Information Center,** which is now investigating the matter.

HELPFUL AGENCIES AND SERVICES

The **Cooling-Off Rule,** under the **Federal Trade Commission,** allows consumers to cancel orders for items costing more than $25 if the purchase was made in a "home" situation, such as a home shopping party.

The Bureau of Consumer Protection, part of the Federal Trade Commission, assists with complaint inquiries related to the **Fair Debt Collection Practices Act.** Call this office at (202) 326-2222.

The **Direct Marketing Association,** P.O. Box 9008, Farmingdale, NY 11735, will direct its members to remove your name from their mailing lists (your request must be in writing).

The **Fair Debt Collections Practices Act** limits the contact debt collectors can have with consumers under certain circumstances. If you believe you are being harassed, contact the Federal Trade Commission at (202) 326-3128.

The **Federal Fair Credit Billing Act** helps to protect consumers against billing errors, unauthorized use of a credit card, goods or services charged but not received, and against paying specific charges for which written proof is sought.

The **Magnuson-Moss Warranty Act** requires manufacturers and dealers to disclose information about warranty options.

The **Mail or Telephone Order Rule** from the **Federal Trade Commission,** (202) 326-2222 or http://www.ftc.gov, protects your rights if merchandise you have ordered doesn't arrive within thirty days.

HELPFUL AGENCIES, AND SERVICES

The **National Association of Consumer Agency Administrators,** (202) 347-7395, enforces consumer laws with regard to the Federal Trade Commission's **Cooling-Off Rule.**

The **National Fraud Information Center,** (800) 876-7060, helps to protect consumers from scams and fraudulent practices.

Though not mentioned earlier in this chapter, the following two organizations can be very useful when your retail-related problem specifically concerns product safety:

Contact the **Product Safety Hotline,** U.S. Consumer Product Safety Commission, Washington, DC 20207, (800) 638-2772, for assistance with retail products other than cars or food. Contact the **U.S. Food and Drug Administration,** Recall and Emergency Coordinator, Washington, DC 20250, (202) 720-3621, for problems with microwave ovens and televisions.

CHAPTER 7

Health Maintenance Organizations (HMOs), Doctors, and Nurses

> He who has health has hope, and he who has hope has everything. —ARAB PROVERB

HEALTH MAINTENANCE ORGANIZATIONS

Perhaps today's preeminent medical disorder is that menacing gang of unseen, unknown, and, as many of us Americans believe, uncaring strangers who dictate decisions about our health and well-being from the top of their ivory towers. We've all heard horror stories about a child being delivered one afternoon and mother and babe being kicked out of the hospital the next day, with subsequent problems occurring simply because the family's HMO refused to pay for more than a twenty-four-hour stay. Thank goodness recent legislation has changed some of these absurd rulings, especially the requirement about newborns and their mothers: the hospital stay for new mothers and their babies is forty-eight hours if the physician feels it necessary. On the other hand, we still have a long, long way to go before we can breathe more easily about receiving quality health care. There have been cries to enact laws to protect the consumer, but Congress faces opposition from groups like the American Association of Health Plans, which is the national trade organization for HMOs. The consensus of the HMOs remains that Congress shouldn't be poking its nose into establishing clinical standards or other guidelines for health plans.

Even if you personally haven't had a reason to complain yet, you can certainly get to work on helping on your friends' or neighbors' behalf. If you (or anyone you know) is denied appropriate care because an HMO screams a resounding, "NO!" follow these steps:

❶ Document the problem just as you would any other complaint. Again, this is fundamental to getting what you seek. Conversations with doctors, nurses, insurance representatives, and the like should all be documented, becoming a part of the running list you're building.

❷ Obtain your medical records. Your medical records are your property even if they are sealed up in your physicians' never-never land of files.

❸ Learn all you can about your particular medical problem. Whether it's a run-of-the-mill operation or some little-known bacterial virus you picked up visiting a Third World country, do some research to try to understand it. Scarily enough, sometimes our doctors simply haven't kept current with the latest medical research and information, and, therefore, they don't have the knowledge required to best treat the disease. Frequently it's even better to consult with a specialist who *isn't* on your plan. His or her expert opinion or diagnosis may be the best ammo you can gather for a later appeal.

One handy organization that can assist you in finding organizations that support particular health issues is **Health Finder;** locate it on the World Wide Web at www.healthfinder.gov. This service can put you in touch with groups such as the American Cancer Society, the Epilepsy Association, United Cerebral Palsy, and the like—organizations that can provide written information on your health conditions, on usual treatments, on experimental treatments and research, as well as on support groups and other help.

Additionally, if you suspect you are the victim of health-care fraud, waste, or abuse, contact the **Inspector General's Hotline,** U.S. Department of Health and Human Services, P.O. Box 23489, Washington, DC 20013-1133. Issues of concern for this agency include but are not limited to Medicare, the **U.S. Food and Drug Administration,** and the U.S. Agency for Health Care Policy and Research.

Many of the insurance regulators can provide you with information to help you make informed decisions about your problem. These agencies and the laws within your home states could be of tremendous assistance if and when you find yourself fighting the giant health insurance companies. You'll find the regulators and their addresses in the appendices. Write them immediately.

We're now lucky to have a number of companies whose sole aim is to assist people who can't seem to get anywhere with those "ivory-tower" health-care tyrants. The **American Medical Consumers,** at (800) 836-5262, helps health-care subscribers with choices of doctors, specialists, and appropriate treatments. **Care-Counsel,** at (800) 227-3334, reviews cancer treatments with oncologist specialists; and **Health Decisions, Inc.,** at (303) 278-1700, offers advice on surgery, prenatal care, and disease management.

As always, get any necessary names and addresses when you call, in the event that it is necessary to cc an organization later if you need to write a poison pen letter.

❹ Find someone who can be your ally when you file your appeal. Your employer just might be the best party to act as an advocate, since most of the hefty HMO bills are coming out of his or her pocket. I expect both your company's leaders and your benefits department want to get their money's worth. State departments of insurance are also a viable connection to make. Each state has its own laws and regulations for *all* types of insurance, as well as people who will enforce the law. You'll find the regulators and their addresses listed in the appendices. Write to your state official immediately when you encounter a problem with your health-care provider. The organizations listed in the previous item can also act as allies.

5 **Alert your insurance company that you're filing a complaint, but be sure to follow the process and procedures set up by your own health plan.** Be sure to contact the most comprehensive national group that does its best to help consumers, **Physicians Who Care** (PWC), at (800) 800-5154, with your concerns; they will advise you on grievance procedures. PWC assists in a variety of ways, from reviewing medical charts, providing second opinions, becoming an additional advocate to appeal to the HMO, and helping you to write the letters I mentioned earlier.

6 **Involve your political representatives.** In addition to writing to the state insurance commission, compose a strong letter to your state and federal senators and representatives whose names and addresses may easily be obtained from the local library. Health care is an especially hot topic in Washington, so political pressure really can be effective. And don't forget the most obvious but often the most overlooked person, the president himself. Health care is definitely a nonpartisan issue for consumers everywhere. Research and research some more; explore every avenue possible.

One of my clients called me when he was experiencing more and more physical pain after being injured in an auto accident but was receiving fewer and fewer benefits from his HMO. When he was feeling the financial pressure and had no sick time left, and the remaining treatments allotted by his HMO were rapidly running out, he could find no one to listen to his pleas for coverage for the extra hours of physical therapy prescribed by his physician. He had tried many times over to cut through the bureaucracy of his plan, yet all he ever received in return was a massive runaround. Armed with all the information, I set out my own shingle, and Dr. Ellen went to work.

998 Hurt Street
Boise, ID 83721
August 26, 1998

Nathan Noodlehead, President/CEO
Hell Motivated Organization
135 Devil Avenue, Suite 666
Chicago, IL 60606

Dear Mr. Noodlehead:

I realize that I am only one individual out
of the hundreds of thousands of Hell Motivated Organization subscribers, but you are
my only hope for resolving a shocking problem I am currently experiencing.

I sustained severe back and neck injuries
in an automobile accident on July 5, 1998.
After my discharge from the hospital, my
physician, Dr. Donald Doctor, prescribed a
series of physical therapy treatments (all
documentation enclosed). As you know, the
HMO allows only fifteen such treatments,
and I have just completed the tenth one.
Dr. Doctor states that a minimum of fifteen
more sessions are mandatory in order for
my pain to diminish and my health to be
restored enough so that I can return to
work. At this point, any further time I
take off from work will be unpaid, and I
will be forced to live off my rapidly dwin-
dling savings account. Under these conditions I cannot afford to pay for the extra
treatments. The sooner I get the treatments
I need, the sooner I can return to work and
resume earning my normal pay.

At this point, I am faced with only two options: (1) I can return to work and run the risk of being fired because I am physically unable to perform my duties; or (2) I can spend the remainder of my savings on physical therapy treatments, thereby leaving me no money for any future needs.

I have attempted many times in the past two weeks to speak with someone at both the local and the national HMO office, in the hopes that an exception could be made in my case. Unfortunately, either no one returns my calls or I am routed to someone who is unable to give me any answers. I have enclosed a listing of the times, dates, and responses I have received.

I beg of you to review my case. As you do so, please do not think of me as simply another number in a vast system but as a human being. Also please note that the HMO has had to pay out very little for my health care over the years that I have been a premium-paying member, with the exception of this past accident.

I know that you are very busy, but I would very much appreciate hearing from you within the next two weeks before I must make a decision about continuing my treatments.

Thank you.

Sincerely,

Patrick Pain

```
cc:  Dr. Donald Doctor
     4377 Physicians Lane
     Boise, ID 83797

     The Honorable Donna Shalala, Secretary
     United States Department of
     Health and Human Services
     200 Independence Avenue, SW
     Washington, DC 20201

     Department of Beneficiary Services
     United States Department of
     Health and Human Services
     6325 Security Boulevard
     Baltimore, MD 21207

     James Alcorn, Director
     Department of Insurance
     700 West State Street
     Boise, ID 83720
```

Believe it or not, in Patrick Pain's case, behind that faceless nonentity we call our insurance companies, there beat the heart of a *real* person. Mr. Noodlehead, the president and CEO, actually came through. Although he didn't approve the prescribed additional sessions, he did authorize five extra ones, leaving Patrick Pain's bank account more or less intact.

⬤ PRESCRIPTIONS

Is there any one of us who doesn't have to take prescription medication at some point or other? If we're lucky, the medicine isn't for a life-threatening condition, but if it is, we must have the assurance that it will be there when we need it. One important source of problem-solving is the **U.S. Food and Drug Administration,** (301) 443-4177. One of its critical responsibilities is to monitor the testing, manufacturing, distributing, and selling of pharmaceuticals and medical equipment. One client, thoroughly (and understandably) outraged because her husband's nemesis, their HMO's prescription center, repeatedly put his health in danger, wanted an equally outraged letter to her HMO's prescription center.

P.O. Box 333
Louisville, KY 89036
April 5, 1998

Betty Bovine, Quality Assurance
Department Manager
Pseudo Prescriptions
108 Prescription Parkway, 6th Floor
Indianapolis, IN 46202

Dear Ms. Bovine:

After I lodged a telephone complaint yesterday, April 4, with Diana Dullard, supervisor at Pseudo Prescriptions, she advised I write directly to you about an appalling situation that has occurred not once, but twice.

My husband, Michael Medication, must take Zestril for high blood pressure. The last two times we have telephoned in a refill request to Pseudo Prescriptions, a shocking mismanagement of our order took place. I might also add that we spoke directly to a representative and did not leave the refill information through the automated option. The first time, not only did the Zestril not arrive when promised, but after repeated calls, when it did come, the enclosed paperwork was for a gentleman in Georgia who takes his medication for cancer! I cannot help but wonder if he ever received his own medicine and is still alive, thanks to Pseudo's slipshod practices.

The last time we ordered the prescription, the result was the same: we did not receive the Zestril. When it became apparent that the order would not arrive on time, we instructed Pseudo to mail the medication via FedEX. My husband called twice as a reminder, and each time he was assured that it would be sent in this manner.

By this past Thursday (April 3), when the medicine had not arrived as promised, he called again and was once again assured that it would be FedEx'ed that day to arrive Friday morning. On Friday, April 4, he repeated his call and attempted to explain again that his supply of Zestril would be taken up by Saturday, and his health would be in jeopardy. Once more, with profuse apologies, the representative promised that the medication would be in my husband's hands the following morning.

No medicine arrived. Once more my husband called, and to our dismay he was informed that an error had been made and that the Zestril had been shipped out by regular mail. Luckily, our local pharmacist was kind enough to give my husband a few pills to tide him over; at least someone cares whether my husband lives or dies.

When we spoke with Ms. Dullard, she reiterated that there never should have been a problem. The order had a number of notes on

it stating that it should be shipped via
Federal Express. It was obvious to her and
to us that somewhere in your order ful-
fillment department you have at least one,
if not many, totally incompetent persons
in charge of life-saving medications. It
is also obvious that you need to investigate
this matter immediately and thoroughly before a death occurs.

I have enclosed the receipt for our copay-
ment for the extra pills, for which we
expect reimbursement, and I also anticipate an immediate reply.

Sincerely,

Rhonda Raging

cc: George Nicholas, Commissioner
    Department of Insurance
    215 West Main Street
    Frankfort, KY 40601

    The Honorable Donna Shalala, Secretary
    United States Department of
    Health and Human Services
    200 Independence Avenue, SW
    Washington, DC 20201

    Consumer Product Safety Commission
    4330 East West Highway
    Bethesda, MD 20207

Following is an excerpt of the response Mrs. Raging received
from Pseudo Prescriptions:

Dear Mrs. Raging:

Unfortunately, at the beginning of the year we experienced some unexpected inventory problems that have been resolved. Your receipts for the medications you purchased while waiting for your mail order have been forwarded to our claims department, and you will be receiving your reimbursement check within seven to ten days. Enclosed are coupons for future mail orders. You are a valued member, and the level of service you received is unacceptable.

Sincerely,

Betty Bovine

⊙ DOCTORS AND NURSES

Writing letters might also be a smart way to shorten the amount of time you have to spend in a doctor's *waiting* room. Many physicians have a policy that if you're either late for or miss your appointment altogether and don't give adequate notice, then you're charged for the office visit anyway. After waiting (and steaming) for almost two hours after his own appointment time, a busy attorney walked up to the receptionist and handed her his business card, on which he had written: "For services *not* rendered, $200" (his rate was $100 per hour). The following is a letter in which he made his displeasure further known.

Allan S. Attorney, PC
8733 Litigation Lane, Suite 211 / Dover, DE 19865
Telephone: (302) 433-8987 / Fax: (302) 433-8968

August 1, 1998

Dr. David Delay
137 Professional Park, Suite 489
Dover, DE 19865

Dear Dr. Delay:

It is absolutely appalling what transpired
in your office on Wednesday, July 30, 1997.

My appointment time was set for 11:00 A.M.
I had deliberately scheduled this particular time because I had scheduled an appointment with a client at 1:30 P.M., and I
thought this slot would give me time to see
you, to eat a quick lunch, and to return to my
office in time to meet with my client. Unfortunately, this did not prove to be the case.

I sat and waited for approximately two hours
after the designated appointment time. I
finally had no choice but to leave without
seeing you. Upon my departure, I left a bill
for $200 (my rate for two hours of work) with
your receptionist, for which I expect immediate payment. My time is equally as valuable
as yours.

I understand that some patients have more
needs than others; what I do not understand, however, is how you can ignore other
patients for such a long time and force them
to wait for you. This is unconscionable.

I expect to hear from you within the next
seven days.

Sincerely,

Allan S. Attorney

Within twenty-four hours after the doctor's office received
this communication, "Allan" got a call from "Doctor Delay."
After a long heart-to-heart, it was mutually agreed that the physician would not pay the $200 bill, but our lawyer friend wouldn't

CONSUMER FEEDBACK

Manufacturers are concerned for their "patients." In
the words of Marylou F. Ulincy, Manager of Customer
Relations for the Bayer Corporation:

*Bayer Consumer Care has set up a consumer relations depart-
ment to ensure that the comments we receive from our consumers are reviewed and responded to. We strongly believe
that consumer satisfaction and loyalty are the foundations to
our business success. As such, we value consumer feedback.*

*We receive numerous consumer comments on a daily
basis. We have a toll-free number on most of our products
to encourage such dialogue. In addition, we are establishing brand-specific sites on the Internet to reach out to our
"cyber consumers."*

*Bayer Consumer Care also incorporates feedback in prod-
uct improvement initiatives. We have made several modifi-
cations to various products over the years based on this
feedback. And it doesn't take thousands or even hundreds
of consumers to get our attention. Often just one comment
is all it takes!*

be responsible for covering his next two office visits. I'll bet that Allan never had to wait again!

Another letter comes to mind concerning a nurse who acted rudely and irresponsibly. Before we look at this case, however, let me state up front that nurses fall into the same category as teachers: they are overworked and underpaid. Most of the men and women in this particular medical role are the finest and most compassionate of people. Too bad my client didn't encounter one of the good ones.

> 901 Suffering Street
> Bismarck, ND 58504
> February 5, 1997
>
> Dr. Peter Physician, Chief of Staff
> Painbreak Hospital
> 173 Epson Lane
> Bismarck, ND 58505
>
> Dear Dr. Physician:
>
> I recently experienced an appalling situation while I was a patient at Painbreak Hospital. I am sure you wish to be made aware of the circumstances.
>
> On January 31, 1997, I fell on the ice and injured my arm. My wife subsequently rushed me to the hospital where I was admitted to the emergency room for treatment. As it turned out, my arm was broken

in three places, so you can imagine the excruciating pain I suffered. First, one of the ER nurses, Thelma Torture, had the audacity to tell me "not to be such a baby" when I requested medication for the pain. Then, after two hours had passed and I still had not been seen by a physician, I asked Nurse Torture if she could check to see when I would be examined. Her response this time was, "This is an emergency room. You're not an emergency, and you'll be seen when a doctor has time and not before."

I understand that patients are triaged based on varying types of emergencies, and I certainly would never condone treating someone with a broken arm before a person in the throes of a heart attack, for example. However, to be spoken to and dealt with in what I believe to be such an unprofessional and rude manner is unconscionable.

I expect a full investigation into this matter, and I ask that an official reprimand be placed into Ms. Torture's personnel file. I expect to hear from you by February 15, 1997.

Thank you.

Sincerely,

Benjamin Break

```
cc: HMO, Inc.
    102 Patient Lane
    Anywhere, CA 65466

    American Medical Association
    1601 Broadway
    New York, NY 10019

    Inspector General's Hotline
    United States Department of
    Health and Human Services
    P.O. Box 23489
    Washington, DC 20013-1133

    Heidi Heitkamp
    Office of the Attorney General
    600 East Boulevard
    Bismarck, ND 58505
```

My client got his wish. The chief of staff at "Painbreak Hospital" immediately responded and informed "Mr. Break" that the nurse in question had been transferred to another department and that her personnel file was now a little fuller.

HELPFUL AGENCIES AND SERVICES

The **American Medical Consumers** (800) 836-5262 helps health-care subscribers with requests regarding choosing doctors, specialists, and the best treatments.

CareCounsel (888) 227-3334 will provide a quality review of cancer treatment in conjunction with oncologists at Memorial Sloan-Kettering Cancer Center.

Health Decisions, Inc. (303) 278-1700 offers advice on surgery, prenatal care, and disease management.

Health Finder assists in researching hospitals, associations, and medical libraries. Find it on the Web at www.healthfinder.gov.

To report health-care fraud, waste, or abuse, contact the **Inspector General's Hotline** (800) 447-8477.

Physicians Who Care (800) 800-5154 is a comprehensive organization that advises consumers on grievance procedures and acts as an advocate to help with appeals to HMOs.

For information on food, drugs, and medical equipment, call the **U.S. Food and Drug Administration** at (202) 720-3631.

CHAPTER 8

Sue or Arbitrate?

> The best laid schemes o' mice an' men . . .
> —ROBERT BURNS

If all my advice has paid off, you can turn to Chapter 9 and learn more about the power of writing letters that are more personal in nature. But who said life is fair? Maybe you've tried the verbal approach, written your share of complaint letters, and you still have not seen a successful resolution of your problem. It can happen. Perhaps the verbal approach ended in a slap across the face get outta here invective, or, heaven forbid, your complaint letters didn't do the trick, and now you're still stuck with the lemon, the overdraft on your bank account, or the extra-extra-large "Sleek and Satin Seduction Promise" nightgown. Before you race off to small claims court or to see your lawyer about filing a class-action suit, consider a couple of other alternatives: arbitration and mediation.

● ARBITRATION VERSUS MEDIATION

Arbitration is strictly defined as "the settlement of a dispute by an impartial person chosen to settle such dispute between parties." Generally, *mediation* is defined as assistance necessary to help

bring agreement between opposing parties in—for our purposes—a controversy over products and/or services. Although
there are differences, in today's world the term *mediator* has
become somewhat synonymous with *arbitrator*. Both mediators
and arbitrators listen to both sides of a complaint and then try to
solve it using their own special brand of expertise. The proceedings may be informal and take the form of a roundtable discus-
sion or be as formal as the cold, stern courtroom environment in
that there are opening statements, rebuttals, and closing arguments. The big difference between mediation and arbitration is
that neither arguing party has to agree to the solution in a mediation, whereas both parties have to agree in advance to abide by
the solution in a binding arbitration (unless a notification is
snuck in, as we'll discuss later).

Take the case of your car's terminal lemonitis (see Chapter 5).
If you can't get satisfaction after a letter campaign, arbitration
may be a viable option, and in a few states it's even mandatory.
The process is usually handled by a panel of auto-industry and
consumer representatives who control the meeting and decide
the results. Section 703 of the Magnuson-Moss Act requires that
the arbitrator make a decision within forty days after you file for
arbitration. This speeds things up a bit for you.

Most automobile manufacturers either endorse their own
third-party dispute resolution program or participate in **AUTO-
CAP** (the American Consumer Action Program) or **AUTO-
LINE** (an arbitration panel under the auspices of the Better
Business Bureaus). The appendices list those manufacturers that
participate in arbitration programs and those that don't.

In some states, arbitration is mandatory for settling disputes in
other areas as well. For example, Kaiser Permanante HMO
patients who live in California, Colorado, and Massachusetts
can expect arbitration if a problem arises with medical treatment; in the other fourteen states where Kaiser is based, including New York, customers can sue for grievances, including
malpractice. My advice is to check with your own insurance
company and your state's attorney general's office to discover the
usual practices.

Don't assume that there's always a *choice* about arbitrating as opposed to suing. Arbitration may be forced on you in a most unsuspected fashion. When you sign a contract, do you always take the time to read the fine print? If not, you may later discover that you've John Hancock'ed away your right to sue in court and to ask for a jury trial. In other words, some contracts stipulate that all disputes will be settled through arbitration. You may still request that a court invalidate the arbitrator's decision if the contract you signed does not stipulate arbitration for the type of dispute you face with the company or if there was some hanky-panky in the proceedings that may have affected the outcome. And if the stakes are really high, you should seriously consider hiring a lawyer to represent you at an arbitration hearing. So be careful: when you are writing letters, don't assume that you have the right to sue.

Many corporations don't require arbitration and insist only that the parties attempt mediation before the parties resort to a lawsuit. But consumers beware! Some companies finagle themselves out of a prospective lawsuit by mailing out low-key, innocuous notices of new company arbitration practices. These letters don't come with messages like LOOK! PAY ATTENTION! YOUR HOME AND ITS ENTIRE CONTENTS ARE AT STAKE! emblazoned on the envelope. No, they're more like the nondescript sort of notice that you usually throw in the trash because the envelope looks like your typical junk-mail notice. Whoops! You've just ditched the one piece of correspondence that lets you know that your right to sue has just been unilaterally snatched away. Who knows, maybe if you read that letter, you might decide to get rid of the company's product before something goes wrong with it, do some investigation of your own, and buy another similar product for which your legal rights are protected.

Consumer advocacy groups, such as **Consumer Action** and others listed under "National Consumer Organizations" in the appendices, have become Davids in the battle against these corporate Goliaths. Most of these organizations develop and distribute consumer education and information materials. Several are primarily or exclusively concerned with improving con-

LAWYERLY ADVICE

Attorney John C. Morrison has some good advice regarding matters of arbitration:

Half a loaf is better than no loaf at all. Good problem-solving skills often include the ability to realize that a satisfactory settlement of a portion of one's claim early in the process may be better than expending all of the time and effort that may be required to end up with the full claim, or possibly nothing at all.

sumer protection or customer service; many advocate for consumer interests before government, the courts, and the news media.

The arbitration process is touted as a fair and low-cost option to litigation, but it is increasingly complicated and is beginning to resemble litigation more and more. Mediators and mediation organizations can still be of enormous help, though. If you find yourself in need of such an expert, look in the phone book under "Mediation Services."

What if the mediation/arbitration proceedings do not solve your problem or complaint? In the case of many products, such as the car with lemonitis, the next step is another system—the courts. Even if you can't afford an attorney, take heart. Some state lemon laws permit the judge to award you attorney's fees if you win, through the Magnuson-Moss Act. Check out the law in your state by contacting your state attorney general's office (see appendices).

● SMALL-CLAIMS COURT

Since the majority of consumer complaints usually involve only a few hundred dollars, small-claims court could be a viable option if you find yourself at loggerheads and you are not required to go through binding arbitration. Small-claims court could be your last hurrah to get your money back for a defective product or maybe even recoup losses that resulted from purchasing a faulty product or service, such as the new toilet that leaked down two stories and ruined the walls of your new sunken living room. The maximum amount for which you can settle varies from state to state and can range from $1,000 all the way up to $10,000.

The only real problem with small-claims court is that you have to be your own lawyer, and that old adage about the person who represents himself in court having a fool for a client could come crashing down on your head if you're not extra careful. Before you walk into small-claims court to try to resolve the matter, be really sure you've got all your information organized and documented, just as was advised in Chapter 3. You might want to consult the free twelve-page booklet *About Taking Legal Action*, which comes with a bonus booklet entitled *About Being Sued* from the **Consumer Information Center,** Department 76, Pueblo, CO 81009.

HELPFUL AGENCIES AND SERVICES

The **American Consumer Action Program (AUTOCAP)** (703) 821-7144 is an automobile dispute resolution program in which many automobile manufacturers participate. See the appendices for a listing of participating automakers.

AUTOLINE at (800) 955-5100 is an arbitration panel directed by the Better Business Bureaus. See the appendices for a listing of participating automakers.

Consumer Action at (415) 777-9635 is one of many consumer advocacy groups that assist consumers with consumer problems.

Write the **Consumer Information Center,** Department 76, Pueblo, CO 81009, or call (719) 948-4000, for free booklets entitled *About Taking Legal Action* and *About Being Sued.*

CHAPTER 9

Letters of a More Personal Nature: From Petitions to Pleas

> What one has, one ought to use: and whatever he does, he should do with all his might.   —CICERO

● PERSONAL PETITIONS

Next to the complaint letter in which you're writing to a company president about a defective product or lousy service or even unfair treatment from an HMO there is the *personal petition* — an appeal for help and special attention from courts of law or government departments and agencies. These might include the Social Security Administration, your state Medicaid program, the Immigration and Naturalization Service, or a number of other government bodies.

You may write to a state or federal department or agency to find out how state or federal regulations relate to your present problem. Perhaps you know what the law is as it relates to your problem, but you can't seem to get a bureaucrat or the system to work for you. Maybe you are mired in red tape and don't know whom to petition. Your state and federal representatives can be of help to put you in touch with someone with the power to make a difference. Also know that most agencies and departments have built-in processes for resolving disputes — such as appeals and investigations — and the ground rules for these processes can be found in state and federal laws and regulations. Also, state and federal government committees have oversight for departments and agencies. State and federal departments also have citizen councils that report to governors and other governmental bodies. If you find the right committee or council member and approach him or her in the right way, you can get advice and help in resolving a problem.

Personal petitions, which can take the form of letters or statements, can address issues as diverse as

- child custody and visitation rights
- child support
- consumer fraud
- environmental issues
- debt management
- subsidized housing problems
- immigration and naturalization
- Medicare and Medicaid issues
- parent care
- state funding for people with disabilities and the elderly
- workers' compensation disability

Petition letters are formal in style, although they contain personal information. The goal of such letters is to personalize your situation in order to distinguish your plea from the scores of others that the official who is appraising your case might come across that day. A good petition letter should get your file moved from the back of a bureaucratic pile to the front, where it will be dealt with promptly.

Petitioning the Court on Child Support

If you're experiencing difficulty collecting child support, there's no corporate boss to whom you can write a poison pen. But a petition to the court might provide relief. After Susan Lust's ex-husband reneged on his court-mandated child support payments and refused to pay a share of the children's medical expenses, she tried for several years to have the support reinstated but always found herself blocked by the system. Her final plan of action was to write the following petition to the judge.

October 1, 1997

To the Knox County Fourth Circuit Court

I am here today as a victim to appeal to and to plead with the court on my children's behalf.

In 1989, the year of my original divorce settlement, my now ex-husband, Mr. Inexcusable, was ordered to pay child support payments. This support has never been fully paid, but, to make things worse, in December 1992 Mr. Inexcusable made an appeal to the Court to discontinue payments altogether. It found in my favor. Mr. Inexcusable appealed this decision the following year, and Judge Y overruled the December decision. Not only did he find for Mr. Inexcusable, but he also decimated the support payments. This decision was not based on my ex-husband's W-2 forms or any tax record but on the testimony of his paid private accountant.

Since this judgment, Mr. Inexcusable has further evaded his responsibilities as a father. I assume that because the judgment against him was lessened, he now feels he is either above the law or can circumvent it.

One particular example stands out. Our eldest son had a skating accident, and his two front teeth were knocked out. His father refused to pay the initial medical bill.

When subsequent infection set in and further treatment was necessary, my attorney sent a second bill to my ex-husband. There was no monetary response, and the only message from his attorney was, "No comment; not our concern." This, too, was apparently the view of the Fourth Circuit Court as I received no response from it either. "Not our concern" has continued to be the message, and what a humiliating and anguishing one it has been for our three boys. My children have already had to pay a terrible toll because their father has not been there for them emotionally or physically; they should not have to suffer further because he refused to be financially responsible.

I have spent thousands of dollars over the years in an attempt to resolve this situation with my former husband, only to be met on all sides with diversions and vengeful tactics. My current husband, who pays $800 a month in child support himself because he is a responsible person and father, has had to take on the extra financial burden for my three children. This he does because of his love for them and for me, even though it leaves him with a financial hardship. I greatly appreciate his efforts, but it is a total injustice that my children's <u>own</u> father remains completely irresponsible.

All that I am asking today is to have the full child support reinstated along with the 50 percent portion of the medical bills and to somehow be assured that this goes no further and that Mr. Inexcusable <u>remains</u> financially responsible. Only then, per-

```
haps, can this family tragedy cease and all
of us can go on with our lives.

Thank you.


Susan Lust
```

Susan Lust's battle continues.

Personal petitions require a strategy that is a bit different from what we have seen in earlier chapters, so there are some points of difference as regards the advice given in Chapter 3. Without repeating the meaning of each, let's recap the steps that are pertinent to this chapter.

1 Calm down. Remember that cold shower? If you really wish to make a positive impression, don't go off half-cocked and write an appeal before you're ready.

2 Document and organize. I can't emphasize this point enough. If you don't have all the necessary information and have it organized, you won't ever see that first disability benefit you're seeking, for example.

3 Discover the name of the person at the highest level. If your appeal needs to go to the secretary of state, then send it to him or her. Make sure you spell the person's name correctly. This person may exercise control over your livelihood (or your life), and you want to be on his or her good side from the outset.

4 Use a standard business letter format. A petition is a much more formal style of business letter; thus it must really appear professional. Though there are a couple of generally accepted styles, I suggest you follow the formal styles of the example letters in this chapter.

5 Grab the reader's attention. As much as the petition properly allows, you should try to use phrases such as, "My life is in your hands," or "You are my final hope," where appropriate. Phrases such as these may make the reader of your letter sit up a little straighter.

6 Summarize the history of your situation. Have you attempted in the past to secure a wheelchair-accessible apartment from your local housing authority? Has this office been unhelpful and uncooperative? Are you living in substandard housing while you wait for a wheelchair-accessible apartment? Have you appealed to the Department of Housing and Urban Development to no avail? Again, use your *documentation* to cite the facts in your case.

7 State your expectations. Do you wish to see a criminal behind bars or your child support increased? Are you asking for Social Security benefits to be reinstated? Be specific.

8 Close politely and firmly. You may want to close with the usual "I expect to hear from you within ten days," but there may be circumstances that call for another tack, such as "As my court date is in two weeks, I appreciate hearing from you before that time," or "My visa expires on January 10, 1998; therefore, I would appreciate your response as quickly as possible."

9 Copy key people. Certainly there are times when you write a personal petition and you want others to see your letter or statement. If the Immigration and Naturalization Service is involved, then do send a copy to the secretary of state; if Judge Tiddlywinks is the recipient and the person to decide if your license is revoked, mail a copy to your state's Department of Motor Vehicles.

10 Proofread for errors. This is the one time that everything you write needs to be better-than-perfect in grammar and mechanics. After all, it may be the president himself who ultimately ends up reading the appeal. Common mistakes for which you should watch out should include but are not limited to the following: being too free with commas; writing incomplete sentences; problems with subject-verb agreement (for instance, Mrs. Jones talk on the telephone); and, of course again, spelling.

In this chapter I've provided sample letters dealing with significant issues: child support, disability, immigration, funding for health care for the elderly, and troubles at a federally subsidized housing complex. Adapt these letters to fit your own circumstances, keeping in mind the general guidelines just listed.

Disability

Let's say you're hurt on the job (and who hasn't been hurt at one time or another?). Sometimes it's a serious injury. It doesn't matter if you stumbled over the wastepaper basket in a corporate office, fell off a truck at a construction site, or tripped over broken pieces of concrete on the sidewalk while you were performing your duties, as did the gentleman in the next example. Bureaucracy still reigns; therefore, sometimes your needs will be denied or even ignored, and getting the system to work on your behalf can take a lot of work, but (famous last words) never give up!

If, indeed, your claim is denied, you do have some recourse. If you appeal the decision and the appeals board rules against you, you can then go to a state district court judge. While in the middle of this process, you have the right to be represented by an attorney whose fees are often set by law as a percentage of the amount of benefits you will receive. Hiring a lawyer may also be a good idea if you believe the amount of your disability check isn't right or if you're fired, suspended, or disciplined in any manner for filing the claim in the first place. When in doubt, contact a workers' compensation attorney or your local office of the **Equal Employment Opportunity Commission** (EEOC). Either should be able to reassure you that you're protected from unfair practices like this under the Americans with Disabilities Act.

105 Sunset Drive
Collingwood, TN 35709
April 16, 1998

Matilda May-Help, Coordinator
Disabilities U.S.A.
432 Stratford Circle, Suite 11
Nashville, TN 37578

Dear Ms. May-Help:

Per your suggestion, I wish to put in writing what I related to you in our recent conversation. As you recall, I suffered a severe injury when I tripped and fell while on school business (a field trip with my students). After applying for workers' compensation I was shocked when my claim was denied.

I must state strongly that even though I began to experience excruciating pain within six hours, because I was not in immediate pain, I attempted to complete the field trip. By the time I began to drive home that afternoon, I could barely concentrate on the highway because I was then in such distress. I saw Dr. Feel Good the next day, and he has written up a report on the nature of my back injury (copy enclosed). I have had to miss several weeks of school. The only reason that I returned to work as quickly as I did was that my sick leave ran out. I am still in continuous pain.

I find it so hard to believe that injuries suffered while one is involved on the job

are not covered. I sincerely ask that my
claim be reviewed and accepted.

Thank you so much, and I look forward to
hearing from you as quickly as possible.

Sincerely,

Arthur Ailing

Not only did this gentleman receive his due compensation, but it turned out that his injury was severe enough that he was able to retire with full disability benefits. Even though he paid a price with his health, I like to envision him lying on the beach, sipping a cold drink, and raising his fist to the sun while he screams, "YES!"

Immigration

On September 30, 1996, President Clinton signed into effect a new immigration law, H.R. 2002, which radically reformed the immigration process as we knew it and led to many new regulations. For the purposes of our example, I'll mention a few of the changes. The first ruling affects a person who holds a temporary visa and is afraid to return to his or her native country. This person must now be able to demonstrate what is known as a "credible fear of persecution." The second ruling affects anyone who sponsors a foreign national. Such persons must now demonstrate proof of income that is at least 20 percent above the poverty level. This means that if the immigrant has no job or job offers in the United States, then the sponsoring relative has to submit for approval an Affidavit of Support, showing that he or she can support the immigrant.

The following petition concerns two sisters separated for

twenty-nine years; one is a naturalized American and the other is still a British subject. The sisters wanted to live together for the remainder of their lives in the United States.

```
                              1457 Doorbell Lane
                              Weeping Falls, MN 80136
                              July 19, 1997

The Honorable Madeleine Albright
United States Department of State
2201 C Street NW
Washington, DC 20520

Dear Madam Secretary:

At this point, I am desperate and I do not
know where else to turn. I was born in En-
gland but have been a naturalized citizen
of America for the past twenty-nine years.
America--the land of freedom and opportu-
nity. Since I have been here, I have bought
my own home, paid my taxes, have always
been employed and have never been on wel-
fare. I have had only myself to depend upon,
and I have done so. I have been a faithful
citizen of this country, never having to use
its social resources because I have always
believed in the American work ethic.

It has not been an easy life for me. I have
had to work two jobs to make ends meet, and
I have reared a daughter and a son com-
pletely alone. However, living in this coun-
try has still been the greatest blessing
of my life, and it is my greatest hope that
I can share that blessing with my best
friend and sister, who still lives in En-
gland. For many years it has been her de-
sire to come to America to live.
```

We have written to both Senators Robb and Warner and to state officials and, even with my limited resources, I contacted an immigration lawyer. He said that he could not help us, as did those previous officials to whom I had written. I cannot believe that there can be no assistance to be found anywhere. Daily I read of illegal immigrants entering this country and, in some cases, being allowed to stay. I am not an illegal. I left the home of my birth, not because of anything that had occurred other than some incidents in my personal life, but because America had always been a beacon of light to me, as it has been and is now to my sister.

She has been offered employment in this country already; she also has people willing to pay her way to get her from England to America. All of this is wonderful, but no one will let her come to stay on a permanent basis. We have been separated for so long, both as sisters and as truly best friends. All we wish is to be together as we enter the twilight of our years, our family once more whole and the two of us together. Surely someone in this great country to which I have given all of my love and loyalty for the last twenty-nine years can find the solution to help us in this matter. We are not asking a great deal. We are only asking that a <u>new American</u> be admitted, that a <u>new American</u> be allowed to enjoy the fruits and the bounty of this country, and that my sister be this new American.

I hope and believe that you can afford us
the opportunity to make this dream possible, and I look forward to hearing from you
at your earliest convenience and, I hope, no
later than September 30, 1997.

Sincerely,

Serena Sister

cc: The Immigration and Naturalization Board
    United States Department of Justice
    425 Eye Street, NW
    Washington, DC 20536

As Napoleon once remarked, "Victory belongs to the most persevering," and these two launched their own victory.

Funding for Social Services

There is another type of issue that faces all too many of us—caring for disabled relatives or our aging parents. We can feel helpless when it comes to finding and funding the appropriate care for our loved ones. Whether the issue is Medicare coverage, state funding, Social Security benefits, nursing homes, or home health care, there often comes a time when we must resort to a personal petition to try to bring about a resolution. Sometimes we must advocate with our legislators to see that special programs have adequate funding. In early 1998 a concerned son wrote to his senator and congresswoman concerning the vote at the federal level to limit home health services. The same letter was mailed to each of the officials. Note, for a current list of members of Congress, call 1-800-659-8708.

7821 Woodbine Road
Arnold, MD 21017
January 4, 1998

The Honorable Barbara Mikulski
United States Senate
World Trade Center
401 East Pratt Street, Suite 253
Baltimore, MD 21202-3041

Dear Senator Mikulski:

Home health care for our nation's elderly is a vital issue. Currently, both my mother and my father are in frail health, necessitating home health care and venipuncture services three times per week. Even though the venipuncture portion of the upcoming bill is not one that presents a problem at this time, the continuation of home health care services is certainly a major concern for us.

My mother is partially bedridden. The home health aides assist her in bathing and toileting, and they place fresh linens on her bed. This along with checking her temperature, blood pressure, and the like are only a few examples of the important chores the aides perform for those who cannot help themselves. Although my father is in somewhat better health, he is increasingly unable to care for my mother, and the time will soon come when he must depend upon home health care himself.

My parents and those of their generation deserve the best care that we can give them.

They are the very ones who took an exhausted America after World War II and
built it into the greatest nation on earth.
America's government must reciprocate that
loyalty. Do not ignore their needs; do not
push them into the background. Our elected
officials must see that our senior citizens
are given the opportunity to live with
the dignity they deserve. This is not possible without adequate assistance from home
health aides.

I trust that you agree with me and that
your vote will demonstrate your allegiance
to what is only the right thing to do.

Thank you,

Sincerely,

Sigmond Son

Housing

One of my poison pen clients needed a personal petition in the
worst way. After writing several letters herself, to no avail, she
turned to me for assistance in helping solve a problem with the
subsidized housing community in which she lived. After she saw
an exchange of drugs in one of the corridors, she realized that all
too soon the complex would become a mecca for drug traffic (if,
in fact, it wasn't already). As the mother of two adolescent boys,
she feared that her sons' lives could be in jeopardy, and she was
determined to make *someone* sit up and take notice. Our letter
did just that.

891 Drug Drive, #109
Spartenburg, SC 29864
May 18, 1998

The Honorable Andrew Cuomo, Secretary
United States Department of
Housing and Urban Development
451 Seventh Street, SW
Washington, DC 20410

Dear Secretary Cuomo:

You are my last resort in my battle to bring
decency, justice, and security to the HUD
housing community in which I live. The Swallows apartment complex is becoming a haven
for drug dealers, and no one wants to listen to my appeals for assistance. The following paragraphs summarize the problem:

- On February 23, 1998, as I was walking to
  the Swallows' office, I noticed several
  young men passing two packages between
  them. One package appeared to hold a white
  powder; the other contained money. That
  these men made no effort to hide their
  transaction caused me deep distress.
- I immediately reported the men and gave
  the names of the two I recognized to Alma
  Apathetic, the resident manager. She was
  so unmoved by the information provided
  and by my concern that I called Ned Nonchalant, the president of the Swallows
  Corporation. I spoke with his assistant,
  Irma Indifferent, who promised to send an
  investigator to take my statement within
  the following three days. Thus far no one
  has come.

- On March 1 I once again contacted Mr.
  Nonchalant's office and followed up the
  telephone call with a letter (copy enclosed). Again my appeal was met with
  total apathy on the part of his personnel. I have yet to receive any response
  to my letter.

I desperately fear for the safety and security of my two sons. At eleven and thir-
teen, they face enough "normal" temptations
without the addition of available drugs
right on their doorstep. HUD is ultimately
responsible for providing safe and non-
threatening environments in its subsidized
housing complexes. I cannot afford to move
to another home at the present time, yet I
am afraid to remain here under the circumstances, especially if the men in question
realize I have undertaken these measures.

I trust that you will launch an immediate
and thorough investigation into this matter before our community is shattered by
violence such as that which we read about
daily in other metropolitan areas.

Because there is no time to waste in eradi-
cating this criminal element, I look forward to hearing from you within the next
seven working days.

Thank you.

Sincerely,

Thelma Threatened

HUD did investigate, and quickly. Statements were taken, reports were filed, and the criminals were arrested. Thelma became a heroine in the eyes of her neighbors, and, as far as I know, her community is a peaceful one once more.

If you are experiencing other housing issues such as poor lighting in public spaces or unsafe playground equipment, consider a letter like Thelma's to help you and your neighbors.

O PERSONAL PLEAS

If you encounter situations that require as much diplomatic savvy as a petition but are of a much more personal nature, you should consider writing a personal appeal or plea. Such letters are from the heart, but with a very definite purpose. Whatever the motive may be for writing such letters—you may just want to be listened to by the other person, or maybe to open up a dialogue, or perhaps to resolve a long-standing unhappiness—you should always give such communications your best effort.

Let's say your grandmother is undermining you in front of other people. She doesn't do it on purpose; in fact, she's probably not even aware that she's doing it. Or perhaps the situation is more serious. You may have a problem with your boss at work or with your neighbors at the apartment house where you live. Even worse, it could be that you're separated from your husband or wife, and you're experiencing problems with your child because his or her other parent is not showing up for scheduled visits. What do you do?

As with poison pen letters and personal petitions, no two plea situations are exactly the same. Before I provide you with templates for letters you could write to address various situations, I'll outline some advice that should be helpful in almost every situation that warrants a personal plea.

❶ Try the verbal approach first. Sit down and attempt a real heart-to-heart with the other party. Some people are not even aware that they're being stubborn or offensive or unreasonable until you point it out to them. If you've tried the verbal approach and have gotten nowhere, it might be time to sit down and write a letter.

2 Remain calm and detached. Regardless of the emotions that are plaguing you, the personal plea you write should be as free of emotion as possible.

3 Document and organize your information. You don't need to go over the entire history of your relationship, but you may want to include a couple of relevant and representative episodes from your shared past to illustrate your point. Remind your grandmother that your feelings are hurt when she makes a comment about your cooking, as she has for the past fifteen family get-togethers. Remind your ex that he or she has skipped out on scheduled weekends four times in the last year.

4 Use polite language. After all, you have a personal relationship with this individual—a friend, a boss, a relative, or a former spouse—and he or she is presumably someone who will more than likely remain a part of your life—like it or not. Calling him or her a scum-sucking jackass might not be the best approach. Polite language applies to both the salutation and the closing—"Dear *#%@le" or "Forever pissed" is most assuredly the quickest way to undermine your petition.

5 State your expectations implicitly. Write a nice paragraph where you let the recipient know what would set your mind at peace, so that your letter leaves no room for ambiguities. Make sure you're as clear as glass to avoid any misinterpretation.

6 Finally, as with the poison pen letters, never give up. It may take a letter or two or a letter followed by a conversation to get the results you desire, but no way on God's green earth should you give up the fight.

To a Difficult Relative

Your dear old Grams is the one member of your family who still thinks you're in diapers and you haven't a grain of sense anywhere in your whole body even though you're thirty-five years old. No matter that you love her and she dotes on you, sometimes enough is enough. Inevitably, after you've worked hard to prepare a family feast, Grandma will bellow at the top of her lungs in front of all your guests, "Ellen, that dinner was delicious. You didn't cook it yourself, did you?" A missive of the following sort is useful when you encounter a similar problem with any of your family members.

May 31, 1997

Dear Grams,

It was so much fun being all together at the reunion last weekend. You just seem to get younger and younger! [A little initial suck-up may come in handy.] I did want to tell you, though, that something has been bothering me.

I know you don't mean to do it, but sometimes when we're around other members of the family, you say things that hurt my feelings. For example, I know I'll never be as good a cook as you are [a little more of the "kiss up"], but I try my best. When you make comments like, "Ellen, I know you didn't cook this meal. It's delicious," it really makes me feel bad.

You are my very favorite person [Lie if you have to!], and we share a special rela-

tionship. I'm sure that in the future you'll
be more careful.
    Thanks as always for listening to me and
my "problems."

                                Much love,

                                Ellen

Problems at Work

One day I received a call from a woman who had just that day
been terminated from her position with no explanation whatsoever. Although she certainly needed the money from this job,
she was more upset because she didn't know why she had been
fired, and she was disturbed by the manner in which the message had been delivered. You'll notice that Hilda Helpless's tone
is both deferential and assertive. I advise that you take this tack
when writing to employers. The letter we wrote to the company
president surely caught his eye, bringing an amazing response.

            9967 Hapless Avenue, Apartment 6
            Minneapolis, MN 27641
            March 21, 1998

Paul Protective, President
Apartments, Inc.
1900 Helpme Street, 7th Floor
Minneapolis, MN 27643

Dear Mr. Protective:

It is with a great deal of grief and anguish that I turn to you for assistance.

On March 18, 1998, I went to work, as usual, at the Neighborly Apartments, where I have been the onsite manager since October 30, 1997. Imagine my horror when Mr. Bouncer approached me that morning and with no explanation whatsoever gave me two weeks' severance pay and terminated my employment with Neighborly.

Because I was so delighted and satisfied with my position with Neighborly, I chose to be responsive to other needs, as well, not necessarily just the contractual ones. Many times I would stay much later in the evenings in order to accommodate people who were unable to view apartments during the normal working-day hours. This has, of course, been of great benefit to your company, as otherwise certain units I supervised might have remained vacant.

The Neighborly Apartments complex is home to a very diverse population, and I am proud that I have been friends with many of the residents; in fact, at one time or another a majority of them have expressed their appreciation of the manner in which I fulfilled my position. I found many times that a simple word or an act of kindness goes a long way in making your tenants happy. Even the owner of the property, Mr. Rich, commented to me that one of the repairmen who lives onsite stated that because of me, the tenants have been easier to deal with than in past years.

I simply cannot believe that you have knowledge of or have approved this shocking de-

cision. I am sure that you will wish to investigate this matter thoroughly and immediately. It is unconscionable that I have
been treated this way, especially that I
was given no forewarning and not even the
simple professional courtesy of being told
why I was being terminated.

Sincerely,

Hilda Helpless

As Mrs. Helpless told me later, she was happy (not shocked, appalled, or dismayed) when she heard a persistent knock on her door one morning after this letter had been posted. After she realized that "whoever" it was wasn't going away anytime soon, she opened the door, and there stood the president of the company! After receiving the letter, he personally had looked into the matter and come to offer his apologies for the manner in which Mrs. Helpless had been treated. He offered her another position within his company.

Tenant/Landlord Dispute

Those of us who live in apartments sometimes have neighbors living above us. If we're lucky, noise isn't a major problem; on the other hand, running, screaming kids, loud parties, and the like may be the norm rather than the exception. One downstairs client found his peace and quiet frequently disturbed, so he wrote the following petition to his landlord.

8903 Apartment Lane, #202
Silver Spring, MD 33981
August 4, 1998

Rob Responsible, Landlord
SS Apartments
8905 Apartment Lane
Silver Spring, MD 33981

Dear Mr. Responsible:

On numerous occasions I have been distressed and dismayed about the disruption above my apartment, in apartment #203, home to Mr. and Mrs. Brown. As the landlord of SS Apartments, you need to be made aware of this problem.

The lease strictly states, "Loud noises in apartments are unacceptable, and tenants will be held accountable for inappropriate behaviors, even to the risk of having the lease terminated." On several occasions I have politely asked the Browns to keep their children from playing loud music and dancing. The last time I made this request was on August 2, 1997. The response was appalling.

Mr. Brown told me to mind my own business and that how his children conducted themselves was none of my affair. When I attempted to explain that I had to arise at 4:30 A.M., he slammed his door in my face.

I expect you to speak with Mr. Brown immediately and remind him of the lease agree-

```
ment. Thank you, and I look forward to hear-
ing from you within five days.

Sincerely,


Sam Sleepless
```

The landlord did just that. The Browns moved soon thereafter.

To an Insensitive Parent

Following is a letter addressed to an ex-husband who didn't seem to care about disappointing his son by not showing up for scheduled visits. If you are in this situation, or know someone else who is, you can probably identify with this woman's concerns. As the primary caretaker she was trying her hardest to instill certain values and attributes in her son, including self-confidence. She was bearing the lion's share of responsibility for rearing him, but once a month, per the custody decision, her ex-husband was scheduled to take the boy for the weekend. Friday, Saturday, and Sunday would come and go, and the boy's father wouldn't show up. Sure enough, the child's response was self-doubt and a handful of hard-to-answer questions, such as "Why doesn't Daddy want to see me"? Here is the letter we wrote to that boy's father.

```
                                June 29, 1997

Dear Martin,

    I know you don't want to receive this let-
ter, but I'm compelled to write it. I've tried
```

to speak with you about the importance of picking up Marty on time for visits or calling in advance if you're not coming at all. Maybe I haven't been clear enough in the past; hence, I write this plea.

Marty loves you very much--you're his dad, and he wants to be with you as much as possible, especially when arrangements have been made. He really looks forward to the weekends when you two go camping or boating or just spending time together. There have been so many times when his excitement has turned to tears and then to anger because you simply didn't show up, and often you didn't even call to tell him you weren't coming.

At ten years old, our son is at a very vulnerable age. He simply doesn't understand (nor do I for that matter) why you treat him this way. All he sees is that you change your mind because "something came up."

As Marty's father, you have the capacity and the responsibility to help ensure that he grows up to be a happy and stable adult. At this point, I'm worried that won't happen. More and more I see him withdraw and become belligerent every time you let him down. This cannot go on.

I know you love our son very much, and I don't wish for the two of you to be estranged later on in life; however, I believe this will certainly happen if the present pattern continues. I provide all the love and support I can, but you are his father--to a boy, that's a very special relationship. You're running a terrible risk of losing it.

> Please think carefully about what I've said in this letter. Our son's future depends upon it.
>
>   Sincerely,
>
>   Martha

As you can ascertain, personal petitions and pleas can be written to address a variety of problems. Once you develop the right process, though, just as you have become proficient in writing complaint letters, you will also find the right words to appeal to the right persons so as to influence your own specific circumstances. In Chapter 11, "Fill in the Blank," I've provided a number of other sample letters of this nature.

HELPFUL RESOURCES

Congress at Your Fingertips is a publication that provides photographs and all vital information, such as addresses, phone numbers, the committees on which they sit, et cetera, for all members of Congress. Copies can be purchased by contacting Capital Advantage at (800) 659-8708.

The **Equal Employment Opportunity Commission**, 1801 L Street NW, Washington, DC 20507, (800) 688-9889, is a federal agency that assists people with job-related disputes.

CHAPTER 10

The Art of the Perfect Thank-You

> Behave yourself a little better than is absolutely necessary. —WILL CUPPY

Those of us who were born in the Deep South are steeped in tradition and in the "proper" manner of behaving. Etiquette—the rules of correct behavior in society or among the members of a profession—has long been a way of life and is ingrained in our culture, particularly for the ladies. Despite my characteristically fierce Scarlett O'Hara disposition, I *do* know how to behave, particularly when it comes to writing proper thank-you letters.

I was reared from infancy on Emily Post's and Amy Vanderbilt's strict rules on the social graces; as a matter of fact, my mother taught me that these rules were etched in stone right up there beside the Ten Commandments. One of the basic rules is to always write a thank-you note after receiving a gift or some other expression of kindness or assistance. Below I've outlined how to write an array of effective thank-you's—and the grande dames of etiquette would approve of all of them.

FORMAL THANK-YOU LETTERS

If you've solved a problem verbally or you've written a poison pen letter that gets the kind of results for which you were looking, you should always write a thank-you letter to or about the person who has helped you. Aside from being a very nice gesture, it may even assure more efficient service and greater employee resourcefulness and politeness in the future.

Just as all of us are delighted to receive a pat on the back for a job well done, so do the oft-neglected people who come to our rescue. Imagine a formal thank-you letter that will go into an individual's personnel file, and word your letter as you would like a letter about you to read. One of my favorite quotes is by William Faulkner: "I believe that man will not merely endure; he will prevail. He is immortal, not because he alone among the creatures has an exhaustible voice, but because he has a soul, a spirit capable of kindness and compassion." This *spirit* is what we're trying to convey with thank-you letters.

Your thank-you letter should be

- written in standard business style;
- typed, not handwritten; and
- sent via regular mail, not by e-mail or fax.

Thank-You for a Job Well Done

The father of Elizabeth Enraged, whose letter of complaint about her terrible experience on Unfeeling Airlines appears in Chapter 5, wrote to acknowledge the assistance his daughter received from one of Unfeeling Airline's agents.

411 Seventh Street NW
Hattiesburg, MS 19000
May 5, 1998

Frederick First-Class, President/CEO
Unfeeling Airlines, Inc.
111 Airline Avenue
Chicago, IL 60606

Re: Carl Comfort

Dear Mr. First Class:

With great appreciation I wish to commend
your agent, Carl Comfort. My daughter was
flying from DCA to Nashville, Tennessee, on
October 4. When it became apparent that the
weather would force cancellations to Nashville, leaving her stranded in Atlanta, Mr.
Comfort provided wonderful assistance. Not
only did he locate her personally; he booked
her on two flights to Columbus, where my
other daughter lives. He did this in the
event that she would be unable to make the
first flight, which, as it turned out, was
what occurred.

I might add that a series of fiascoes
happened because of the fault of several
other Unfeeling personnel. My daughter
was left without luggage for three days
and encountered several abusively rude people, especially in your baggage handling
department. It is fortunate for us, however, that Unfeeling has at least one help-

ful and professional employee--Carl Comfort.

Thank you.

Sincerely,

Frazzled Father

"Carl Comfort" probably received a boost in pay or a promotion when this dad's letter landed on the desk of his supervisor.

It never hurts to write and acknowledge a public official for helping you in a time of need. It feels good, and heaven knows these nice people need to get the credit they deserve.

123 Laurel Parkway
Springfield, IL 60707
November 30, 1997

Captain Bill Big Cheese
District Commander
Station 24
Springfield Police Department
344 Forest Road
Springfield, IL 60708

Re: Officer On-the-Spot

Dear Captain Big Cheese:

I wish to commend Officer Johnny On-the-
Spot for his quick assistance and his kindness last week.

My toddler swallowed almost an entire bottle of cough medicine, and Officer On-the-Spot was the initial responding officer, arriving along with the ambulance. Even at the hospital where my little boy (and I) underwent the trauma of having his stomach pumped, Officer On-the-Spot continued his help. He took it upon himself to take care of and to entertain my six-year-old daughter the entire time that the medical team was attending to my son.

This was a frightening experience, and I am so grateful that I could depend on the Springfield police force. I will never forget Officer On-the-Spot's compassion and kindness.

Please forward my thanks to him, and congratulations to you for having such a fine young man in your district.

Thank you.

Sincerely,

Michele Mother

Michele Mother was amazed when she received a letter from the district captain with *his* thanks to her (us) for writing the commendation. The captain stated that her letter would be placed in Officer On-the-Spot's file. One polite deed is usually rewarded by another.

Thank-You in Response to Personal Petitions

A similar letter can be written to acknowledge officials and people involved in solving problems that were brought to the fore by personal petitions. These top folks often go the extra mile for us when we're in dire straits. Not only does a thank-you letter express our thanks for their humanity; it demonstrates our own as well. Consider the following letter written to a Very Big Cheese.

```
                              8770 Grateful Lane
                              Grand Rapids, MI 11220
                              October 15, 1997

The Honorable William J. Clinton
President of the United States
1600 Pennsylvania Avenue, NW
Washington, DC 20500

Dear Mr. President:

I wish to express my gratitude for both
your personal understanding and your in-
tervention with my Social Security appeal.
You were my very last recourse for resolving
an almost impossible situation. Your per-
sonal decision to accelerate the arduous
process has quite literally saved my life,
and I am deeply grateful.

Thank you again from the bottom of my
heart.

Sincerely,


Rebecca Respect
```

⦿ FORMAL THANK-YOU NOTES

Just as a thank-you *letter* is a wonderful follow-up after problems have been resolved by poison pen letters, a thank-you *note* is a gracious way to acknowledge the attention that a colleague, a friend, or a loved one has paid to an issue that has been resolved as a result of a personal plea letter. In fact, thank-yous are a courteous and distinguished method to show appreciation for just about any good deed that's been rendered unto you. Did someone give you and your new spouse a towel set for your wedding gift? Write him or her a note. Did you get invited to a dinner party? Write the host a thank-you. If you really want the job for which you interviewed, write the person with whom you interviewed a polite note.

Unlike thank-you letters, formal thank-you notes can be handwritten. There are also several other rules:

1 Always write on a note card. That expensive specially monogrammed note card some of you keep on hand for such occasions is lovely, but there are plenty of assorted types available from the drugstore just for this purpose.

2 Write your thank-you in black ink. If you don't have a black pen on hand, go out and spend the 69 cents to buy one.

3 Begin on the bottom half of the note card. Some of you may have to write a tad or even a whole lot smaller than usual, but you won't be writing more than a very few sentences.

4 Don't print. Unless your handwriting resembles that of your doctor when he writes prescriptions, use *cursive* writing.

5 Spell out the date in the top right-hand corner.

6 Begin the salutation on the left-hand side a couple of spaces below the date. If you are writing to someone other than a friend or relative, use the recipient's title, such as Dear Mrs. (Ms.) Brown (**comma**). Don't make the mistake of addressing someone you barely know by his or her first name. Remember the old adage, "Familiarity breeds contempt," and an error like this could cost you that new career. If you are writing to a couple to acknowledge a gift or an event, the salutation is addressed to the female.

7 Single-space your note and indent each of your short paragraphs.

8 Begin with the reason for the thanks. This first sentence should express your appreciation for the job interview, the dinner party, the assistance your child's teacher provided, and so forth. When writing to a couple as mentioned earlier, this first sentence (or at least the second one) should include the spouse's name as well. When writing on *behalf* of a couple, include the other person's name in your thanks: "Bob and I would like to thank you . . ."

9 Next write a sentence or two about the job/position/act/gift. "This job is one that I find both exciting and innovative." "You have really helped Penny to explore her potential this school year." "The diamond earrings made my birthday even more special."

10 In the last paragraph, express once again your appreciation to the addressee.

11 Align your final closing ("Sincerely," and so forth) directly under the date. Use informal closings such as "Love" or "Fondly" only if you are writing to someone you're close to.

12 Sign your first *and* last name. If you're writing to someone you know in a professional capacity or to your brand-new wife's friend in Outer Mongolia who doesn't know you from Adam's house cat, you need to include your last name.

Thank-You in Response to a Personal Plea

Remember the divorced mom who appealed to her ex-husband to be more considerate about showing up for scheduled visits with their son in Chapter 9? Her plea did the trick, so she wrote this letter to thank her ex for cooperating.

July 30, 1998

Dear Martin,

I really wanted to let you know how much I appreciate the efforts you've made in picking Marty up for your weekend visits together. Not only have you been on time, but the one occasion you were not able to make it, you called him in advance to let him know.

The change in our son is nothing short of miraculous, and for that I do thank you.

Sincerely,

Martha

Thank-You for a Job Interview

Make it a practice to thank the person who interviews you for a job. You'll make a good impression, and maybe that will be just the added something that lands you the position.

January 19, 1998

Dear Mrs. Smith,

Thank you for providing the opportunity
to meet with you on Tuesday. As we talked,
I realized that writing letters of complaint is certainly the career in which I
would excel, and your company is most
intriguing in its development of this service.

I appreciate the time you spent with me,
and I certainly hope that you will afford
me the chance to demonstrate my talents as
part of your team.

Thank you again, and I look forward to
hearing from you.

Sincerely,

Ellen H. Phillips

Thank-You for a Gift

And regardless of whether one is a child or simply a child at
heart, we all love receiving presents—holiday, wedding, birthday, whatever—and these, too, must be recognized with a formal
note. A verbal thanks is fine initially, but follow it up with a note.

December 3, 1998

Dear Aunt Betsy,

You are such a dear to think of me with
the beautiful diamond earrings. A twenty-

first birthday is special in itself, but
your unexpected gesture made it a birthday I will always remember.
    Thank you again for your generosity and
thoughtfulness.

                   Love,

                   Debi

PEGGY POST ON THE NEED
FOR COURTEOUS LETTERS

Emily Post's great book on etiquette has been up-dated by two subsequent generations of Posts, Eliza-beth Post and Peggy Post. The seventy-fifth anniversary edition of *Emily Post's Etiquette* has been recently authored by Peggy Post, Emily's great-granddaughter-in-law, who also writes etiquette columns for *Good Housekeeping* and *Parents* magazines.

Peggy Post agrees that a complaint letter coupled with manners receives a far more positive response. After all, in order to have and to maintain a civilized society, the individuals within that society must them-selves be civilized.

Etiquette, civility, courtesy, decorum—whatever title we bandy about—it all comes down to being mannerly and kind toward others. Furthermore, by being additionally aware of our manners, we are paving the road for a more successful complaint or request when the need arises. We'll sound as profes-sional and as cordial as possible to get the job done the way we want it.

Peggy Post reaffirms:

Kindness and consideration toward others—the very es-sence of etiquette—never go out of style. Nor do courteous letters, it must be added. Emily Post wrote in 1938: "It is these messages of kindly thought that not only renew old friendships, but little by little build new ones which other-wise might never have developed."

Today, more than ever, the kind words spoken through our letters stand out and are remembered by their recipients. Letters not only matter in our personal lives; they impact our business dealings, as well. When we send carefully-written and cordial correspondence, we create good impressions of ourselves—an excellent start toward positive results.

CHAPTER 11

Fill in the Blank

> For they can conquer who believe they can.
> — JOHN DRYDEN

For many people it's nearly impossible to find the time or the energy to write a letter of complaint. In this chapter I've provided you with a few time-saving templates that can be adjusted to suit your own specific situation. But don't be tempted to dash off a helter-skelter dispatch, just by copying the text of a particular letter. Even though at first glance you're now a proficient complainer and letter writer, it's monumentally important to use the standard forms and all the skills you have learned from Chapter 3, "How to Write an Effective Complaint Letter," to tailor the perfect letter to suit your purposes.

Airlines

[Your street address]
[Your city/town, state, zip code]
[Today's date]

[Inside Address]

Dear Mr./Ms. _____:

As a faithful and long-standing customer of _____ Airlines, I am certain that you wish to be made aware of the appalling experience I recently suffered with your airline.

On [date], I traveled from [city and airport] on flight #_____ to my destination, [city and airport] (copies of tickets/boarding passes enclosed). Imagine my shock when [here, state the problem: flight canceled, luggage didn't arrive with you, unhelpful personnel, stale peanuts; and so forth].

When I first attempted to solve the problem myself, I [state what you did, to whom you spoke, when, and so forth]. However, no one seemed the least bit sympathetic to my very real plight. [If there are applicable regulations, such as the ones I mentioned earlier in the book, state them here. For example, "Even though I brought Rule 240 to the attention of your agent, he failed to book me on the next flight" or "Even though my flight would be two hours later than the original arrival time, your agent refused to discuss the $200 or the cost of the flight owed to me as determined on page 17 in the U.S. Department of Transportation's publication, *Fly-Rights*."]

I cannot believe that you are aware of or condone what I believe to be unprofessional [rudeness, unfeeling or unhelpful treatment, and so forth—whatever fits your particular circumstances] service on the part of your airline and its employees. I am certain you will wish to investigate this matter immediately and thoroughly.

I look forward to hearing from you within thirty days with the resolution that is fairly owed to me: [first-class tickets, new luggage, fresh peanuts, and so forth].

Thank you.

Sincerely,

[Your Name]

cc: The Honorable Rodney Slater, Secretary
United States Department of Transportation
400 Seventh Street, SW
Washington, DC 20590

Office of Intergovernmental and Consumer Affairs
United States Department of Transportation
400 Seventh Street, SW
Washington, DC 20590

Federal Aviation Administration
Aviation Consumer Protection Division
800 Independence Avenue, SW
Washington, DC 20591

[Leyser Q. Morris
Special Assistance Attorney General
Director, Office of Consumer Protection
P.O. Box 22947
Jackson, MS 39225-2947]*

*We're using the contact name and address for the state of Mississippi as an example here. Please consult the appendices to find the contact and address for your state.

Automobiles

[Your street address]
[Your city/town, state, zip code]
[Today's date]

[Inside Address]

Dear Mr./Ms. _____:

The trust and loyalty I have placed in [_____] Motors for many years has shockingly not been merited with regard to my current model, [name of car and ID number]. The [harassment, ill-mannered employees, and so forth] I have experienced in dealing with your company besmirches the fine name of [name of corporation].

I purchased my vehicle on [date] from [dealership] in [city and state]. Imagine my dismay when the following problems began to occur: [Document the date, problem, what you did, to whom you spoke, and so forth, and include copies of repair tickets, estimates, and so forth.]

1.

2.

3.

4.

5.

This horrendous problem has caused me a great deal of emotional, physical, and financial hardship [one, two, or all three, if applicable]. I might add that all of my family and friends who have observed what I have suffered are equally appalled at what has transpired as a result of your company's practices (implied threat).

All I ask is what I am duly and fairly owed: [state what this is]. I am sure you will wish to investigate this matter promptly and thoroughly, and I look forward to hearing from you by [date].

Thank you.

Sincerely,

[Your Name]

cc: Manager, Consumer Affairs
     Automotive Consumer Action Program
     8400 West Park Drive
     McLean, VA 22102

     Auto Safety Hotline
     National Highway Traffic Safety Administration
     United States Department of Transportation
     Washington, DC 20590

     [Mark S. Herr, Director
     New Jersey Division of Consumer Affairs
     P.O. Box 45027
     Newark, NJ 07101]*

*We're using the contact name and address for the state of New Jersey as an example here. Please consult the appendices to find the contact and address for your state.

Automobile Insurance

[Your street address]
[Your city/town, state, and zip code]
[Today's date]

[Inside Address]

Dear Mr./Ms. _____:

Having been a [name of company] policyholder for [x number of years], I am shocked to find that when I have to call on your services, your company ignores my needs.

I was recently involved in a [fender bender?, major automobile wreck?, accident in which I ran over the neighbor's cat that always sleeps under my left tire?]. As the enclosed police statement documents, this episode was not my fault; therefore I cannot understand why the insurance money is not forthcoming for [repairing my fender?, painting the car? burial for the cat?] (estimates enclosed).

I expect that you will investigate this matter immediately and transmit the amount of [a reasonable sum to cover your necessary expense] to me within the next two weeks.

Thank you.

Sincerely,

[Your Name]
[Be sure to include your policy number under your name if you don't include it within the letter itself.]

cc: [Dennis Wright, Chief Director
     Consumer Affairs Division
     Office of the Attorney General

> 11 South Union Street
> Montgomery, AL 36130]*
>
> [Michael DeBellis, Acting Commissioner
> Department of Insurance
> 135 South Union Street, #200
> Montgomery, AL 36130]*

This letter could also be easily revised to reflect dissatisfaction with a store's or a company's goods and services, problems with service contracts, mechanic's mistakes, and a whole range of other *appalling* gripes, including petitions and appeals.

Cybershopping

As a reminder, letters regarding commerce on the Internet should be *mailed* not e-mailed.

> [Your street address]
> [Your city/town, state, and zip code]
> [Today's date]
>
> [Inside Address]
>
> Dear Mr./Ms. _____:
>
> My very first Cybershopping experience is a total disaster. On [date] I purchased a Very-Fast modem from your on-line company for $59.00 plus $8.00 shipping and handling, for a total of $67.00. This was charged to my Master Card #11111111555555.

*We're using the contact name and address for the state of Alabama as an example here. Please consult the appendices to find the contact and address for your state.

Not only was the modem shockingly inadequate, it also [ate my hard drive or blew up my computer]. Because I believe your company to be a reputable one, it is obvious that this particular model somehow slipped past your quality control department.

Enclosed find the Very-Fast modem and its invoice. I expect a letter of explanation and a credit to my bank card for $67.00 within the next ten business days.

Thank you.

Sincerely,

[Your Name]

cc: Federal Trade Commission
    Sixth Street and Pennsylvania Avenue, NW
    Room 240
    Washington, DC 20580

    [Indiana Consumer Protecton Division
    Office of the Attorney General
    219 State House
    Indianapolis, IN 46204]*

Health or Disability Insurance

So you broke your neck (probably in an automobile accident!), and you or your insurance company owes the hospital and all thirty-three consulting doctors lots and lots of money. You patiently await the statements showing that all the medical costs have been paid except for your deductible; instead you get nothing but dunning notices from the hospital for the $47,635.92

*We're using the contact name and address for the state of Indiana here. Please consult the appendices to find the contact and address for your state.

you owe (the 92 cents is for the one tissue you used to wipe your tears after the nurse gave you an enema—for your *neck!*). Pen ready, please.

[Your street address]
[Your city/town, state, and zip code]
[Today's date]

[Inside Address]

Dear Ms./Mr. _____:

It has now been [number of weeks, months, years] since I submitted my claim [#] for [disability benefits, workers' compensation, a doctor's visit, a hospital stay] (see attached copies of my claim). Not only have I not received an acknowledgment of this claim, but the unpaid bill(s) for my treatment continue to accumulate.

I would very much appreciate your investigating this matter as soon as possible so that the [amount of the bill, or, in the case of the latter, the benefits themselves] may be immediately paid and my credit reputation does not suffer.

I look forward to hearing from you within the next two weeks.

Thank you.

Sincerely,

[Your Name]

cc: The Honorable Donna Shalala, Secretary
    United States Department of
    Health and Human Services
    200 Independence Avenue, SW, Room 615F
    Washington, DC 20201

Department of Beneficiary Services
United States Department of
Health and Human Services
6325 Security Boulevard
Baltimore, MD 21207

[James Alcorn, Director
Department of Insurance
700 West State Street
Boise, ID 83720]*

And here is an extra HMO letter simply because these organizations are so "popular."

[Your street address]
[Your city/town, state, and zip code]
[Today's date]

[Inside Address]

Dear Ms./Mr. _____:

As president of [health-care company name] only you can assist me with a horrific and shocking problem I have recently experienced with my health plan.

On [date], I entered the [name] Hospital for [describe the treatment: surgery on my tonsils? hemorrhoids? ingrown toenail?). The total cost for this procedure was [amount] (copy of bill enclosed); however, when the claim was filed I was reimbursed only [$1065? $125? fifty cents?]. When I contacted the claims supervisor, [name], on [date], s/he informed me that the bill was beyond what is considered to be "reasonable and customary" fees.

*We're using the contact name and address for the state of Idaho as an example here. Please consult the appendices to find the contact and address for your state.

As you know, prior to any surgery a subscriber must receive approval from [health-care company name]. I obtained this approval on [date], and at that time there was no mention of "reasonable and customary" fees. To think that most people have available funds to personally make up the difference of [$amount] is nothing short of ludicrous. I am on a fixed income, and to have to pay this enormous difference would completely deplete my savings. Also it must be noted that I have been a subscriber for [number] years, and this is the very first claim for this type of service that I have submitted.

I expect an immediate and thorough investigation into this matter, and I expect my hospital and physician's fees to be paid immediately. Be advised, too, that my employer, [employer name], with its [number] employees will receive notice of this barbarous situation.

Thank you, and I look forward to hearing from you within the next ten working days.

Sincerely,

[Your Name]

Enclosure

cc: [Mark Boozell, Director
     Department of Insurance
     320 West Washington Street
     Springfield, IL 62767]*

     The Honorable William J. Clinton, President
     United States of America
     1600 Pennsylvania Avenue, NW
     Washington, DC 20500
     ATTN: Ann F. Lewis, Communications Director

*We're using the contact name and address for the state of Illinois as an example here. Please consult the appendices to find the contact and address for your state.

The Honorable Donna Shalala, Secretary
United States Department of
Health and Human Services
200 Independence Avenue, SW, Room 615F
Washington, DC 20210

Department of Beneficiary Services
United States Department of
Health and Human Services
6325 Security Boulevard
Baltimore, MD 21207

The Honorable Carol Mosely-Braun
United States Senate
Second and C Streets, NE
Washington, DC 20510

The Honorable Richard J. Durbin
United States Senate
First and C Streets, NE
Washington, DC 20510

Hotels/Restaurants

[Your street address]
[Your city/town, state, and zip code]
[Today's date]

[Inside Address]

Dear Mr./Ms. _____:

I have enjoyed the fine services of your [hotel or restaurant], [name], in [city, state], for many years and have, until this point, been more than satisfied. However, I recently had the most appalling experience at your [hotel or restaurant], of which you need to be made aware, and it is now doubtful that I will continue my patronage of your business.

On [date], I [and friends? family? the entire college graduating class?] entered the [name of hotel or restaurant], and naturally I was [we were] expecting the identical accommodations from your staff to which I am [we are] accustomed. To my [our] shock, however, what actually occurred fell far short of my [our] expectations. [State the nature of the problem.]

Over the years I have spent a great deal of money [hundreds? thousands? millions?] at this [restaurant, hotel]. Unless I receive an immediate response from you, I will take my business elsewhere. I believe that I should also receive [what do you want?].

Thank you for looking into this matter, and I hope to hear from you no later than [date]. I also anticipate receiving the [what you asked for/demanded].

Sincerely

[Your Name]

cc: [Robert F. Tongren
Office of Consumers' Counsel
State Consumer Protection Office
77 South High Street, 15th Floor
Columbus, OH 43266-0550]*

[Helen McMurray
Consumer Frauds and Crimes Section
Office of the Attorney General
30 East Broad Street

*We're using the contact name and address for the state of Ohio as an example here. Please consult the appendices to find the contact and address for your state.

State Office Tower, 25th Floor
Columbus, OH 43266-0410]*

[Levon Hays
Youngstown Office of Consumer Affairs
26 South Phelps Street
City Hall
Youngstown, OH 44503-1318]*

American Hotel and Motel Association
1201 New York Avenue, NW, Suite 600
Washington, DC 20005-3931

Moving Companies

How many of us have safely moved to a new address and, to our
dismay, discovered that some of our belongings didn't arrive in
the same condition? Perhaps some of the fine china was chipped
or Great-Aunt Beth's antique mirror was shattered. A letter to the
moving company could read like this:

[Your street address]
[Your city/town, state, and zip code]
[Today's date]

[Inside Address]

Dear Mr./Ms. _____:

When I researched moving companies to find the most
economical and reliable one, I decided that [name of

*We're using the contact name and address for the state of Ohio as an example
here. Please consult the appendices to find the contact and address for your
state.

company] would best suit my needs. However, your workers' appalling disregard for my furnishings was not what I expected based on your advertisements.

When the boxes were unloaded on [date] (see enclosed copy of invoice and list), I immediately realized something was terribly wrong. My [expensive china? antique mirror? rubber spatula?] was damaged beyond repair. As my [husband? wife? entire set of cousins on my mother's side?] looked on in shock, your supervisor, [name of person], accused me of breaking the [item] myself in order to obtain a free replacement. To add further insult to injury, he refused to unload the remainder of my belongings from the van until I immediately paid the moving charges. Boxes including [clothing? bedroom furniture? my baby's dirty diapers?] were still sitting in the moving truck. I had no choice but to give in to his demands.

I have contacted stores within the surrounding vicinity to determine the most equitable costs to replace the items that were damaged by your workers. I certainly anticipate your response and a check in the amount of [$109.95? $2005.87? 59 cents?] within the next ten working days.

Thank you.

Sincerely,

[Your Name]

cc: [George Weber, Chief
     Consumer and Antitrust Division
     Department of the Attorney General
     1 Ashburton Place
     Boston, MA 02108]*

*We're using the contact name and address for the state of Massachusetts as an example here. Please consult the appendices to find the contact and address for your state.

[Priscilla H. Douglas, Secretary
Executive Office of Consumer Affairs
and Business Regulation
1 Ashburton Place, Room 1411
Boston, MA 02108]*

The Honorable William Daley, Secretary
United States Department of Commerce
15th Street and Constitution Avenue, NW
Washington, DC 20230

Neighbors

[Today's date]

Dear_____:

I certainly wish to maintain our congenial relationship,
but I am dismayed at what continues to occur.

[State the problem. This could be a multitude of complaints, including such sore spots as children trampling
through your flower beds, loud music disturbing your
evening rest, dogs barking continuously—and don't forget "Stinky," the pooping dog.]

I do hope that you will give this problem your prompt
attention. While I wish to maintain a neighborly relationship, I also wish to [preserve my expensive flowers, get a
good night's sleep, avoid stepping in poop, and so forth].

I would be more than happy to reach some amicable agreement in the hopes of settling the matter. I don't mind [if

*We're using the contact name and address for the state of Massachusetts as an
example here. Please consult the appendices to find the contact and address for
your state.

you really don't] if [your children walk through my yard to get to their destination, but please see that they avoid the flowers; or please keep the music/dog howls lowered after 9:00 P.M., your animal on a leash; whatever].

I really appreciate your assistance.

Sincerely,

[Your Name]

Now, I'm going to assume two things here: one, you have tried the verbal approach and for whatever reason it didn't work; and two, you're not yet in gear for launching a *real* complaint. Maybe you don't care if you're never bosom buddies with the other person again, but you still don't want to wade into a potentially messy legal situation. If, on the other hand, either this "nice" complaint doesn't work or you simply don't give a rat's patootie, then you can change the tone of your letter to reflect such.

Depending on the problem you're having with a neighbor, there may be neutral agencies to consult. If it's a problem with the neighbor's pet, try consulting your town's animal control officer or the police. If the problem is noise, your community probably has a noise ordinance on its law books, too. Call your town hall and inquire. As for the children and your stomped-on petunias, my only suggestion is that you string an invisible wire across your flower beds, hide, and enjoy the fun! (I'm kidding, I'm kidding! As I've mentioned before, don't dish out nastiness unless you are prepared to get it back double.)

Postal Service

Through rain and sleet and snow, etc., etc., etc. While most of our mail carriers are reliable (and I would hate to have a killer dog launching itself at *my* kneecaps!), a lot of us have a beef with the postal service, particularly regarding delays, lost mail, or mail delivered to our house or apartment erroneously. Meanwhile, the rates continue to rise, penny by penny. If you continue to find yourself in this type of situation, consider the following:

[Your street address]
[Your city/town, state, and zip code]
[Today's date]

[Inside address to the U.S. Postal Service Big Daddy]
Kenneth Huntly, Chief Postal Inspector
475 L'Enfant Plaza, SW
Washington, DC 20260

Dear Inspector Huntly:

Once again I have experienced an appalling problem with my mail delivery. The [letter from my sick mother? $10,000 lottery check? ice chest containing my new liver?] arrived [ten days? one month? five years?] after the post date. This type of service is, unfortunately, what I have come to expect from the postal service as late deliveries such as this occur [daily? weekly? bi-weekly?].

I have spoken with [U.B. Useless], the local postmaster, on many occasions, but he cannot seem to provide me with any concrete answers to this dilemma, and the situation only continues to worsen. I do not mind increased payment for mail deliveries; however, I do object to decreasing service. I am certain that important correspondence is floating around the post offices of [my city? my state? the Free World? the solar system?], and I would like you to investigate this matter immediately, at least as it pertains to me.

Thank you, and I look forward to hearing from you within the next thirty business days.

Sincerely,

[Your Name]

Retail

[Your street address]
[Your city/town, state, and zip code]
[Today's date]

[Inside Address]

Dear Mr./Ms._____:

I purchased a [item] from your store, [name of store], on [date]. The following day this item went on sale, but my requests for a credit for the difference between the price I paid and the sale price were refused by [name of person(s) and his/her (their) title(s)]. As you can see from the enclosed copy of the receipt, the difference in the amount is _____.

I have been a loyal patron of your store for [number of weeks, years, a lifetime], and I expect that loyalty to be reciprocated.

Please immediately credit my account [or, send me a check] in the amount of the difference in price: _____ plus tax for a total of _____.

I look forward to receiving [the credit or the money] within the next thirty days.

Thank you.

Sincerely,

[Your Name]

For this type of letter, it's best to carbon copy the product manufacturer (La-Z-Boy Chair Company, for example), whose address can be found either in the appendices or in directories at your local library.

And what about that item you purchased that promises to do everything but wash windows? You brought it home, plugged it in, and all it did was wheeze and cough. Again, try the verbal approach first, and if you have no success, it's letter time.

[Your street address]
[Your city/town, state, and zip code]
[Today's date]

[Inside Address]

Dear Ms./Mr. _____:

On [date] I purchased the [name of product] at your store [or, from your catalog] for [price] (receipt enclosed), and I was appalled the very first time I attempted to use it.

[Describe what went wrong, how the product acted, any damage it may have caused, such as destroyed my home, injured me and all my neighbors within a thirty-mile radius.]

I am immediately returning this shoddy product to you, and I expect [a new one, my money back, a credit to my account] within the next seven days.

Thank you.

Sincerely,

[Your Name]

cc: Federal Trade Commission
Consumer Response Center, Room 285
Sixth Street and Pennsylvania Avenue, NW
Washington, DC 20580

Kenneth Huntly, Chief Postal Inspector
U.S. Postal Service
475 L'Enfant Plaza West, SW
Washington, DC 20260-2100

Direct Marketing Association
1111 Nineteenth Street, NW, Suite 1100
Washington, DC 20036

The Honorable William Daley, Secretary
United States Department of Commerce
Fifteenth Street and Constitution Avenue, NW
Washington, DC 20230

Vacation Scams

[Your street address]
[Your city/town, state, and zip code]
[Today's date]

[Inside address to your attorney or to the office's fraud division]
[Frank Seales, Jr., Chief
Antitrust and Consumer Litigation Section
Office of the Attorney General
Commonwealth of Virginia
900 East Main Street
Richmond, VA 23219]*

Dear Mr. Seales:

I have recently become the victim of travel fraud, and I turn to you in the hope that justice will prevail. On [date],

*We're using the contact name and address for the Commonwealth of Virginia as an example here. Please consult the appendices to find the contact and address for your state.

I received a letter (copy enclosed) from Gotcha! Travel Bureau in Reston, Virginia, which offered a vacation trip [around the world? touring the local animal shelter?]. I immediately mailed in a check for [$300? $2,000? $100,000?]. This amount was to include airfare for two, transfers, and hotel accommodations.

It has now been six weeks and I have received nothing from Gotcha! After my check was cashed on [date], I called and called this company on [dates], and on each occasion was promised that a Freddy Fraud would return my call. Upon no response from Mr. Fraud, I called again on [date] and a recording informed me that the number _____ had been disconnected.

Please investigate this matter promptly and thoroughly. I wish to receive my money, and am very much afraid that others have been duped as well.

Thank you, and I look forward to hearing from you within the next ten business days.

Sincerely,

[Your Name]

Enclosure

cc: Louis Freeh, Director
     Federal Bureau of Investigation
     945 Pennsylvania Avenue, NW
     Washington, DC 20535-0001

     National Fraud Information Center
     815 Fifteenth Street, NW
     Suite 928-N
     Washington, DC 20005

EPILOGUE

So now we come to the close of *Shocked, Appalled, and Dismayed!* Just as the subtitle suggests, I expect that you're all now accomplished in writing complaint letters. Let us never forget that the art of correspondence—the correct and proper way to write—is a fundamental means of obtaining the results we desire. John Adams, the second U.S. president, once wrote, "A pen is an excellent instrument to fix a man's attention and to influence his ambition." Take the information you have in your possession and use it in the methods to which I ascribe, and you can attain your own aims. Ultimately, *your own* personal brand of poison will strike while the pen is hot!

APPENDICES

THE ATTORNEYS GENERAL OF THE UNITED STATES AND STATE CONSUMER PROTECTION OFFICES

State Consumer Protection Offices provide consumers with important services. They might mediate complaints, conduct investigations, prosecute offenders of consumer laws, license and regulate a variety of professionals, promote strong consumer legislation, provide educational materials, and advocate in consumers' interest. State offices, sometimes in a separate department of consumer affairs or the attorney general's or governor's office, are familiar with state laws and look for statewide patterns of problems. *The Consumer's Resource Handbook*, government publication, also contains useful listings of names and addresses.

Alabama Consumer Protection Division
Office of the Attorney General
11 South Union Street
Montgomery, AL 36130
(334) 242-7334
(800) 392-5658

Alaska Attorney General
1031 West Fourth Avenue, Suite 200
Anchorage, AK 99501
(907) 276-3550
(Alaska's Consumer Protection Office was closed in 1995).

Arizona Consumer Protection Division
Office of the Attorney General
1275 West Washington Street
Room 259
Phoenix, AZ 85007
(602) 542-3702
(800) 352-8431

Arkansas Consumer Protection Division
Office of the Attorney General
200 Tower Building

4th and 323 Center Streets
Little Rock, AR 72201
(501) 682-2341
(800) 482-8982

California Department of Consumer Affairs
Office of the Attorney General
1020 N Street
Sacramento, CA 95814
(916) 445-0660
(800) 344-9940

Colorado Consumer Protection Unit
Office of the Attorney General
110 Sixteenth Street, 10th Floor
Denver, CO 80202
(303) 620-4581

Connecticut Department of Consumer Protection
State Office Building
165 Capitol Avenue
Hartford, CT 06106
(203) 566-4999
(800) 842-2649

Delaware Division of Consumer Affairs
Department of Community Affairs
820 North French Street, 4th Floor
Wilmington, DE 19801
(302) 577-3250

District of Columbia
Department of Consumer and
Regulatory Affairs
614 H Street, NW
Washington, DC 20001
(202) 727-7000

Florida Division of Consumer Services
Mayo Building
407 South Calhoun Street
Tallahassee, FL 32399
(904) 488-2226
(800) 327-3382

Georgia Office of Consumer Affairs
2 Martin Luther King Jr. Drive
Plaza Level, East Tower
Atlanta, GA 30334
(404) 656-3790
(800) 869-1123

Hawaii Office of Consumer Protection
Department of Commerce and
Consumer Affairs
828 Fort Street Mall
Honolulu, Hawaii 96813
(808) 587-3222

Idaho Consumer Protection Unit
Office of the Attorney General
700 West Jefferson, Room 119
Boise, ID 83720
(208) 334-2424
(800) 432-3545

Illinois Governor's Office of Citizen Assistance
222 South College, 401 FLR
Springfield, IL 62706
(217) 782-0244
(800) 642-3112

Indiana Consumer Protection Division
Office of the Attorney General
219 State House
Indianapolis, IN 46204
(317) 232-6330
(800) 382-5516

Iowa Citizens' Aid Ombudsman
Capitol Complex
215 East Seventh Street
Des Moines, IA 50319
(515) 281-3592
(800) 358-5510

Kansas Consumer Protection Division
Office of the Attorney General
Kansas Judicial Center
301 West Tenth Street
Topeka, KS 66612
(913) 296-3751
(800) 432-2310

Kentucky Consumer Protection Division
Office of the Attorney General
209 St. Clair Street
Frankfort, KY 40601
(502) 564-2200
(800) 432-9257

Louisiana Consumer Protection Section
Office of the Attorney General
State Capitol Building

P.O. Box 94005
Baton Rouge, LA 70804
(504) 342-7013

**Maine Consumer Assistance
Service**
Office of the Attorney General
State House Station No. 6
Augusta, ME 04333
(207) 289-3716

**Maryland Consumer Protection
Division**
Office of the Attorney General
200 St. Paul Place
Baltimore, MD 21202
(301) 528-8662

**Massachusetts Consumer
Protection Division**
Office of the Attorney General
131 Tremont Street
Boston, MA 02111
(617) 727-7780

**Michigan Consumer Protection
Division**
Office of the Attorney General
P.O. Box 30213
Lansing, MI 48909
(517) 373-1140

**Minnesota Office of Consumer
Services**
Office of the Attorney General
117 University Avenue
Room 124, Ford Building
St. Paul, MN 55155
(612) 296-2331

**Mississippi Consumer Protection
Division**
Office of the Attorney General
P.O. Box 22947
Jackson, MS 39225
(601) 354-6018

**Missouri Public Protection
Division**
Office of the Attorney General
P.O. Box 899
Jefferson City, MO 65102
(314) 751-3321
(800) 392-8222

**Montana Office of Consumer
Affairs**
Department of Commerce
1424 Ninth Avenue
Helena, MT 59620
(406) 444-4312

**Nebraska Consumer Protection
Division**
Department of Justice
2115 State Capitol, Room 2115
Lincoln, NB 68509
(402) 417-4723

Nevada Consumer Affairs Division
Department of Commerce
4600 Kietezke Lane
Building M, Suite 245
Reno, NV 89502
(702) 688-1800
(800) 992-0900

**New Hampshire Consumer
Protection and Antitrust Bureau**
Office of the Attorney General
33 Capitol Street
Concord, NH 03301
(603) 271-3641

**New Jersey Department of the
Public Advocate**
25 Market Street, CN850
Trenton, NJ 08625
(609) 292-7087
(800) 792-8600

**New Jersey Division of Consumer
Affairs**
P.O. Box 45027
Newark, NJ 07101

**New Mexico Consumer and
Economic Crime Division**
Office of the Attorney General
P.O. Drawer 1508
Santa Fe, NM 87504
(505) 827-6060
(800) 432-2070

**New York Bureau of Consumer
Frauds and Protection**
Office of the Attorney General
The Capitol
Albany, NY 12224
(518) 474-5481

**North Carolina Consumer
Protection Division**
Office of the Attorney General
P.O. Box 629
Raleigh, NC 27602
(919) 733-7741

**North Dakota Consumer Fraud
Division**
Office of the Attorney General
600 East Boulevard
Bismarck, ND 58505
(701) 224-3404
(800) 472-2600

**Ohio Consumer Frauds and
Crimes Section**
Office of the Attorney General
30 East Broad Street, 25th Floor
Columbus, OH 43266-0410
(614) 466-4986
(800) 282-0515

**Oklahoma Consumer Protection
Unit**
Office of the Attorney General
112 State Capitol Building
Oklahoma City, OK 73105
(405) 521-3921

Oregon Financial Fraud Section
Consumer Complaints
Department of Justice
Justice Building
Salem, OR 97310
(503) 378-4320

**Pennsylvania Bureau of Consumer
Protection**
Office of the Attorney General
Strawberry Square, 14th Floor
Harrisburg, PA 17120
(717) 787-9707
(800) 441-2555

**Puerto Rico Department of
Consumer Affairs**
Department of Consumer Affairs
Minillas Station, P.O. Box 41059
Santurce, PR 00940
(809) 722-7555

**Rhode Island Consumer
Protection Division**
Office of the Attorney General
72 Pine Street
Providence, RI 02903
(401) 277-2104
(800) 852-7776

South Carolina Department of Consumer Affairs
P.O. Box 5757
Columbia, SC 29250
(803) 734-9452
(800) 922-1594

South Dakota Division of Consumer Affairs
Office of the Attorney General
500 East Capitol Building
Pierre, SD 57501
(605) 773-4400

Tennessee Division of Consumer Affairs
500 James Robertson Parkway
5th Floor
Nashville, TN 37243
(615) 741-4737
(800) 342-8385

Texas Consumer Protection Division
Office of the Attorney General
Capitol Station
P.O. Box 12548
Austin, TX 78711
(512) 463-2070

Utah Division of Consumer Protection
Department of Commerce
160 East Third South
Salt Lake City, UT 84145
(801) 530-6601

Vermont Public Protection Division
Office of the Attorney General
109 State Street
Montpelier, VT 05609-1001
(802) 828-3171

Virgin Islands Department of Licensing and Consumer Affairs
Property and Procurement Building
Subbase #1, Room 205
St. Thomas, VI 00802
(809) 774-3130

Virginia Division of Consumer Affairs
P.O. Box 1163
Richmond, VA 23209
(804) 786-2042

Washington Consumer and Business Fair Practice Division
Office of the Attorney General
900 Fourth Avenue, Suite 2000
Seattle, WA 98164
(206) 464-6684
(800) 551-4636

West Virginia Consumer Protection Division
Office of the Attorney General
812 Quarrier Street, Sixth Floor
Charleston, WV 25301
(304) 348-8986
(800) 386-8808

Wisconsin Office of Consumer Protection and Citizen Advocacy
Department of Justice
P.O. Box 7856
Madison, WI 53707
(608) 266-1852
(800) 362-8189

Wyoming Consumer Affairs
Office of the Attorney General
123 State Capitol Building
Cheyenne, WY 82002
(307) 777-7841

AUTOMOBILE DISPUTE RESOLUTION PROGRAMS

AUTOCAP

Acura
Acura Division
American Honda Motor Company,
Inc.
(800) 382-2238

BMW
BMW of North America, Inc.
(800) 831-1117

Honda
American Honda Motor Company,
Inc.
(310) 783-3260

Infiniti
Infiniti Division
Nissan Motor Corporation in the
USA
(800) 662-6200

Isuzu
American Isuzu Motors, Inc.
(800) 255-6727
(310) 699-0500

Jaguar
Jaguar Cars
(201) 818-8100

Mitsubishi
Mitsubishi Motor Sales of America,
Inc.
(800) 222-0037

Nissan
Nissan Motor Corporation in the USA
(800) 647-7261

Rolls-Royce
Rolls-Royce Motor Cars, Inc.
(201) 967-9100

Volvo
Volvo Cars of North America
(800) 458-1552
(201) 767-4737

AUTOLINE

AUTOLINE, an arbitration program sponsored by the Council of Better Business Bureaus, (800) 955-5100, covers cars made by the following manufacturers:

Alfa Romeo
AM General
Audi
General Motors Corporation (including the **Buick, Cadillac, Chevrolet/ Geo, GMC Truck, Oldsmobile, Pontiac** Divisions, and the **Saturn Corporation**)
Honda (including the **Acura** Division)
Hyundai
Isuzu
Kia
Land Rover
Nissan (including the **Infiniti** Division)
Peugeot
Porsche
Saab (AUTOLINE is available to owners of 1991 model-year Saab vehicles only in California, Florida, Kentucky, Minnesota, and Oregon)
Sterling
Subaru
Toyota (including the **Lexus** Division)
Volkswagen

Chrysler: Chrysler Motors Corporation sponsors a third-party dispute resolution program, the Chrysler Customer Arbitration Board (CAB). If your car is a **Chrysler, Dodge, Jeep/Eagle,** or **Plymouth,** contact Chrysler's Customer Relations and Surveys Manager at (800) 992-1997.
Ford: Ford Motor Company (including **Lincoln, Mercury,** and **Merkur** Divisions) sponsors a third-party dispute resolution program, the Ford Dispute Settlement Board (DSB). For more information call (800) 392-3673.

The following motor companies **do not** participate in any mediation or arbitration program for resolution of disputes. For further assistance, contact the national customer relations office of your manufacturer as listed below.

Daihatsu
Daihatsu America, Inc.
(714) 761-7000

Fiat
FIAT USA, INC.
(212) 207-0947

Lotus
Lotus Cars USA, Inc.
(404) 822-4566

Mazda
Mazda Motor of America, Inc.
(800) 222-5500

Mercedes-Benz
Mercedes-Benz of North America, Inc.
(800) 367-6372

Suzuki
American Suzuki Motor Corporation
(800) 934-0934

NATIONAL CONSUMER ORGANIZATIONS

These organizations define their missions as consumer assistance, protection and/or advocacy. Most develop and distribute consumer education and information materials; several are professional associations primarily or exclusively concerned with improving consumer protection or customer service, and many are engaged in advocacy of consumer interests before government, the courts and the news media.

Alliance Against Fraud in Telemarketing (AAFT)
1701 K Street, NW, Suite 1200
Washington, DC 20006
(202) 835-3323
Promotes cooperative educational efforts to alert potential victims to the threat of telemarketing fraud and steps consumers can take to protect themselves.

American Association of Retired Persons
601 E Street, NW
Washington, DC 20049
(202) 434-6030
AARP's Consumer Affairs Section advocates on behalf of mid-life and older consumers.

American Council on Consumer Interests (ACCI)
240 Stanley Hall
University of Missouri
Columbia, MO 65211
(573) 882-3817
E-mail: acci@showme.missouri.edu
Promotes publications and educational programs related to consumer issues and family economics.

American Council on Science and Health (ACSH)
1995 Broadway, 2nd Floor
New York, NY 10023-5860
(212) 362-7044
ACSH's goal is to provide up-to-date, sound information about health and chemicals, foods, lifestyles, and the environment.

Manager, Consumer Affairs
Automotive Consumer Action Program
8400 Westpark Drive
McLean, VA 22102
(703) 821-7144
A service of the National Automobile Dealer's Association. Provides information on handling dealer disputes and problems with vehicles, as well as safety and recall information.

Aviation Consumer Action Project
(202) 638-4000
Founded by Ralph Nader, ACAP researches consumer issues and publishes the brochure *Facts and Advice for Airline Passengers*. Advises passengers about rights and safety issues over the phone.

Bankcard Holders of America (BHA)
524 Branch Drive
Salem, VA 24153
(540) 389-5445
BHA assists consumers in saving money on credit, getting out of debt, and resolving credit problems.

Call for Action
5272 River Road,
Suite 300
Bethesda, MD 20816
(Network info) (301) 657-8260
Assists consumers with marketplace problems and helps consumers and small businesses through mediation of marketplace disputes.

Center for Auto Safety (CAS)
2001 S Street, NW, Suite 410
Washington, DC 20009
(202) 328-7700
CAS assists consumers with auto-related problems and advocates on behalf of consumers in auto safety and quality, fuel efficiency, emissions and related issues.

Citizen Action
1730 Rhode Island Avenue, NW
Washington, DC 20036
(202) 775-1580
Works on behalf of consumers on health care reform, environment, energy, transportation and civil rights issues.

Congress Watch
215 Pennsylvania Avenue, SE
Washington, DC 20003
(202) 546-4996
E-mail: congresswatch@citizen.org

An arm of Public Citizen, Congress Watch works for consumer-related legislation, regulation and policies in such areas as trade, health and safety, and campaign financing.

Consumer Action (CA)
116 New Montgomery, Suite 233
San Francisco, CA 94105
(415) 777-9635
Assists consumers with marketplace problems; specializes in credit, finance, and telecommunications issues.

Consumer Federation of America (CFA)
1424 Sixteenth Street, NW
Suite 604
Washington, DC 20036
(202) 387-6121
A consumer advocacy and education organization which represents consumer interests, including telephone service, insurance and financial services, product safety, indoor air pollution, health care, product liability and utility rates.

Consumers for World Trade (CWT)
2000 L Street, NW, Suite 200
Washington, DC 20036
(202) 785-4835
E-mail: cwt@ids2.idsonline.com
Promotes economic growth and increase of consumer choice and price competition in the marketplace.

Consumers Union of U.S., Inc. (CU)
101 Truman Avenue
Yonkers, NY 10703-1057
(914) 378-2000

Researches and tests consumer goods and services and disseminates the results in its monthly magazine, *Consumer Reports*.

Council of Better Business Bureaus, Inc. (CBBB)
4200 Wilson Boulevard
Arlington, VA 22203
(703) 276-0100
E-mail: bbb@bbb.org
Website: www.bbb.org
See also Appendix for Professional and Trade Associations

Families USA Foundation
1334 G Street, NW, Suite 300
Washington, DC 20005
(202) 628-3030
E-mail: info@familiesusa.org
Website: epn.org/families.html
Organization committed to comprehensive reform of health and long-term care.

Health Research Group (HRG)
1600 Twentieth Street, NW
Washington, DC 20009
(202) 588-1000
A division of Public Citizen; works for protection against unsafe foods, drugs, medical devices, and workplaces, and advocates for greater consumer control over personal health decisions.

National Association of State Utility Consumer Advocates (NASUCA)
1133 Fifteenth Street, NW, Suite 550
Washington, DC 20005
(202) 727-3908

Represents millions of consumers served by investor-owned gas, telephone, electric, and water companies.

National Coalition for Consumer Education (NCCE)
295 Main Street, Suite 200
Madison, NJ 07940
(201) 377-8987
Educates consumers about such important issues as financial management, health, and safety, and the environment.

National Consumers League (NCL)
1701 K Street, NW, Suite 1200
Washington, DC 20006
(202) 835-3323
Works for health, safety, and fairness in the marketplace and workplace. Current principal issue areas include consumer fraud, food and drug safety, fair labor standards, child labor, health care, the environment, financial services, and telecommunications.

National Foundation for Consumer Credit, Inc. (NFCC)
8611 Second Avenue, Suite 100
Silver Spring, MD 20910
(800) 388-2227
Educates and counsels individuals and families on credit issues.

National Fraud Information Center (NFIC)
P.O. Box 65868
Washington, DC 20035
(800) 876-7060
E-mail: nfic@internetmci.com
Website: www.fraud.org
Assists consumers with recognizing and filing complaints about telemarketing and Internet fraud.

National Insurance Consumer Organization (NICO) see Consumer Federation of America

Project OPEN (Online Public Education Network)
Interactive Services Association
8403 Colesville Road, Suite 865
Silver Spring, MD 20910
(301) 495-4955
E-mail: project-open@isa.net
Primarily helps consumers understand how to use online and Internet services in an informed and responsible way.

Public Citizen, Inc.
1600 Twentieth Street, NW
Washington, DC 20009
(202) 588-1000
Represents consumer interests through lobbying, litigation, research, and publications. Primary current areas of interest include product liability, health-care delivery, safe medical devices and medications, open

and ethical government and safe and sustainable energy use.

Public Voice for Food and Health Policy
1101 Fourteenth Street, NW
Suite 710
Washington, DC 20005
(202) 371-1840
E-mail: pvoice@ix.netcom.com
Website: publicvoice.org/pvoice.html
Works for food and agriculture policies and practices that improve the safety, health, and affordability of the food supply and protect the environment.

The Sierra Club
Legislative Offices
408 C Street, NE
Washington, DC 20002
(202) 547-1141
Advocates for environmental issues.

U.S. Public Interest Research Group (USPIRG)
218 D Street, SE
Washington, DC 20003-1900
(202) 546-9707
E-mail: pirg@pirg.org
Website: www.pirg.org/pirg
Battles corporate power and consumer abuses, especially in the areas of rising bank fees, financial identity theft, dangerous products, and children's products.

CORPORATE CONSUMER CONTACTS

This section lists the names and addresses of more than six hundred corporate headquarters and, in some cases, the name of the president, CEO, or executive of the company. If not listed, you can address your letter to the Customer Relations Department. Many listings also include toll-free 800 numbers. Additionally TDD (Telecommunications Devices for the Deaf) numbers are made available by a number of companies.

In some cases, you will see a company name or brand name listed with the instructions to see another company listed elsewhere in this section, for example, "Max Factor, see Procter and Gamble." This means that questions about Max Factor products should be directed to the consumer contact at Procter and Gamble. If a company has changed its name recently or is popularly known by another name, you will be directed to the company name listed. Remember that executives' names may change, so always call to confirm the name of the person who is currently in charge.

If you do not find the product name in this section, check the product label or warranty for the name and address of the manufacturer. If you cannot find the name of the manufacturer, the *Thomas Register of American Manufacturers* lists the manufacturers of thousands of products.

A

AAMCO Transmissions, Inc.
One Presidential Boulevard
Bala Cynwyd, PA 19004-1034
(800) 523-0401

AETNA Life and Casualty
151 Farmington Avenue
Hartford, CT 06156
(800) 872-3862

AJAY Leisure Products, Inc.
1501 East Wisconsin Street
Delavan, WI 53115
(800) 558-3276

Michael Armstrong, CEO
A T & T
295 North Maple Avenue
Basking Ridge, NJ 07920
(908) 221-5311

David Hodnik, President/CEO
Ace Hardware Corporation
2200 Kensington Court
Oak Brook, IL 60521
(708) 990-6600

Acura
1919 Torrance Boulevard
Torrance, CA 90501-2746
(800) 382-2238

Airwick Industries, Inc. (see Reckitt & Colman, Inc.)

Andrea Cohan, Senior Manager
Alamo Rent A Car
P.O. Box 22776
Ft. Lauderdale, FL 33335
(800) 445-5664

Alaska Airlines
P.O. Box 68900
Seattle, WA 98168
(206) 431-7286

Alberto Culver Company
2525 Armitage Avenue
Melrose Park, IL 60160
(708) 450-3163

Alfa-Romeo Distributors of North America, Inc.
6220 South Orange Blossom Trail
Suite 209
Orlando, FL 32809
(407) 856-5000

Allied Van Lines
P.O. Box 4403
Chicago, IL 60680
(800) 470-2851
www.alliedvan.net

Allstate Insurance Company
2775 Sanders Road
Northbrook, IL 60062
(847) 402-5448

Denise Yates, Manager
Customer Relations
Aloha Airlines
P.O. Box 30028
Honolulu, HI 96820
(800) 803-9454

Dixie Trout, Vice President
Consumer Relations
Amana Refrigeration, Inc.
Amana, IA 52204
(800) 843-0304

Koichi Miya, CEO
American Honda Motor Company, Inc.
1919 Torrance Boulevard
Torrance, CA 90501-2746
(310) 783-3260

American Motors Corporation (see Chrysler Corporation)

American Suzuki Motor Corporation
P.O. Box 1100
Brea, CA 92822-1100
(Motorcycles) (714) 996-7040
(Automobiles) (800) 934-0934

Richard Goodmanson
President/CEO
America West Airlines
4000 East Sky Harbor Boulevard
Phoenix, AZ 85034
(800) 235-9292

Donald J. Carty, President/CEO
American Airlines, Inc.
P.O. Box 619612 MD 2400
DFW International Airport, TX 75261-9612
(817) 967-2000

American Automobile Association
Mailspace 15
1000 AAA Drive
Heathrow, FL 32746-5063
(Written inquiries only)

Harvey Golub, CEO
American Express Company
American Express Tower C
World Financial Center
200 Vesey Street
New York, NY 10285

(Gold card) (800) 327-2177
(Platinum card) (800) 525-3355
(Green card) (800) 528-4800

American Greetings Corporation
One American Road
Cleveland, OH 44144
(800) 321-3040

Sue Holiday, Consumer
Correspondent
American Home Food Products, Inc.
5 Giralda Farms
Madison, NJ 07940
(800) 544-5680

Richard Nicolosi, President/CEO
American Tourister, Inc.
11200 East Forty-fifth Avenue
Denver, CO 80239
(800) 635-5505

America's Favorite Chicken Company
6 Concourse Parkway, Suite 1700
Atlanta, GA 30328-5352
(404) 391-9500

Richard Smith, Customer Relations
Amoco Oil Company
200 East Randolph Drive
Chicago, IL 60601
(800) 333-3991

Martha Tancil, Director
Customer Satisfaction
Amtrak
Washington Union Station
60 Massachusetts Avenue, NE
Washington, DC 20002
(800) USA-RAIL

Robin Koop, Director
Customer Service
Amway Company
7575 East Fulton Road
Ada, MI 49355
(616) 787-7717

Ken Chapman, President/CEO
Andersen Windows, Inc.
100 Fourth Avenue, North
Bayport, MN 55003
(612) 430-5564

August Busch, III, CEO
Anheuser-Busch, Inc.
One Busch Place
St. Louis, MO 63118-1852
(800) 342-5283

Aon Corporation
123 North Wacker Drive
Chicago, IL 60606
(312) 701-3000

Gill Amelio, CEO
Apple Computer, Inc.
20525 Mariani Avenue
Cupertino, CA 95014
(800) 776-2333

Aramis, Inc. (see Estee Lauder Companies)

Arizona Mail Order
3740 East Thirty-fourth Street
Tucson, AZ 85713
(520) 748-8600

Arm & Hammer (see Church & Dwight Co., Inc.)

Tim Harris, President/CEO
Armour Swift Eckrich
2001 Butterfield Road
Downers Grove, IL 60515
(800) 325-7424

Fred Fuest, Manager
Customer Affairs
Armstrong Tire Division
Pirelli/Armstrong Tire Corporation
500 Sargent Drive
New Haven, CT 06536
(800) 243-0167

Robert Shannon, President/CEO
Armstrong World Industries
P.O. Box 3001
Lancaster, PA 17604
(800) 233-3823

Gary Tramiel, Vice President
Dealer Sales
Atari Video Game Systems
455 South Milhilda Avenue
Sunnyvale, CA 94086
(408) 328-0900

April Richards, Manager
Customer Relations
Atlantic Richfield Company
ARCO Products Company

1055 West Seventh Street
Los Angeles, CA 90017
(800) 322-2726

Glen Dunkers, Vice President
Customer Service
Atlas Van Lines
P.O. Box 509
Evansville, IN 47703-0509
(800) 252-8885

Audi of America, Inc.
3800 Hamlin Road
Auburn Hills, MI 48326
(800) 822-2834

Barbara Pearson, Manager
Customer Service
Avis Rent-A-Car System
4500 South 129th East Avenue
Tulsa, OK 74134-3802
(800) 352-7900

Avon Fashions, Inc. (see Newport News, Inc.)

Lynn Baron, Consumer Information Center
Avon Products, Inc.
9 West Fifty-seventh Street
New York, NY 10019
(800) 367-2866

B

BMW of North America, Inc.
P.O. Box 1227
Westwood, NJ 07675-1227
(800) 831-1117

Frederick J. Wilson, General Counsel
Bacardi-Martini USA, Inc.

2100 Biscayne Boulevard
Miami, FL 33137
(800) BACARDI

Bali/Sara Lee Intimate Apparel
Sara Lee Corporation
3330 Healy Drive
P.O. Box 5100 (23113)

Winston-Salem, NC 27103
(800) 225-4872

Bank of America, NT & SA
Box 37000
San Francisco, CA 94137
(415) 622-6081

The Bank of New York Company, Inc.
48 Wall Street, 16th Floor
New York, NY 10286
(212) 495-2066

Barnett Banks, Inc.
P.O. Box 40789
Jacksonville, FL 32231
(904) 791-7720

Johnny Morris, President/CEO
Bass Pro Shop
1935 South Campbell
Springfield, MO 65898
(800) BASS-PRO

Rick Fersch, President
Eddie Bauer
P.O. Box 97000
Redmond, WA 98073-9700
(800) 426-6253

Darla J. Elkin, Manager
Regulatory and Consumer Affairs
Bausch and Lomb
1400 North Goodman Street
Rochester, NY 14692
(800) 553-5340

Marylou F. Ulincy, Manager
Consumer Relations
Bayer Corporation
36 Columbia Road
Morristown, NJ 07962-1910

(800) 331-4536
(also Sterling Health, Glenbrook, & Winthrop Products)

Leon Gorman, President
L. L. Bean, Inc.
Casco Street
Freeport, ME 04033-0001
(800) 341-4341

Bear Creek Corporation
2518 South Pacific Highway
P.O. Box 299
Medford, OR 97501
(541) 776-2400

Beatrice Cheese, Inc.
770 North Springdale Road
Waukesha, WI 53186
(414) 782-2750

Beech Holdings Corporation (see Budget Rent-A-Car Corp.)

Ivan Seidenberg, Chairman
Bell Atlantic
1095 Avenue of the Americas
New York, NY 10036
(800) 772-2300
TDD: (800) 342-4181

Benihana of Tokyo
8685 Northwest Fifty-third Terrace
Miami, Fl 33166
(800) 327-3369

Adair Sampogna, Director
Consumer Communications
Best Foods
CPC International, Inc.
P.O. Box 8000 International Plaza
Englewood Cliffs, NJ 07632
(201) 894-2324

Peggy Yoder, Manager
Customer Service
Best Western International
P.O. Box 42007
Phoenix, AZ 85080-2007
(800) 528-1238

BIC Corporation
500 Bic Drive
Milford, CT 06460
(203) 783-2000

Birds Eye (see General Foods)

Michael Hoopis, President
Archibald Nolan, CEO
Black and Decker Household Products
6 Armstrong Road
Shelton, CT 06484
(800) 231-9786

Barbara B. Lucas, Senior Vice
President
Public Affairs
Black and Decker Power Tools
701 East Joppa Road TW 245
Towson, MD 21286
(800) 762-6672

Blockbuster Entertainment Corporation
One Blockbuster Plaza
Ft. Lauderdale, FL 33301
(954) 832-3000

Lori Hunt, Customer Affairs
Representative
Block Drug Company, Inc.
257 Cornelison Avenue
Jersey City, NJ 07302
(800) 365-6500

Bloomingdale's by Mail, Ltd.
475 Knotter Drive
P.O. Box 593
Cheshire, CT 06410-9933
(203) 271-1313

Blue Bell, Inc. (see Wrangler)

Patrick Hayes, President/CEO
Blue Cross and Blue Shield Association
1310 G Street, NW, 12th Floor
Washington, DC 20005
(202) 626-4780

Karen Braswell, Marketing Director
Bojangles
P.O. Box 240239
Charlotte, NC 28224
(800) 366-9921

Borden, Inc.
180 East Broad Street
Columbus, OH 43215
(614) 225-4511

Stephanie Whelan, Manager
Consumer Affairs
Bradlees Discount Department Stores
One Bradlees Circle
P.O. Box 9015
Braintree, MA 02184-9015
(781) 380-5377

Breck Hair Care Products (see The Dial Corporation)

Bridgestone/Firestone, Inc.
P.O. Box 7988
Chicago, IL 60680-9534
(800) 367-3872

Brights Creek
5000 City Lane Road
Hampton, VA 23661
(804) 827-1850

Bristol-Myers Products
1350 Liberty Avenue
Hillside, NJ 07205
(800) 468-7746

Robert Laverty, Director
Public Affairs
Bristol-Myers Squibb
Pharmaceutical Group
P.O. Box 4000
Princeton, NJ 08543-4000
(800) 332-2056

Brita, USA (see Clorox Company)

British Airways
75-20 Astoria Boulevard
Jackson Heights, NY 11370
(718) 397-4000

Dianne Hall, Manager
Consumer Services Administration
Brown-Forman Beverage Company
P.O. Box 1080
Louisville, KY 40201
(800) 753-1177

Budget Gourmet
P.O. Box 10
Boise, ID 83707
(800) 488-0050

Budget Rent-A-Car Corporation
P.O. Box 111580
Carrollton, TX 75011-1580
(800) 621-2844

Bob Coletta, President
Buick Motor Division
General Motors Corporation
902 East Hamilton
Flint, MI 48550
(800) 521-7300

Bull & Bear Group, Inc.
11 Hanover Square
New York, NY 10005
(800) 847-4200

Herbert Hosmann, CEO
Bulova Watch Company
One Bulova Avenue
Woodside, NY 11377
(718) 204-3300

Monroe Milstein, President
Burlington Coat Factory
Warehouse Corporation
1830 Route 130 North
Burlington, NJ 08016
(609) 387-7800

Burlington Hosiery (see Kayser-
Roth Corporation)

George Henderson, President/CEO
Burlington Industries
P.O. Box 21207
3330 West Friendly Avenue
Greensboro, NC 27420
(910) 379-2276

C

CIBA Corporation
Pharmaceuticals Division
556 Morris Avenue
Summit, NJ 07901-1398
(908) 277-5000

CIBA Corporation
Plant Protection
410 Swing Road
Greensboro, NC 27409
(800) 334-9481

CIBA Self-Medication, Inc.
581 Main Street
Woodbridge, NJ 07095
(908) 602-6800

CIE Terminals (see CIE America)

Mark A. Whiter, Director
Customer Services
**CIGNA Property and Casualty
Companies**
1601 Chestnut Street
Philadelphia, PA 19192
(215) 761-4555

CPC International, Inc.
International Plaza
Box 8000
Englewood Cliffs, NJ 07632
(201) 894-4000

Neil Dinerman, President
Chairman of the Board
C & R Clothiers
8660 Hayden Place
Culver City, CA 90232
(310) 559-8200

CVN (see QVC Network)

C V S
One CVS Drive
Woonsocket, RI 02895-9988
(800) 555-4771

Cadbury Beverages, Inc. (see Motts, USA)

Caloric Modern Maid Corporation
(see Amana Refrigeration, Inc.)

David Johnson, President
Campbell Soup Company
Campbell Place
Camden, NJ 08103-1799
(800) 257-8443

Susan Read, Manager
Quality Control
Canandaigua Wine Company
116 Buffalo Street
Canandaigua, NY 14424
(716) 394-7900

Hauro Murase, President/CEO
Canon U.S.A., Inc.
One Canon Plaza, Building C
Lake Success, NY 11042
(800) 828-4040

Marcia King-Gamble, Director
Guest Relations
Carnival Cruise Lines
3655 Northwest Eighty-seventh
Avenue
Miami, FL 33178-2428
(800) 438-6744

Guy Fanconneau, President/CEO
Carrier Air Conditioning Company
P.O. Box 4808

Syracuse, NY 13221
(800) 227-7437

   Bryant Heating and Air
   Conditioning
   (800) 428-4326

   Payne Heating and Air
   Conditioning
   (800) 428-4326

Carte Blanche (see Diners Club
International)

Carter-Wallace, Inc.
1345 Avenue of the Americas
New York, NY 10105
(212) 339-5000

Carvel Corporation
20 Batterson Park Road
Farmington, CT 06032-2502
(written inquiries only)

Casio, Inc.
570 Mount Pleasant Avenue
Dover, NJ 07801
(800) 962-2746

Ron Dohr, Supervisor
Customer Service
Champion Spark Plug Company
P.O. Box 910
Toledo, OH 43661
(419) 535-2002

Arie Kopelman, President/CEO
Chanel, Inc.
9 West Fifty-seventh Street
44th Floor
New York, NY 10019-2790
(212) 688-5055

Chase Manhattan Bank
270 Park Avenue
New York, NY 10017
(212) 270-9300

Walter Dabek, Director
Consumer Information
Cheesebrough-Pond's, USA
55 Merritt Boulevard
Trumbull, CT 06611
(800) 243-5804

ChemLawn Services Corporation
(see TruGreen Limited Partnership)

W.P. Howell, Supervisor
Consumer Affairs
Chevron Products Company
P.O. Box H
Concord, CA 94524
(800) 962-1223

Chi-Chi's, Inc.
10200 Linn Station Road
Louisville, KY 40223
(502) 426-3900

Roger Eaton, President/Chairman of
the Board
Corporate Office
Chrysler Corporation
P.O. Box 21-8004
Auburn Hills, MI 48321-8004
(800) 763-8422

Chuck E. Cheese (see ShowBiz
Pizza Time, Inc.)

Church's Fried Chicken, Inc. (see
America's Favorite Chicken Co.)

Cincinnati Microwave
One Microwave Plaza
Cincinnati, OH 45249-9502
(800) 433-3487

Richard Sharp, President/CEO
Circuit City Stores, Inc.
9950 Mayland Drive
Richmond, VA 23233
(800) 627-2274

John S. Reed, CEO
Sanford I. Weill, CEO
Citicorp/Travelers
599 Lexington Avenue, 24th Floor
New York, NY 10043
(212) 559-0043

Tina Sherritt, Executive Secretary
**Citizen Watch Company of
America, Inc.**
8506 Osage Avenue
Los Angeles, CA 90045
(800) 321-1023

Steve Sandove, CEO
Clairol, Inc.
40 West Fifty-seventh Street
23rd Floor
New York, NY 10019
(800) 223-5800

Clinique Laboratories, Inc. (see
Estee Lauder Companies)

Sandy Stewart, Manager
Consumer Services
**Clopay Building Products
Company**
312 Walnut Street, Suite 1600
Cincinnati, OH 45202-4036
(800) 225-6729

Susan Silva, Manager
Consumer Services
Clorox Company
1221 Broadway
Oakland, CA 94612-1888
(510) 271-7283

Club Med Sales, Inc.
40 West Fifty-seventh Street
New York, NY 10019
(212) 977-2100

Roberto Giodueta, CEO
The Coca-Cola Company
P.O. Drawer 1734
Atlanta, GA 30301
(800) 438-2653
TDD: (800) 262-2653

Coldwell Banker Corporation
339 Jefferson Road
Parsippany, NJ 07054
(800) 733-6629

Reuben Marx, CEO
**Colgate, Palmolive, Mennen
Company**
300 Park Avenue
New York, NY 10022
(800) 228-7408

Gregory Barsteas, President
Colonial Penn Group, Inc.
399 Market Street, 5th Floor
Philadelphia, PA 19181
(215) 928-8000

Columbia House
P.O. Box 4450
New York, NY 10101-4450
(Records and tapes) (800) 457-0500
(Videos) (800) 457-0866

Combined Insurance Company of America (see Aon Corp.)

Compaq Computer Corporation
P.O. Box 692000
Houston, TX 77269-2000
(800) 345-1518

Comprehensive Care Corporation
16305 Swingley Ridge Drive
Suite 100
Chesterfield, MO 63017
(800) 678-2273

Roger Morris, President/CEO
Congoleum Corporation
3705 Quakerbridge Road
P.O. Box 3127
Mercerville, NJ 08619
(609) 584-3000

Contempo Casuals
5433 West Jefferson Boulevard
Los Angeles, CA 90016
(213) 936-2131

Gordon Bethune, CEO
Gregory Brenneman, President
Continental Airlines, Inc.
2929 Allen Parkway
P.O. Box 4607
Houston, TX 77210
(713) 987-6500

Converse, Inc.
One Fordham Road
North Reading, MA 01864-2680
(800) 428-CONS

Coors Brewing Company
Consumer Information Center
NH 475

Golden, CO 80401
(800) 642-6116

Coppertone (see Schering-Plough HealthCare Products, Inc.)

Roger G. Ackerman,
Chairman/CEO
Corning, Inc.
Administrative Headquarters
One Riverfront Plaza
Corning, NY 14831-0001
(800) 999-3436

Craftmatic Organization
2500 Interplex Drive
Trevose, PA 19053-6998
(800) 677-8200

Jenny Craig International
445 Marine View Avenue
Del Mar, CA 92014
(619) 259-7000

Gail Compagnone, Manager
Customer Relations
A. T. Cross Company
One Albion Road
Lincoln, RI 02865
(800) AT CROSS

Steve Stevens, President/CEO
Crown Books
3300 Seventy-fifth Avenue
Landover, MD 20785
(800) 831-7400

Peter Cammarata, Director
Sales and Marketing Operations
Cuisinarts Corporation
One Cummings Point Road
Stamford, CT 06904
(800) 726-0190

Culligan International Company
One Culligan Parkway
Northbrook, IL 60062
(847) 205-5757

Marvin E. Eisenstadt, President
Cumberland Packing Corporation
Two Cumberland Street
Brooklyn, NY 11205
(718) 858-4200

Cunard Line
555 Fifth Avenue
New York, NY 10017
(800) 528-6273

Dan Roth, Department Head
Customer Service
Current, Inc.
P.O. Box 2559
Colorado Springs, CO 80901
(800) 525-7170

D

d-Con (see Reckitt and Colman,
Inc.)

Daihatsu America, Inc.
4422 Corporate Center Drive
Los Alamitos, CA 90720
(800) 777-7070

Dairy Queen (see International
Dairy Queen)

Eileen O'Gorman, Director
Customer Relations
Dannon Company, Inc.
1111 Westchester Avenue
White Plains, NY 10604
(Written inquiries only)

Mary Ann Domuracki, President
Danskin
111 West Fortieth Street, 18th Floor
New York, NY 10018
(800) 288-6749

Terry Pitra, Manager
Guest Relations
**Dayton's, Hudson's, Marshall
Field's Department Stores**

Box 1197
700 Nicollet Mall
Minneapolis, MN 55402
(612) 375-3382

**Dean Witter
Discover and Company**
2 World Trade Center, 66th Floor
New York, NY 10048
(800) 733-2307

Dearfoam (see R. G. Barry Corp.)

Deere & Company
John Deere Road
Moline, IL 61265-8098
(309) 765-8000

Del Laboratories, Inc.
565 Broad Hollow Road
Farmingdale, NY 11735
(516) 293-7070

Brian Haycox, CEO
Paul Mullan, President
Del Monte Foods
P.O. Box 193575
San Francisco, CA 94119-3575
(800) 543-3090

Del Pharmaceuticals, Inc. (see Del Laboratories, Inc.)

Delphi Auto Systems
2401 Columbus Avenue
Mail Code 18-109
Anderson, IN 46016
(317) 646-3000

Ronald W. Allen, President/CEO
Delta Air Lines
Hartsfield Atlanta International Airport
Atlanta, GA 30320
(404) 715-1402

Barbara Ashley, Assistant Manager
Product Services
Delta Faucets
P.O. Box 40980
Indianapolis, IN 46280
(317) 848-1812

Denny's, Inc.
203 East Main Street
Spartanburg, SC 29319-0001
(864) 597-8000

George Andrassy, Vice President
Research and Development
Dep Corporation
2101 East Via Arado
Rancho Dominguez, CA 90220-6189
(800) 367-2855

Malcolm Jozoff, President/CEO
The Dial Corporation
1850 North Central Avenue
Phoenix, AZ 85004
(800) 258-DIAL

Diet Center, Inc.
395 Springdale Drive
Akron, OH 44333
(330) 665-5861

Digital Equipment Corporation
111 Powder Mill Road
Maynard, MA 01754
(800) 332-4636

Dillard Department Stores, Inc.
1600 Cantrell Road
Little Rock, AR 72201
(501) 376-5200

Jim Scherman, Vice President
Customer Service
Diners Club International
183 Inverness Drive West
Englewood, CO 80112
(800) 234-6377
TDD: (303) 643-2155

Discover (see Dean Witter, Discover and Company)

Helen Robinson, Manager
Consumer Response
Dole Packaged Foods
5795 Lindero Canyon Road
Westlake Village, CA 91362-4013
(800) 232-8888

Thomas F. Monaghan, President/CEO
Domino's Pizza, Inc.
P.O. Box 997
Ann Arbor, MI 48106-0997
(313) 930-3030

Robert J. Posch, Jr., Vice President
Legal Affairs
Doubleday Book & Music Clubs, Inc.
401 Franklin Avenue
Garden City, NY 11530-5806
(516) 873-4628

Sharon Clark, Manager
Consumer Affairs
Dow Brands
P.O. Box 68511
Indianapolis, IN 46268-0511
(800) 428-4795

Jim Ball, Vice President
Corporate Communications
Dr. Pepper/Cadbury North America, Inc.
P.O. Box 655086
Dallas, TX 75265-5086
(214) 360-7000

Walter Drake & Sons, Inc.
Drake Building
Colorado Springs, CO 80940-0001
(719) 596-3140

Jane Lagusch, Vice President
Drug Emporium, Inc.
155 Hidden Ravines Drive
Powell, OH 43065
(614) 548-7080

Dulcolax
CIBA Consumer Pharmaceuticals
581 Main Street
Woodbridge, NJ 07095
(908) 602-6780

Robert M. Rosenberg, CEO
Dunkin Donuts of America/Baskin Robbins
P.O. Box 317
Randolph, MA 02368
(617) 961-4000

Steven Wyanacek, Manager
Consumer Affairs
Dunlop Tire Corporation
P.O. Box 1109
Buffalo, NY 14240-1109
(800) 548-4714

Jack Krol, President/CEO
DuPont Company
1007 Market Street
Wilmington, DE 19898
(800) 548-4714

Duracell USA
Duracell Drive
Bethel, CT 06801
(800) 551-2355

Durkee-French Foods (see Reckitt & Colman, Inc.)

E

Daniel Carp, President/COO
George M. C. Fisher
Chairman/ CEO
Eastman Kodak Company
343 State Street

Rochester, NY 14650-0229
(800) 242-2424

Nancy J. Avino, Customer Service
Eckerd Drug Company

8333 Bryan Dairy Road
P.O. Box 4689
Clearwater, FL 34618
(813) 399-6000

Edmund Scientific Company
101 East Gloucester Pike
Barrington, NJ 08007-1380
(609) 573-6260

Electrolux Corporation
2300 Windy Ridge Parkway
Suite 900
Marietta, GA 30067
(800) 243-9078

Emery Worldwide
A CF Company
One Lagoon Drive
Redwood City, CA 94065
(800) 227-1981

Sonia Franklin, Director
Consumer Affairs
**Encore Marketing International,
Inc.**
4501 Forbes Boulevard
Lanham, MD 20706
(800) 638-0930

Norman Braun, Vice President
Public Affairs
Encyclopedia Britannica, Inc.
310 South Michigan Avenue
Chicago, IL 60604-4293
(312) 347-7200

Labat R. Yancey, Vice President
Customer Relations
Equifax
P.O. Box 105139
Atlanta, GA 30348
(800) 685-1111

Carolann V. Mathews
Vice President
Customer Relations
Equitable Life Assurance Society
787 Seventh Avenue
New York, NY 10020
(212) 554-1749

Esprit de Corps
900 Minnesota Street
San Francisco, CA 94107-3000
(415) 648-6900

Theresa Sullivan, Vice President
Customer Relations
Estee Lauder Company
767 Fifth Avenue
New York, NY 10153-0003
(212) 572-4200

Francine Recine-Quinn, Corporate
Manager
Consumer Affairs
Ethan Allen, Inc.
Ethan Allen Drive
Danbury, CT 06813
(203) 743-8668
E-mail: ethanadv@ethanallen.com

Rick Gremer, Manager
Customer Relations
The Eureka Company
1201 East Bell Street
Bloomington, IL 61701-6902
(800) 282-2886

Bob Evans Farms, Inc.
3776 South High Street
Columbus, OH 43207
(800) 272-7675

Sharon L. Plummer, Manager
Consumer Assistance
Exxon Company, U.S.A.

P.O. Box 2180
Houston, TX 77252-2180
(800) 243-9966

F

**Faultless Starch – Bon Ami
Company**
1025 West Eighth Street
Kansas City, MO 64101-1200
(816) 842-1230

Fayva Shoe Stores (see Morse Shoe,
Inc.)

Jean H. Ward-Jones, Manager
Quality and Process Improvement
Federal Express Corporation
P.O. Box 727, Department 1845
Memphis, TN 38194-1845
(800) 238-5355

Paula S. Coffey, Assistant
Consumer Affairs
Federated Department Stores
7 West Seventh Street
Cincinnati, OH 45202
(513) 579-7000

Ferrari North America, Inc.
250 Sylvan Avenue
Englewood Cliffs, NJ 07632
(201) 816-2684

Maurice Altham, President
Fieldcrest Cannon, Inc.
204 West Stadium Street
Eden, NC 27288
(212) 957-2500

Finast
17000 Rockside Road

Cleveland, OH 44137-4390
(216) 587-7100

Mary Luethmers, Manager
Customer Relations
Fingerhut Corporation
11 McLeland Road
St. Cloud, MN 56395
(612) 259-2500

L.A. Mann, Sr., Director
Quality Assurance
First Brands Corporation
88 Long Hill Street
East Hartford, CT 06108
(800) 835-4523

First Interstate Bank of California
707 Wilshire Boulevard, W35-13
Los Angeles, CA 90017
(213) 614-3103

Thomas J. Metz, Sr., Vice President
Customer Services
First Union National Bank
100 Constitution Drive
Upper Darby, PA 19082-4603
(800) 225-5332
TDD: (800) 835-7721

Byron Davis, President/CEO
Fisher Price
636 Girard Avenue
East Aurora, NY 14052
(800) 432-5437
TDD: (800) 382-7470

Bob Norton, President/CEO
**Florist Transworld Delivery
Associates (FTD)**
29200 Northwestern Highway
P.O. Box 2227
Southfield, MI 48037-4077
(800) 669-1000

Phil Hurwitz, Customer Service
Florsheim Shoe Company
130 South Canal Street
Chicago, IL 60606-3999
(800) 633-4988

Heeth Varnedoe, President
Flowers Industries, Inc.
P.O. Box 1338
Thomasville, GA 31799-1338
(912) 226-9110

Scott R. Yablon, Vice President
Finance Administrator
Forbes, Inc.
60 Fifth Avenue
New York, NY 10011
(212) 620-2409

Alex Trotman, President/CEO
Ford Motor Company
300 Renaissance Court
P.O. Box 43360
Detroit, MI 48243
(800) 392-3673
TDD: (800) 232-5952

Linda Yocum, Customer Service
Frank's Nursery and Crafts, Inc.

6501 East Nevada
Detroit, MI 48234
(313) 366-8400

The Frigidaire Company
P.O. Box 7181
Dublin, OH 43017-0781
(800) 451-7007

Jackie Wolfe
Office of Consumer Affairs
Friskies PetCare Company
800 North Grand Boulevard
Glendale, CA 91203
(818) 543-7749

Dick Lappin, President
Fruit of the Loom, Inc.
P.O. Box 90015
Bowling Green, KY 42102-9015
(502) 781-6400

Maryanne Salimbene, Associate
Manager
Customer Service
Fuji Photo Film U.S.A., Inc.
400 Commerce Boulevard
Carlstadt, NJ 07072-3009
(800) 659-3854

Fuller Brush Company
P.O. Box 1247
Great Bend, KS 67530-0729
(800) 523-3794

G

Tony Nicely, CEO
GEICO Insurance Corporation
One GEICO Plaza

5260 Western Avenue
Washington, DC 20076
(301) 986-3077

G T E Corporation
One Stamford Forum
Stamford, CT 06904
(800) 548-2389

Teddi Burris, Manager
Customer Relations
Ernest and Julio Gallo Winery
P.O. Box 1130
Modesto, CA 95353
(209) 579-3161

J. S. Welch, CEO
General Electric Company
3135 Easton Turnpike
Fairfield, CT 06431
(800) 626-2000

Harris Ashton, President/CEO
General Host Corporation (General Foods)
P.O. Box 10045
Stamford, CT 06904
(800) 431-1001

General Mills, Inc.
P.O. Box 1113
Minneapolis, MN 55440-1113
(Bakery) (800) 328-6787
(Cereals) (800) 328-1144
(Gortons) (800) 222-6846
(Snacks) (800) 231-0308

John F. Smith, Jr., President/CEO
General Motors Acceptance Corporation (GMAC)
3044 West Grand Boulevard
Room AX348
Detroit, MI 48202
(800) 441-9234
TDD: (800) TDD-GMAC

Buick Motor Division
(800) 521-7300
TDD: (800) 832-8425

Cadillac Motor Car Division
(800) 458-8006
TDD: (800) 833-2622

Chevrolet/Geo Motor Division
(800) 222-1020
TDD: (800) 833-2438

GMC Truck Division
(800) 462-8782
TDD:(800) 462-8583

Oldsmobile Division
(800) 442-6537
TDD: (800) 833-6537

Pontiac Division
(800) 762-2737
TDD: (800) 833-7668

Saturn Corporation
(800) 553-6000
TDD: (800) 833-6000

Joyce Bowman, Customer Service
General Tire, Inc.
One General Street
Akron, OH 44329-0007
(800) 847-3349

Genesee Brewing Company, Inc.
445 St. Paul Street
Rochester, NY 14605
(716) 546-1030

Georgia-Pacific Corporation
P.O. Box 105605
Atlanta, GA 30348-5605

(Paper products) (404) 652-4000
(Building products) (770) 953-7000

Al Piergalline, President/CEO
Gerber Products Company
Corporate Headquarters
445 State Street
Freemont, MI 49413-1056
(800) 443-7237

Pete Manons, President/CEO
Giant Food, Inc.
P.O. Box 1804
Washington, DC 20077
(301) 341-4365
TDD: (301) 341-4327

Gibson Appliances (see The
Frigidaire Company)

Beverly Smith, Manager
Consumer Affairs
Gillette Company
P.O. Box 61
Boston, MA 02199
(617) 463-3337

James Sainsburg, Manager
Product Regulations
The Glidden Company
925 Euclid Avenue
Cleveland, OH 44115
(216) 344-8818

Golden Grain Company
4576 Willow Road

Pleasanton, CA 94588
(800) 421-2444

A.L. Finlry, Director
Consumer Relations
Goodyear Tire & Rubber Company
1144 East Market Street
Akron, OH 44316
(330) 796-3909
TDD: (216) 796-6055

Michael Legrand, Senior President
Operations
Gordon's Jewelers
A Subsidiary of Zale Corporation
901 West Walnut Hill Lane
Irving, TX 75038-1003
(214) 580-4924

Julie Churchill, Manager
Customer Relations
Greyhound Lines, Inc.
P.O. Box 660362
Dallas, TX 75266-0362
(214) 849-8000

Paul Marciano, President
Morrice Marciano, CEO
Guess? Inc.
1444 South Alameda Street
Los Angeles, CA 90021
(800) 394-8377

Guinness Import Company
Six Landmark Square
Stamford, CT 06901-2704
(800) 521-1591

H

Marti Johnson, Director
Client Relations
H & R Block, Inc.

4410 Main Street
Kansas City, MO 64111-9986
(800) 829-7733

H V R Company (see Clorox
Company)

Dan Freberg, Manager
Customer Service
Hallmark Cards, Inc.
P.O. Box 419034
Kansas City, MO 64141-6034
(800) 425-6275

John Schultz, Manager
Customer Service
Halston Borghese, Inc.
767 Fifth Avenue, 49th Floor
New York, NY 10153
(212) 572-3100

Hanes (see L'eggs)

Hanover-Direct, Inc.
340 Poplar Street
Hanover, PA 17333-9989
(717) 637-6000

Bonnie Fisher, Supervisor
Consumer Affairs
Hasbro, Inc.
P.O. Box 200
Pawtucket, RI 02862-0200
(800) 255-5516

Hathaway Shirts (see Warnaco
Men's Apparel)

Tom Wise, Marketing Manager
Heath Company
Benton Harbor, MI 49022
(616) 925-6000

Michael Foley, President
Heineken USA
50 Main Street

White Plains, NY 10606
(914) 681-4100

Donna Elliot, Manager
Consumer Affairs
Heinz U.S.A.
P.O. Box 57
Pittsburgh, PA 15230
(412) 237-5740

Paula Cisar, Manager
Consumer Affairs
Helene Curtis, Inc.
325 North Wells Street
Chicago, IL 60610-4713
(800) 682-8301

Mindy Soleman, Manager
Customer Relations
Hershey Foods Corporation
100 Crystal A Drive
Hershey, PA 17033
(717) 534-6799

Frank Gonzalez, Manager
Customer Relations
Hertz Corporation
225 Brae Boulevard
Park Ridge, NJ 07656-0713
(201) 307-2000
TDD: (800) 654-2280

Hewlett-Packard Company
19310 Prune Ridge Avenue
Mail Stop 49AU25
Cupertino, CA 95014-0604
(800) 752-0900

Stephen Bollenbach, CEO
Hilton Hotels Corporation
9336 Civic Center Drive
Beverly Hills, CA 90209-5567
(310) 278-4321

Mike Rudman, Vice President
Human Resources
Hit or Miss
100 Campanelli Parkway
Stoughton, MA 02072
(617) 344-0800

Bruce Schoenogge
Director of Marketing
**Hitachi Home Electronics
(America), Inc.**
3890 Steve Reynolds Boulevard
Norcross, GA 30093
(800) 241-6558

Randall Smith, Manager
Holiday Inn Worldwide
Three Ravenia Drive, Suite 2000
Atlanta, GA 30346
(404) 604-2000

Bernard Marcus, CEO
Arthur Blank, President
Home Depot, Inc.
2455 Paces Ferry Road, NW
Atlanta, GA 30339
(800) 553-3199

Home Shopping Network
P.O. Box 9090
Clearwater, FL 34618-9090
(800) 284-3900

Honda Motor Corporation (see
American Honda Motor
Corporation)

Ray Gwin, Manager
Consumer Affairs
Honeywell, Inc.
Honeywell Plaza
P.O. Box 524
Minneapolis, MN 55440-0524
(800) 468-1502

Larry Calder, Manager
Consumer Response Center
Hoover Company
101 East Maple
North Canton, OH 44720
(800) 944-9200

Terry Gradite, Customer Service
The Horchow Collection
111 Customer Way
Irving, TX 75039
(800) 395-5397

Cheryl Cook, Director
Consumer Affairs
Hormel Foods Company
One Hormel Place
Austin, MN 55912-9989
(800) 523-4635

Kevin Koesters, Consumer Relations
Huffy Bicycle Company
P.O. Box 1204
Dayton, OH 45401
(800) 872-2453

Humana, Inc.
500 West Main Street
P.O. Box 1438
Louisville, Ky 40201-1438
(502) 580-1000

Hunt-Wesson, Inc.
P.O. Box 4800
Fullerton, CA 92634-4800
(714) 680-1431

Hyatt Hotels & Resorts
200 West Madison Street, 39th Floor
Chicago, IL 60606
(800) 228-3336

Hyundai Motor America
10550 Talbert Avenue
P.O. Box 20850

Fountain Valley, CA 92728-0850
(800) 633-5151

I

Lewis Gerstner, CEO
IBM International Services Center
Old Orchard Road
Armonk, NY 10504
(800) 426-3333

Integra International
5200 Keller Springs Road, Suite 1131
Houston, TX 75248
(214) 233-0966

Dean Peters, Manager
Communications Department
International Dairy Queen, Inc.
P.O. Box 39286
7505 Metro Boulevard
Minneapolis, MN 55439-0286
(612) 830-0200

Isuzu (see American Isuzu Motors, Inc.)

J

Michael Bomba, Manager
Customer Service
J R T
5000 City Line Road
Hampton, VA 23661
(804) 827-6000

Jackson & Perkins Nursery Stock
2518 South Pacific Highway
Medford, OR 97501
(800) 348-3222

Jaguar Cars, Inc.
U. S. National Headquarters
555 MacArthur Boulevard
Mahwah, NJ 07430-2327
(800) 452-4827

Ophelia R. Millon, Manager
Consumer Affairs
James River Corporation
P.O. Box 6000

Norwalk, CT 06856-6000
(800) 243-5384

Jeep/Eagle Division of Chrysler Corporation (see Chrysler Corp.)

Jockey International, Inc.
2300 Sixtieth Street
Kenosha, WI 53140
(414) 658-8111

John Hancock Financial Services
P.O. Box 111
Boston, MA 02117
(617) 572-6272
TDD: (619) 572-9986

Virginia Mellace
Johnny Appleseed's, Inc.
30 Tozer Road
Beverly, MA 01915
(800) 767-6666

Ralph Larson, CEO
**Johnson & Johnson Consumer
Products, Inc.**
One Johnson and Johnson Plaza
New Brunswick, NJ 08933
(908) 874-1000

Tom Conrardy, Director
Consumer Resource Center
S. C. Johnson and Sons
1525 Howe Street
Racine, WI 53403
(800) 558-5252

Howard Johnson, Inc.
3400 NW Grand Avenue
Phoenix, AZ 85017
(602) 264-9164

Kaaryn Denig, Vice President
Marketing and Advertising
Jordache Enterprises, Inc.
1411 Broadway
New York, NY 10018
(800) 289-5326

K

Lisa Brown, Manager
Customer Service
K-mart Corporation
3100 West Big Beaver Road
Troy, MI 48084
(810) 643-1643

Wayne Wilson, Manager
Customer Relations
Karastan Rugmill
Division of Mohawk Industries, Inc.
P.O. Box 129
Eden, NC 27289
(800) 476-7113

**Kawasaki Motor Corporation,
U.S.A.**
P.O. Box 25252
Santa Ana, CA 92799-5252
(714) 770-0400

Keebler Company, Inc.
One Hollow Tree Lane
Elmhurst, IL 60126
(708) 833-2900

Arnold G. Langbo, CEO
Thomas A. Knowlton, President
Kellogg Company
P.O. Box CAMB
Battle Creek, MI 49016
(800) 962-1413

Robert A. Shower, Manager
Product Services
Kelly Springfield Tire Company
12501 Willow Brook Road, SE
Cumberland, MD 21502-2599
(301) 777-6635

Nancy Brebmar, Supervisor
Consumer Relations
Kelvinator Appliance Company
(see the Frigidaire Company)

**Kemper National Insurance
Company**
One Kemper Drive
Long Grove, IL 60049-0001
(800) 833-0355

Bonnie Bolduc, Supervisor
Consumer Affairs
Kenner Products
P.O. Box 200
Pawtucket, RI 02862-0200
(800) 327-8264

Kia Motor America, Inc.
6220 South Orange Blossom Trail,
Suite 209
Orlando, FL 32809
(407) 856-5000

Wayne Sanders, President/CEO
Kimberly-Clark Corporation
P.O. Box 619100
Dallas, TX 75261
(800) 544-1847

Kingsford Products Company (see
Clorox Company)

KitchenAid
2000 M-63 North
Benton Harbor, MI 49022
(800) 422-1230

Denise Fegler, Assistant to the
Senior Vice President
Calvin Klein Industries, Inc.

205 West Thirty-ninth Street
10th Floor
New York, NY 10018
(212) 326-6800

Mark Grunow, Manager
Consumer Affairs
Kohler Company
Kohler, WI 53044
(414) 457-4441

Robert S. Morrison, President/CEO
Kraft, Inc.
One Kraft Court
Glenview, IL 60025
(800) 323-0768

Judy Holland, Manager
Customer Relations
Kroger Company
1014 Vine Street
Cincinnati, OH 45202
(800) 632-6900

Rody Davenport, IV, President/CEO
Krystal Company
One Union Square
Chattanooga, TN 37402
(453) 757-1550

L

LA Gear
2850 Ocean Boulevard
Santa Monica, CA 90405
(800) 786-7800

Leon Gorman, President
L. L. Bean
Freeport, ME 04033
(800) 221-4221

LaCoupe (see Playtex Family
Products Group)

Ann P. Gallagher, Manager
Consumer Services
La-Z-Boy Chair Company
1284 North Telegraph Road
Monroe, MI 48162-3309
(313) 242-1444

Lydie Botham, Director
Consumer Affairs
Land O'Lakes, Inc.
P.O. Box 116
Minneapolis, MN 55440-0116
(800) 328-4155

Michael Smith, President
Lands End
One Lands End Lane
Dodgeville, WI 53595
(800) 332-4700
(800) 356-4444

Bill West, Vice President
Customer Service
Lane Furniture
East Franklin Avenue
P.O. Box 151
Altavista, VA 24517
(804) 369-5641

Tim Kellerman, Customer Service
Lee Apparel
9001 West Sixty-seventh Street
Merriam, KS 66202
(913) 384-4000

L'eggs Products
5660 University Parkway
Winston-Salem, NC 27105
(910) 768-9540

Leichtung, Inc.
23279 Thomas Park
Beechwood, OH 44122
(800) 654-7817

Lennox Industries
P.O. Box 799900
Dallas, TX 75379-9900
(214) 497-5000

Lever Brothers Company
390 Park Avenue
New York, NY 10022-4698
(800) 598-1223

Pete Jacobi, President
Levi Strauss & Company
1155 Battery Street
San Francisco, CA 94111
(800) 872-5384

Eleanor Eckardt, Vice President
Consumer Relations
Levitz Furniture Corporation
6111 Broken Sound Parkway, NW
Boca Raton, FL 33487-2799
(800) 631-4601

Levolor Home Fashion
4110 Premier Drive
High Point, NC 27265
(800) LEVOLOR

Davis Hoffman
Assistant Vice President
Liberty Mutual Insurance Group
175 Berkeley Street
Boston, MA 02117
(800) 225-2390

Lillian Vernon Corporation
2600 International Parkway
Virginia Beach, VA 23452
(800) 285-5555

Eli Lilly & Company
Lilly Corporate Center
Indianapolis, IN 46285
(317) 276-8588

The Limited, Inc.
Three Limited Parkway
Columbus, OH 43230
(614) 479-7000

Long John Silver's
315 South Broadden
Lexington, KY 40508
(606) 388-6000

L'Oreal (see Cosmair, Inc.)

Lorillard Tobacco Company
2525 East Market Street
P.O. Box 21688
Greensboro, NC 27420-1688
(910) 373-6669

Lucky Stores, Inc.
P.O. Box 5008
San Leandro, CA 94577
(510) 678-5444

M

MAACO, Inc.
381 Brooks Road
King of Prussia, PA 19406
(800) 523-1180
(800) 521-6282

Jane King, Senior Manager
Consumer Affairs
MCI Communications
1200 South Hayes Street, 11th Floor
Arlington, VA 22202
(800) 677-6580

M & M/Mars, Inc.
High Street
Hacketstown, NJ 07840
(908) 852-1000

R. H. Macy & Company, Inc.
151 West Thirty-fourth Street
New York, NY 10001
(212) 695-4400

Mannington Mills, Inc.
P.O. Box 30
Salem, NJ 08079
(800) 356-6787

Manor Care Corporation
10770 Columbia Pike
Silver Spring, MD 20901
(800) 833-7696

**Manville Corporation/Schuller
International, Inc.**
P.O. Box 5108
Denver, CO 80217-5108
(800) 654-3103

Marine Midland Bank, N.A.
One Marine Midland Center
Buffalo, NY 14203
(716) 841-1000

Marion Merrell Dow, Inc.
North American Headquarters
P.O. Box 9627
Kansas City, MO 64134-0627
(800) 552-3656

J. W. Marriott, Jr., President/CEO
Marriott Corporation
One Marriott Drive
Washington, DC 20058
(301) 380-3000

Karen Fuller, Director
Consumer Relations
**Massachusetts Mutual Insurance
Company**
1295 State Street
Springfield, MA 01111
(800) 828-4902

Gene Lockheart, CEO
MasterCard International
200 Purchase Street
Purchase, NY 10577
(800) 826-2181

Anthony Lopes, President
Matsushita Services Company
50 Meadowlands Parkway
Secaucus, NJ 07094
(201) 348-7000

Jill Barad, CEO
Mattel Toys, Inc.
333 Continental Boulevard
El Segundo, CA 90245-5012
(800) 524-TOYS

Max Factor (see Procter & Gamble
Company)

Maxicare Health Plans, Inc.
1149 South Broadway
Los Angeles, CA 90015
(213) 742-0900

Maxwell House (see General Foods)

James F. Harner,
Senior Vice President
Customer Service
May Department Stores Company
611 Olive Street
St. Louis, MO 63101
(314) 342-6300

Guy Peyrelonge, President/CEO
Maybelline, Inc.
P.O. Box 1010
Clark, NJ 07066-1010
(800) 944-0730

Mayflower Transit, Inc.
P.O. Box 107
Indianapolis, IN 46206
(800) 428-1234

George Toyama, President/CEO
Mazda Motors of America, Inc.
Box 19734
Irvine, CA 92713-9734
(800) 222-5500

Mary Randisi, Director
Consumer Affairs
McCormick and Company, Inc.
211 Schilling Circle
Hunt Valley, MD 21031
(800) 632-5847

McCrory Stores, Inc.
2955 East Market Street
York, PA 17402
(717) 757-8181

Jack Greenberg, President/CEO
McDonald's Corporation
One Kroc Drive
Oak Brook, IL 60521
(708) 575-6198

McKee Foods Corporation
P.O. Box 750
Collegedale, TN 37315
(800) 522-4499

**McKesson Water Products
Company**
3280 East Foothill Boulevard, #400
Pasadena, CA 91107
(818) 585-1000

**McNeil Consumer Products
Company
Johnson & Johnson**
7050 Camp Hill Road
Fort Washington, PA 19034
(215) 233-7000

Marshall Morton, Senior Vice
President
Media General, Inc.
333 East Grace Street
Richmond, VA 23219
(804) 649-6000

Nancy Little, Customer Service
Meineke Discount Muffler
128 South Tryon Street
Suite 900
Charlotte, NC 28202
(704) 377-3070

Paul S. Videman
Executive Vice President
Mellon Bank Corporation
One Mellon Bank Center
Room 5135
Pittsburgh, PA 15258-0001
(412) 234-8552

Mennen Company (see Colgate,
Palmolive, Mennen Company)

Mentholatum Company, Inc.
1360 Niagara Street
Buffalo, NY 14213
(716) 882-7660

**Mercedes Benz of North America,
Inc.**
One Glenview Road
Montvale, NJ 07645
(800) 222-0100
(800) 367-6372

Patricia Royer, Vice President
Consumer Affairs
Merck Medco Manage Care, Inc.
100 Summit Avenue
Montvale, NJ 07645
(201) 358-5530

Mercruiser
3003 North Perkins Road
Stillwater, OK 74075
(405) 377-1200

Mercury Marine
P.O. Box 1939
Fond Du Lac, WI 54936-1939
(414) 929-5000

Merillat Industries
5353 West U.S. 223
Adrian, MI 49221
(517) 263-0771

**Merrill Lynch Pierce Fenner &
Smith**
265 Davidson Avenue, 4th Floor
Somerset, NJ 08873
(908) 563-8777

Harry Kamen, CEO
**Metropolitan Life Insurance
Company**
One Madison Avenue, Area 1-Z
New York, NY 10010-3690
(212) 578-2544

Michelin Tire Corporation
P.O. Box 19001
Greenville, SC 29602
(800) 847-3435

Cindy Rosenbrook, Manager
Customer Service
Michigan Bulb Company
1950 Waldorf, NW
Grand Rapids, MI 49550
(616) 771-9500

Louis Gergits, Manager
Consumer Relations
Midas International Corporation
225 North Michigan Avenue
Chicago, IL 60601
(800) 621-8545

Mid-Michigan Surgical Supply
595 North Avenue
Battle Creek, MI 19017
(800) 445-5820

Miles Kimball
41 West 8
Oshkosh, WI 54906
(Written inquiries only)

Debra K. Wood, Coordinator
Consumer Services
Milton Bradley Company
443 Shaker Road
East Long Meadow, MA 01028
(413) 525-6411

Hiro Fujii, CEO
Minolta Corporation
101 Williams Drive
Ramsey, NJ 07446
(201) 825-4000

Minwax, Inc.
10 Mountain View Road
Upper Saddle River, NJ 07458-1934
(800) 523-9299

Miracle Gro Products, Inc. (see
Scotts Miracle Gro Products, Inc.)

Suketaka Tachibana,
President/CEO
**Mitsubishi Electronics America,
Inc.**
6100 Atlantic Boulevard
P.O. Box 5025
Norcross, GA 30091-5025
(800) 332-2119

Motohiko Numaguchi, President
**Mitsubishi Motor Sales of America,
Inc.**
6400 West Katella Avenue
Cypress, CA 90630-0064
(800) 222-0037

Lou Noto, President/CEO
Mobil Oil Corporation
3225 Gallows Road
Fairfax, VA 22037
(800) 662-4592

Jim Lorberbaum, President
Mohawk Industries, Inc.
P.O. Box 2208
2001 Antioch Road
Dalton, GA 30722
(706) 277-1100

Monet Group, Inc.
Crystal Brand Jewelry Group
Number Two Lonsdale Avenue
Pawtucket, RI 02860
(401) 728-9800

Monsanto Company
800 North Lindbergh Boulevard
St. Louis, MO 63167
(314) 694-1000

Cindy Mace, Manager
Customer Relations
Montgomery Ward
One Montgomery Ward Plaza, 9-S
Chicago, IL 60671
(800) 695-3553

Morton International
Morton Salt Division
100 North Riverside Plaza
Chicago, IL 60606
(312) 807-2694

Chris Galvin, CEO
Motorola, Inc.
1303 East Algonquin Road
Schaumburg, IL 60196
(847) 576-2108

Darlene Stovall-Hendricks
Supervisor
Consumer Affairs
Motts, U S A
6 High Ridge Park
Stamford, CT 06905
(800) 426-4891

**Mutual Life Insurance Company
of New York (MONY)**
Glenpoint Center West
500 Frank W. Burr Boulevard
Teaneck, NJ 07666
(401) 342-7600

Elizabeth Powell, Manager
Customer Relations
**Mutual of Omaha Insurance
Company**
Mutual of Omaha Plaza
Omaha, NE 68175
(402) 342-7600

N

Linda Middleton, Manager
N B C
30 Rockefeller Plaza
New York, NY 10112
(212) 664-2333

NEC Technologies, Inc.
1255 Michael Drive
Wood Dale, IL 60191-1094
(800) 366-9500

John Greenius, CEO
Nabisco Foods Group
7 Campus Drive, Box 311
Parsippany, NJ 07054-0311
(800) NABISCO

William Tobeck, President/CEO
National Car Rental System, Inc.
7700 France Avenue South
Minneapolis, MN 55435
(800) 468-3334

National Media Corporation
1700 Walnut Street
Philadelphia, PA 19103
(215) 772-5000

National Presto Industries, Inc.
3925 North Hastings Way
Eau Claire, WI 54703-3703
(715) 839-2121

Glen W. Soden, Manager
Customer Relations
Nationwide Insurance Companies
One Nationwide Plaza, 1-22-01
Columbus, OH 43215-2220
(614) 249-6985
TDD: (800) 622-2421

Near East Food Products
797 Lancaster Street
Leominster, MA 01453
(800) 822-7423

Neiman-Marcus
P.O. Box 729080
Dallas, TX 75372
(800) 685-6695

Nestlé Beverage Company
345 Spear Street
San Francisco, CA 94105
(Written inquiries only for all Nestlé
companies)

Nestlé Food Company
P.O. Box 29055
Glendale, CA 91209-9055

**Nestlé Frozen, Refrigerated and Ice
Cream Companies, Inc.**
P.O. Box 39487
Solon, OH 44139-0487

Nestlé USA, Inc.
P.O. Box 29055
Glendale, CA 91209-9055

Alene Lain, Consumer Affairs
Neutrogena Corporation
5760 West Ninety-sixth Street
Los Angeles, CA 90045
(800) 421-6857

Newport News, Inc.
5000 City Line Road
Hampton, VA 23661
(804) 827-7010

News America Publishing, Inc.
Four Radnor Corporate Center
Radnor, PA 19088
(800) 866-1400

Barbara Fagnano
Assistant Vice President
New York Life Insurance Company
51 Madison Avenue
New York, NY 10010
(212) 576-5081

Robert P. Smith, Manager
New York Times Company
229 West Forty-third Street
New York, NY 10036
(212) 556-7171

Nexxus Products Company
P.O. Box 1274
Santa Barbara, CA 93116-9976
(805) 968-6900

Lynda Danovitz, Manager
Customer Advocacy
**Niagara Mohawk Power
Corporation**
Dey's Centennial Plaza
401 South Salina Street
Syracuse, NY 13202
(315) 460-7015

Tom Clarke, President
Phil Knight, CEO
Nike, Inc.
Nike/World Campus
One Bowerman Drive
Beaverton, OR 97005
(800) 344-6453

Nine West Group Corporate Headquarters
9 West Broad Street
Stamford, CT 06902
(203) 324-7567

Nine West-Easy Spirit
One Eastwood Drive
Cincinnati, OH 45227-1197
(800) 285-9955

Nine-West Selby
One Eastwood Drive
Cincinnati, OH 45227-1197
(800) 284-9949

Nile Spice Food
P.O. Box 20581
Seattle, WA 98102
(800) 265-6453

Nintendo of America, Inc.
4820 150th Avenue, NE
Redmond, WA 98052
(800) 255-3700
TDD: (800) 422-4281

Minoru Nakamura, President/CEO
Nissan Motors Corporation USA
Box 191
Gardena, CA 90214-0191
(800) 647-7261

Julie Brown, Manager
Customer Relations
Norelco Consumer Products Company
A Division of Philips Electronics
North America Corporation
1010 Washington Boulevard
P.O. Box 120015
Stamford, CT 06912-0015
(800) 243-7884

Roslyn DeTasquale, Manager
Marketing Service
North American Watch Corporation
125 Chubb Avenue
Lyndhurst, NJ 07071
(201) 460-4800

Northwest Airlines
C6590
5101 Northwest Drive
St. Paul, MN 55111-3034
(612) 726-2046
TDD: (800) 328-2298

Thomas W. Towers
Assistant Director
Public Relations
Northwestern Mutual Life Insurance Company
720 East Wisconsin Avenue
Milwaukee, WI 53202
(414) 299-7179

Alice Kain-Moore, Manager
Customer Relations
Norwegian Cruise Line
95 Merrick Way
Coral Gables, FL 33134
(800) 327-7030

Mike Walsh, Director
Consumer Relations
Nu Tone, Inc.
Madison and Redbank Roads
Cincinnati, OH 45227
(513) 527-5231

The NutraSweet Company
The Merchandise Mart, Suite 900
200 World Trade Center
Chicago, IL 60654
(NutraSweet) (800) 321-7254
(Equal) (800) 323-5316

Nutri/System, Inc.
410 Horsham Road

Horsham, PA 10944
(215) 445-5300

O

Linda Compton, Manager
Consumer Affairs
Ocean Spray Cranberries, Inc.
One Ocean Spray Drive
Lakeville/Middleboro, MA 02349
(800) 662-3263

O'Keefe & Merit Appliances (see
The Frigidaire Company)

Olan Mills, II, CEO
Robert McDowell, President
Olan Mills, Inc.
4325 Amnicola Highway
P.O. Box 23456
Chattanooga, TN 37422-3456
(800) 251-6323

Barbara Abe, Manager
Customer Support
Olympus America
2 Corporate Center Drive
Melville, NY 11747
(800) 622-6372

Denise Armstrong, Supervisor
Consumer Relations

Oneida, Ltd.
The Telemarketing Center
Sherrill, NY 13461
(800) 877-6667

Merine Heberger, Manager
Consumer Affairs
Ore-Ida Foods, Inc.
P.O. Box 10
Boise, ID 83707
(800) 842-2401

Orkin (see Rollins, Inc.)

Henry Hegal, Director
Corporate Services
Outboard Marine Corporation
100 Sea Horse Drive
Waukegan, IL 60085
(847) 689-6200

**Owens Corning World
Headquarters**
Fiberglass Tower
Toledo, OH 43659-0001
(419) 248-8000

P

Beny Alegem, President/CEO
Packard Bell NEC
One Packard Bell Way
Sacramento, CA 95828
(800) 689-6465

Donald Marron, Chairman/CEO
PaineWebber, Inc.
1285 Avenue of the Americas
New York, NY 10019
(800) 354-9103

Panasonic (see Matsushita Services Company)

Parke-Davis (see Warner-Lambert Company)

Noreen MacConchi, Manager
Customer Relations
Pathmark Stores, Inc.
301 Blair Road
Woodbridge, NJ 07095
(908) 499-3500

James Oesterricher, CEO
J. C. Penney Company, Inc.
P.O. Box 10001
Dallas, TX 75301-8212
(214) 431-8500

Bill Hover, Manager
Customer Relations
Pennzoil Products Company
P.O. Box 2967
Houston, TX 77252-2967
(800) 990-9811

Peoples Drug Stores, Inc. (see CVS)

Pepperidge Farm, Inc.
595 Westport Avenue
Norwalk, CT 06851
(203) 846-7276

Brenda Barnes, President
Pepsi-Cola Company
One Pepsi Way
Somers, NY 10589-2201
(800) 433-2652

Frank Perdue, Jr., President
Perdue Farms
P.O. Box 1537

Salisbury, MD 21802
(800) 442-2034

Lisa Drucker, Marketing Group
The Perrier Group
777 West Putnam Avenue
Greenwich, CT 06830
(203) 531-4100

Peugeot Motors of America, Inc.
P.O. Box 607
One Peugeot Plaza
Lyndhurst, NJ 07071-3498
(800) 526-6377

Mark E. Wooley, Manager
Consumer Affairs
Pet, Inc.
P.O. Box 66719
St. Louis, MO 63166-6719
(800) 325-7130

Pfizer, Inc.
235 East Forty-second Street
New York, NY 10017
(212) 573-2323

**Pharmacia and UpJohn
Corporation**
7000 Portage Road
Kalamazoo, MI 49001
(800) 253-8600

Susan A. Strausser, Supervisor
Consumer Affairs
Philip Morris Companies, Inc.
120 Park Avenue
New York, NY 10017
(800) 343-0975

Toni J. Honkisz, Corporate Quality
Administrator
Philips Lighting Company

200 Franklin Square Drive
P.O. Box 6800
Somerset, NJ 08875-6800
(908) 563-3081

Phillips Petroleum Company
16 Phillips Building
Bartlesville, OK 74004
(918) 661-1215

Piaget (see North American Watch
Corporation)

Paul Walsh, CEO
Pillsbury Company
MS 2866
200 South Sixth Street
Minneapolis, MN 55440
(800) 767-4466

Al Segal, Division Manager
Customer Service
Pioneer Electronics Service, Inc.
P.O. Box 1760
Long Beach, CA 90810
(800) 421-1404

Bonnie Bolduc, Supervisor
Consumer Affairs
Playskool
P.O. Box 200
Pawtucket, RI 02862-0200
(800) 752-9755

Theresa B. Thomas, Manager
Consumer Affairs
Playtex Apparel, Inc.
P.O. Box 631
Mail Stop 1526
Dover, DE 19903-0631
(800) 537-9955

**Playtex Family Products
Corporation**
215 College Road
P.O. Box 728
Paramus, NJ 07652
(800) 222-0453

Polaroid Corporation
201 Burlington Road
Bedford, MA 01730
(800) 343-5000

Daisy Modernel, Manager
Consumer Relations
Polo/Ralph Lauren Corporation
4100 Beachwood Drive
Greensboro, NC 27410
(800) 775-7656

Popeye's (see America's Favorite
Chicken Company)

Porsche Cars North America, Inc.
100 West Liberty Street
P.O. Box 30911
Reno, NV 89520-3911
(800) 545-8039

Prescriptives, Inc. (see Estee Lauder
Companies)

Princess Marcella (see Halston
Borghese, Inc.)

**Princeton Pharmaceutical
Products** (see Bristol-Myers Squibb
Group)

Kathleen Fitzsimmons Braun
Manager
Consumer Services
Procter & Gamble Company
Cosmetic and Fragrance Division
11050 York Road
Hunt Valley, MD 21030-2098
(800) 426-8374

Patti Shively, Associate Director
Consumer Relations
Procter & Gamble Company
P.O. Box 599
Cincinnati, OH 45201-0599
(513) 945-8787
Toll-free numbers appear on all Procter & Gamble product labels.

Progresso (see Pet Inc.)

Diane Koken, General Counsel
Provident Mutual Life Insurance
1600 Market Street

P.O. Box 7378
Philadelphia, PA 19101
(800) 523-4681

Prudential Insurance Company of America
Prudential Plaza, 24th Floor
Newark, NJ 07101
(201) 802-6000

Prudential Property & Casualty Company
23 Main Street
P.O. Box 419
Holmdel, NJ 07733
(800) 437-5556

Patricia Lucey, Vice President
Client Relations
Prudential Securities, Inc.
One New York Plaza
New York, NY 10292
(800) 367-8701

Q

QVZ Incorporated
Goshen Corporate Park
1365 Enterprise Drive
West Chester, PA 19380
(800) 367-9444

Quaker Oats Company
P.O. Box 049003
Chicago, IL 60604-9003
(312) 222-7111
Check product package for toll-free number.

Steven Blum, Vice President
Corporate Relations
Quaker State Corporation
P.O. Box 989
Oil City, PA 16301
(800) 759-2525

Quasar (see Matsushita Services Company)

R

Leonard Roberts, President
Radio Shack (see Tandy
Corporation)
P.O. Box 17180
Ft. Worth, TX 76102
(817) 390-3218

Ralston Purina Company
Pet Products Group
Checkerboard Square
St Louis, MO 63164
(800) 788-7462

Orville Redenbacker (see Hunt-
Wesson, Inc.)

Robert Meers, President
Paul Simone, CEO
Reebok International, Ltd.
100 Technology Center Drive
Stoughton, MA 02072
(800) 843-4444

Richard Jones, Manager
Customer Service
The Regina Company
P.O. Box 638
Long Beach, MS 39560
(800) 847-8336

Cass Carroll, Director
Consumer Relations
Reliance Insurance Company
Four Penn Center Plaza
Philadelphia, PA 19103
(800) 441-1652

Remco America, Inc.
8200 Thorn Drive
Wichita, KS 67226
(316) 646-7389

Remington Arms (see DuPont
Company)

Remington Products Company
60 Main Street
Bridgeport, CT 06004
(800) 736-4648

Renaissance Hotels International
29800 Bainbridge Road
Cleveland, OH 44139
(216) 498-9090

George Fellows, CEO
Revlon Consumer
625 Madison Avenue
New York, NY 10022
(800) 473-8566

Carol Owen, Director
Consumer Services
Reynolds Metals Company
6603 West Broad Street
Richmond, VA 23230
(800) 433-2244

**Rhone-Poulenc Rorer
Pharmaceuticals** (see Ciba Self-
Medication)

Richardson-Vicks, Inc. (see Procter
and Gamble Company)

Rockport
220 Donald Lynch Boulevard
Marlboro, MA 01752
(800) 343-9255

Michael Baviello, Service Manager
Rolex Watch U.S.A., Inc.
665 Fifth Avenue
New York, NY 10022
(212) 758-7700

Lawrence Beverley, Jr., Manager
Customer Service
Rollins, Inc.
2170 Piedmont Road, NE
Atlanta, GA 30324
(800) 346-7546

Larry Rothman, Director
Franchise Administration
Roto-Rooter Corporation
300 Ashworth Road
West Des Moines, IA 50265
(800) 575-7737

Roundup Lawn and Garden
P.O. Box 50108
San Ramon, CA 94583-0808
(800) 225-2883

Royal Oak Enterprises, Inc.
900 Ashwood Parkway, Suite 800

Atlanta, GA 30338
(800) 241-3955

Deborah Poole, Manager
Customer Service
Royal Silk
800-A Thirty-first Street
Union City, NJ 07087
(800) 962-6262

Royal Viking Line (see Cunard
Line)

Wolfgang R. Schmitt, CEO
Rubbermaid, Inc.
1147 Akron Road
Wooster, OH 44691-0800
(330) 264-6464

Rustler Jeans (see Wrangler)

Carol Yannone, Group Manager
Customer Service
Ryder Truck Rental
P.O. Box 020816
Miami, FL 33102-0816
(800) 327-7777

S

7 Eleven Food Stores (see The
Southland Corporation)

SFS Corporation
1200 West Artesia Boulevard
Compton, CA 90220
(800) 421-5013

Saab Cars USA, Inc.
4405-A Saab Drive
P.O. Box 9000

Norcross, GA 30091
(800) 955-9007

Steve Burd, President/CEO
Safeway, Inc.
5918 Stoneridge Mall Road
Pleasanton, CA 94588-3229
(510) 891-3267

Donna Lane Swaap, Manager
Corporate Customer Relations

Saks Fifth Avenue
12 East Forty-ninth Street, 3rd Floor
New York, NY 10021
(800) 239-3089

Sandoz Company
Sandoz Pharmaceuticals Corporation
59 Route 10
East Hanover, NJ 07936
(201) 503-7500

Sanyo Electric, Inc. (see SFS
Corporation)

Sara Lee Corporation
Three First National Plaza
70 West Madison Street
Chicago, IL 60602-4260
(800) 621-5235

Watson Brooks, Manager
Customer Relations
**Schering-Plough HealthCare
Products, Inc.**
3030 Jackson Avenue
Memphis, TN 38151-0001
(800) 842-4090

Scholl (see Schering-Plough
HealthCare Products, Inc.)

Penny Sass, Manager
Consumer Relations
Scott Paper Company
Scott Plaza One
Philadelphia, PA 19113-1510
(800) 835-7268

Rose B. Zosuls, Consumer Affairs
Scotts Miracle Gro Products, Inc.
800 Port Washington Boulevard
Port Washington, NY 11050
(516) 883-6550

Scudder Investor Services, Inc.
160 Federal Street
Boston, MA 02110
(800) 225-5163

Alice Bauer, Consumer Relations
Joseph E. Seagram & Sons, Inc.
800 Third Avenue
New York, NY 10022
(212) 572-7335

**Sealy Mattress Manufacturing
Company**
1228 Euclid Avenue, 10th Floor
Cleveland, OH 44115
(216) 522-1310

Donald Leibowitz, Director
Customer Affairs
Seamans Furniture Company, Inc.
300 Crossways Park Drive
Woodbury, NY 11797
(800) 445-2503

**G. D. Searle and Company
Pharmaceuticals**
P.O. Box 5110
Chicago, IL 60680
(800) 323-1603

Arthur Martinez, CEO
Sears and Roebuck Company
3333 Beverly Road
Hoffman Estates, IL 60179
(847) 286-5188

Seiko Corporation of America
27 McKee Drive
Mahwah, NJ 07430
(201) 529-3311

Serta, Inc.
325 Spring Lake Drive
Itasca, IL 60143
(800) 426-0371

Seven-Up (see Pepper/Seven-Up
Companies, Inc.)

Greg Vanzandt, General Manager
Customer Service
Sharp Electronics Corporation
1300 Naperville Drive
Romeville, IL 60441
(Written inquiries only)

Richard Thalheimer, President
The Sharper Image
650 Davis Street
San Francisco, CA 94111
(800) 344-5555

Shell Oil Company
Box 4650
Houston, TX 77252
(800) 248-4257

**Sherwin-Williams Company Paint
Stores Group**
101 Prospect Avenue, NW
Cleveland, OH 44115-1075
(216) 566-2151

Shoney's, Inc.
1717 Elm Hill Pike, Suite B3A
Nashville, TN 37210
(615) 391-5201

Deborah Slaughter, Manager
Consumer/Marketing Services
Simmons Company
6424 Warren Drive
P.O. Box 2768

Norcross, GA 30093
(800) 654-9258

Singer Sewing Company
P.O. Box 1909
Edison, NJ 08818-1909
(800) 877-7762

Slim-Fast Foods Company
777 South Flager Drive
West Tower, Suite 1400
West Palm Beach, FL 33401
(800) 223-1248

Smith Barney
388 Greenwich Street
New York, NY 10013
(800) 421-8609

Snapper Power Equipment
McDonough, GA 30253
(Written inquiries only)

Snapple Beverages
333 West Merrick Road
Valley Stream, NY 11580
(800) 762-7753

Stephanie Sonnabend, President
**Sonesta International Hotels
Corporation**
200 Clarendon Street
Boston, MA 02116
(617) 421-5432

Sony Corporation of America
One Sony Drive
Park Ridge, NJ 07656
(800) 282-2848

Janey Camacho, Manager
Customer Relations
The Southland Corporation
P.O. Box 711
Dallas, TX 75221-0711
(800) 255-0711

Herb Kelleher, CEO
Southwest Airlines
Love Field
P.O. Box 36611
Dallas, TX 75235-1611
(214) 904-4223
TDD: (800) 533-1305

Southwestern Bell Corporation
175 East Houston
San Antonio, TX 78205
(210) 351-2604

Shirley Brisbois, Manager
Consumer Relations
Spalding & Evenflo, Inc.
425 Meadow Street
P.O. Box 901
Chicopee, MA 01021-0901
(800) 225-6601

Speed Queen Company (see
Amana Refrigeration, Inc.)

Spencer Gifts
6826 Black Horse Pike
Egg Harbor Township, NJ 08234
(800) 762-0419

Judith P. Luken, Director of
Customer Satisfaction
Spiegel, Inc.
P.O. Box 927
Oak Brook, IL 60522-0927
(708) 986-8800

Springs Industries, Inc.
Springmaid/Performance
787 Seventh Avenue
New York, NY 10019
(800) 537-0115

David Thornhill
Executive Consumer Services
Sprint
1603 LBJ Freeway, Suite 300
Dallas, TX 75234
(800) 347-8988

Squibb (see Bristol-Myers Squibb
Pharmaceutical Group)

Jack Gauthier, Marketing Manager
Stanley Hardware
Division Stanley Works
480 Myrtle Street
New Britain, CT 06050
(800) 622-4393

Ed Rust, CEO
**State Farm Mutual Automobile
Insurance Company**
One State Farm Plaza
Bloomington, IL 61710
(309) 766-2714

Sterling Health (see Bayer
Corporation)

J. P. Stevens (see WestPoint Stores)

Stokley U.S.A., Inc.
1055 Corporate Center Drive
P.O. Box 248
Oconomowoc, WI 53066-0248
(800) 872-1110

Matthew Cook, Director
**Stop & Shop Supermarket
Company, Inc.**
P.O. Box 1942
Boston, MA 02105
(617) 770-6040

Customer Relations
Strawbridge & Clothier
801 Market Street, 7th Floor
Philadelphia, PA 19107
(215) 629-6722

The Stroh Brewery Company
9399 West Higgins Road
Rosemont, IL 60018
(847) 292-2100

George Muller, President/CEO
Subaru of America, Inc.
P.O. Box 6000
Cherry Hill, NJ 08034
(800) 782-2783

**Sunbeam/Oster Household
Products**
P.O. Box 247

Laurel, MS 39441-0247
(Written inquiries only)

Donna Samelson, Manager
Consumer Affairs
**Sun Diamond Growers of
California**
P.O. Box 1727
Stockton, CA 95201
(209) 467-6267

Supermarket General Corporation
(see Pathmark Stores, Inc.)

Suzuki (see American Suzuki Motor
Corporation)

Doug Williams, Customer Service
Swatch Watch USA
1817 William Penn Way
Lancaster, PA 17604
(800) 937-9282

The Swiss Colony
1112 Seventh Avenue
Monroe, WI 53566
(608) 324-4000

T

Nancy Sperling, Supervisor
Consumer Affairs
3M
3M Center
Building 225-5N-04
St. Paul, MN 55144-1000
(800) 364-3577

Ben Cammarata, CEO
Richard Lesser, President
TJX Companies (T. J. Maxx)

P.O. Box 9123
770 Cochituate Road
Framingham, MA 01701
(800) 926-6299

TRW Information Services
P.O. Box 949
Allen, TX 75002-0949
(214) 235-1200

Talbots
175 Beal Street
Hingham, MA 02043
(800) 992-9010
TDD: (800) 624-9179

Leonard Roberts, President
Tandy Corporation/Radio Shack
P.O. Box 17180
Fort Worth, TX 76102
(817) 390-3218

Tappan Appliance Company, Inc.
(see the Frigidaire Company)

Target Stores
33 South Sixth Street
P.O. Box 1392
Minneapolis, MN 55440-1392
(612) 304-4996

Technics (see Matsushita Services
Company)

George White, Director
Consumer Affairs
Teledyne Water Pik
1730 East Prospect Road
Fort Collins, CO 80553-0001
(800) 525-2774

Cathy Laffin, Director
Customer Service
Teleflora
12233 West Olympic, Suite 140
Los Angeles, CA 90064-0780
(800) 421-2815

Tenneco, Inc.
1275 King Street
Greenwich, CT 06831
(203) 863-1000

Tetley, Inc.
100 Commerce Drive
P.O. Box 856
Shelton, CT 06484-0856
(800) 732-3027

W.D. Kistler, Manager
Customer Relations
Texaco
P.O. Box 790001
Houston, TX 77094
(713) 647-1500

Tom Engibous, CEO
Texas Instruments, Inc.
P.O. Box 655474, MS 236
Dallas, TX 75266
(800) 842-2737
(Tech support) (817) 774-6827

Thom McAn Shoe Company
67 Millbrook Street
Worcester, MA 01606-2804
(508) 791-3811

Thompson & Formby, Inc.
825 Crossover Lane, Suite 240
Memphis, TN 38117
(800) 367-6297

Thrift Drug, Inc.
615 Alpha Drive
Pittsburgh, PA 15238
(800) 284-8212

Gerald White, President/CEO
Timex Corporation
P.O. Box 1676
Little Rock, AR 72203-2740
(800) 448-4639

Bonnie Fisher, Supervisor
Consumer Affairs
Tonka Products
P.O. Box 200
Pawtucket, RI 02861-0200
(800) 248-6652

Mary Elliot, Director
Communications and Public Affairs
The Toro Company
8111 Lyndale Avenue South
Minneapolis, MN 55420
(612) 887-8900

Toshiba America
82 Totowa Road
Wayne, NJ 07470
(800) 631-3811

Helen Baur, Manager
Consumer Affairs
Totes, Inc.
10078 East Kemper Road
Loveland, OH 45140
(513) 583-2300

Yoshio Ishizaka, President/CEO
Toyota Motor Sales USA, Inc.
Box 2991
Torrance, CA 90509-2991
(800) 331-4331
TDD: (800) 443-4999

Michael Goldstein, CEO
Toys "Я" Us
461 From Road
Paramus, NJ 07652
(201) 599-7897

Bob Thomas, Manager
Control Center
Trak Auto
3300 Seventy-fifth Avenue

Landover, MD 20785
(800) 835-7300

Trane/CAC, Inc.
(Residential) (903) 581-3200
(Commercial) (608) 787-2000

Trans Union Corporation
National Disclosure Center
P.O. Box 390
Springfield, PA 19064
(Written inquiries only)

Gerald Gitner, CEO
Trans World Airlines, Inc.
One City Center
515 North Sixth Street
St. Louis, MO 63101
(314) 589-3600
TDD: (800) 421-8400

True Value Hardware Stores (see
Cotter & Company)

Penny Lake, Supervisor
Consumer Services
Tupperware
P.O. Box 2353
Orlando, FL 32802-2353
(800) 858-7221

Patricia Arvidson, Consumer
Correspondence Representative
Turtle Wax, Inc.
5655 West Seventy-third Street
Chicago, IL 60638-6211
(800) 323-9883

Judy Rowley, Director
Customer Service
Tyco Toys
P.O. Box 490
Portland, OR 97207
(800) 367-8926

Willie D. Barber, Manager
Consumer Relations
Tyson Foods

P.O. Box 2020
Springdale, AZ 72765-2020
(800) 233-6332

U

Mary Kaup, Senior Supervisor
Customer Service
U-Haul International
Phoenix, AZ 85036-1120
(800) 528-0463

**Union Fidelity Life Insurance
Company** (see Aon Corporation)

Jim Wilkins, Manager
Consumer Relations
Uniroyal Goodrich Tire Company
P.O. Box 19001
Greenville, SC 29602-9001
(800) 521-9796

UNISYS Corporation
P.O. Box 500
Blue Bell, PA 19424-0001
(800) 328-0440

Gerry Greenwald, CEO
United Airlines
1200 Algonquin Road
P.O. Box 66100
Chicago, IL 60666
(800) 323-0710

**United Parcel Service of America,
Inc.**
55 Glenlake Parkway
Atlanta, GA 30328
(404) 828-6000

**United States Fidelity and
Guarantee Company (USF&G)**
100 Light Street

Baltimore, MD 21202
(410) 547-3000

Shirley Stewart, Director
Customer Service
United Van Lines, Inc.
One United Drive
Fenton, MO 63026
(Service) (800) 325-9980
(Claims) (800) 325-9970

Dawn Windholz, Supervisor
Customer Service
Unocal Corporation
17700 Castleton Street, Suite 500
City of Industry, CA 91748
(Station problems) (800) 527-5476
(Credit cards) (800) 944-7676

The Upjohn Company (see
Pharmacia and UpJohn
Corporation)

Steven Wolf, CEO
U. S. Airways Group
Crystal Park 4
2345 Crystal Drive
Arlington, VA 22227
(Written inquiries only)

U. S. Shoe Corporation (see Nine
West)

U.S. Sprint (see Sprint)

V

Michael Cornett, Director
Customer Service
Valvoline Oil Company
3499 Dabney Drive
P.O. Box 14000
Lexington, KY 40512
(800) 354-9061

Van Camp Seafood Company
4510 Executive Drive, Suite 300
San Diego, CA 92121
(619) 597-4275

Van Heusen Company
1001 Frontier Road
Bridgewater, NJ 08807
(908) 685-0050

Vicorp Restaurants, Inc.
400 West Forty-eighth Avenue
Denver, CO 80216
(303) 296-2121

VISA USA, Inc.
P.O. Box 8999
San Francisco, CA 94128-8999
(415) 432-3200

Volkswagen United States, Inc.
3800 Hamlin Road
Auburn Hills, MI 48326
(800) 822-8987

Volvo Cars of North America
P.O. Box 914
Rockleigh, NJ 07647-0914
(800) 458-1552

W

Wagner Spray Tech Corporation
1700 Fernbrook Lane
Plymouth, MN 55447
(800) 328-8251

Walgreen Company
200 Wilmot Road
Deerfield, IL 60015
(800) 289-2273

David Glass, CEO/President
Wal-Mart Stores, Inc.
702 SW Eighth Street
Bentonville, AR 72716-0117
(501) 273-4000

Rebecca Pierce, Manager
Consumer Affairs

Wamsutta Pacific
1285 Avenue of the Americas
34th Floor
New York, NY 10019
(800) 344-2142

Wang Laboratories, Inc.
600 Technology Park Drive
Billerca, MA 01821-4130
(800) 639-9264

Daniel Pruolx
Manufacturing Vice President
Warnaco Men's Apparel
10 Water Street
Waterville, ME 04901
(207) 873-4241

Mitch Rosalsky, Director
Consumer Affairs Division
Warner-Lambert Company
201 Tabor Road
Morris Plains, NJ 07950
(800) 223-0182
TDD: (800) 343-7805

Weider Health and Fitness
21100 Erwin Street
Woodland Hills, CA 91367
(818) 884-6800

Weight Watchers Food
P.O. Box 10
Boise, ID 83707
(800) 651-6000

Welch's (see Dr. Pepper/Seven-Up
Companies, Inc.)

Dave Thomas, CEO
Gordon Fteter, President
Wendy's International, Inc.
P.O. Box 256
Dublin, OH 43017-0256
(614) 764-6800

Joanne Turchany, Manager
Consumer Information
West Bend Company
400 Washington Street
West Bend, WI 53095
(414) 334-2311

Karen Walters
Senior Operations Manager
**Western Union Financial Services,
Inc.**
13022 Hollenberg Drive
Bridgeton, MO 63044
(314) 291-8000

Jackie McWhorter, Coordinator
Consumer Affairs
WestPoint Stores
P.O. Box 609
West Point, GA 31833-0609
(800) 533-8229

David Whitwam, CEO
Whirlpool Corporation
Executive Maildrop 0120
2303 Pipestone Road
Benton Harbor, MI 49022-2427
(800) 253-1301

White Westinghouse Appliances
(see The Frigidaire Company)

Marc Seim, Manager
Consumer Affairs
Whitehall-Robins Health Care
1405 Cummings Drive
Richmond, VA 23261-6609
(800) 762-4672

Williams-Sonoma
100 North Point Street
San Francisco, CA 94133
(800) 541-1262

C.H. McKellar, Executive Vice
President
Winn Dixie Stores, Inc.
Box B
Jacksonville, FL 32203
(904) 783-5000

Steven R. Evenson
Service Operations Manager
Winnebago Industries
P.O. Box 152
Forest City, IA 50436-0152
(515) 582-6939

Winthrop Consumer Products (see Bayer Corporation)

World Book Educational Products
101 Northwest Point Boulevard
Elk Grove Village, IL 60007-1192
(800) 621-8202

Pam Daugherty
Consumer Relations
Wrangler

P.O. Box 21488
Greensboro, NC 27420
(910) 332-3564

Barbara Zibell, Administrator
Consumer Affairs
Wm. Wrigley, Jr., Company
410 North Michigan Avenue
Chicago, IL 60611
(312) 644-2121

X

Paul Allaire, President/CEO
Xerox Corporation
800 Long Ridge Road

Stamford, CT 06094-1600
(716) 423-5490

Y

Lindsey Foster, Manager
Customer Relations
Yamaha Motor Corporation
6555 Katella Avenue
Cypress, CA 90630-5101
(714) 761-7439

Lori L. Wren, Manager
Consumer Relations
The Yardley Limited Company
P.O. Box 372
Memphis, TN 38101-0372
(901) 320-2166

Z

Laura Moore, Vice President
Zale Corporation
901 West Walnut Hill Lane
Irving, TX 75038-1003
(214) 580-5104

Peter Willmott, President/CEO
Zenith Electronics Corporation
1000 Milwaukee Avenue

Glenview, IL 60025-2493
(800) 488-8129

Benny Alegem, President/CEO
Zenith Packard Bell
Packard Bell NEC
Department A
P.O. Box 9118
Canaga Park, CA 91309
(800) 689-6465

STATE INSURANCE REGULATORS

Each state has its own laws and regulations for all types of insurance, including car, homeowner, and health insurance. The officials listed in this section enforce these laws. Many of these offices can provide you with information to help you make informed insurance buying decisions. Be sure to check the current names of the regulators as they become updated in your state.

Alabama
Michael De Bellis, Acting
Commissioner
Department of Insurance
135 South Union Street, #200
Montgomery, AL 36130
(334) 269-3550

Alaska
Marianne K. Burke, Director
Department of Commerce and Economic Development
Division of Insurance
P.O. Box 110805
Juneau, AK 99811-0805
(907) 465-2515

Thelma Walker, Deputy Director
Division of Insurance
3601 C Street, Suite 1324
Anchorage, AK 99503-5948
(907) 269-7900

American Samoa
Albert Atuatsi
Insurance Commissioner
Office of the Governor
Pago Pago, AS 96799
011-684-633-4116

Arizona
John King, Director
Department of Insurance

2910 North Forty-fourth Street
Suite 210
Phoenix, AZ 85018-7256
(602) 912-8444

Arkansas
Lee Douglas, Commissioner
Department of Insurance
1200 West Third Street
Little Rock, AR 72201-1904
(800) 852-5494

California
Charles Quackenbush
Commissioner
Department of Insurance
300 Capitol Mall, Suite 1500
Sacramento, CA 95814
(800) 927-4357

Colorado
Jack Ehnes, Commissioner
1560 Broadway, Suite 850
Denver, CO 80202
(303) 894-7499

Connecticut
George M. Reider, Jr., Commissioner
Department of Insurance
P.O. Box 816
Hartford, CT 06142-0816
(860) 297-3800

Delaware
Donna Lee H. Williams
Commissioner
Department of Insurance
841 Silver Lake Boulevard
P.O. Box 7007
Dover, DE 19903-1507
(800) 282-8611

District of Columbia
Patrick Kelly, Acting Commissioner
Insurance Administration
441 Fourth Street, NW
8th Floor North
Washington, DC 20001
(202) 727-8000

Florida
Bill Nelson, Commissioner
Department of Insurance
State Capitol
Plaza Level Eleven
Tallahassee, FL 32399-0300
(800) 342-2762

Georgia
John Oxendine, Commissioner
Department of Insurance
2 Martin Luther King, Jr., Drive
Atlanta, GA 30334
(404) 656-2070

Guam
Joseph T. Duenas, Commissioner
Department of Revenue and
Taxation
Government of Guam
378 Chaian San Antonio
Tamuning, GU 96911
011-671-445-5000

Hawaii
Wayne C. Metcalf, Commissioner
Insurance Division
Department of Commerce and
Consumer Affairs
250 South King Street, 5th Floor
Honolulu, HI 46813-3614
(800) 586-2790

Idaho
James Alcorn, Director
Department of Insurance
700 West State Street
Boise, ID 83720
(800) 721-3272

Illinois
Mark Boozell, Director
Department of Insurance
320 West Washington Street
Springfield, IL 62767
(217) 782-4515

100 West Randolph Street
Suite 15-100
Chicago, IL 60601
(312) 814-2420

Indiana
Majorie Maginn, Commissioner
Department of Insurance
311 West Washington Street
Suite 300
Indianapolis, IN 46204-2787
(800) 622-4461

Iowa
Theresa Vaughan, Commissioner
Division of Insurance
Lucas State Office Building
6th Floor
Des Moines, IA 50319
(515) 281-5705

Kansas
Kathleen Sebelius, Commissioner
Department of Insurance
420 SW Ninth Street
Topeka, KS 66612
(800) 432-2484

Kentucky
George Nicoles, Commissioner
Department of Insurance
215 West Main Street
Frankfort, KY 40601
(502) 564-6088

Louisiana
James H. Brown, Jr., Commissioner
Department of Insurance
P.O. Box 94214
Baton Rouge, LA 70801-9214
(504) 342-1259

Maine
Brian Atchinson, Superintendent
Bureau of Insurance
State House Station 34
Augusta, ME 04333-0034
(800) 300-5000

Maryland
Dwight K. Bartlett, III
Commissioner
Insurance Administration
501 St. Paul Place, 7th Floor
Baltimore, MD 21202
(800) 492-6116

Massachusetts
Linda Ruthardt, Commissioner
Division of Insurance
470 Atlantic Avenue, 6th Floor
Boston, MA 02210-2223
(617) 521-7777

Michigan
D. Joseph Olson, Commissioner
Insurance Bureau
Second Floor, North
611 West Ottawa Street
Lansing, MI 48933
(517) 373-0240

Minnesota
David B. Gruenes, Commissioner
Department of Commerce
133 East Seventh Street
St. Paul MN 55101
(612) 296-2488

Mississippi
George Dale, Commissioner
Department of Insurance
1804 Water Sillers Building
Jackson, MS 39205
(800) 562-2957

Missouri
Jay Angoff, Director
Department of Insurance
301 West High Street, 6 North
Jefferson City, MO 65102-0690
(800) 726-7390

Montana
Mark O'Keefe, Commissioner
Department of Insurance
126 North Sanders Mitchell Building, Room 270
Helena, MT 59601
(800) 332-6148

Nebraska
Robert Lange, Director
Department of Insurance
941 O Street, Suite 400
Lincoln, NE 68508
(402) 471-2201

Nevada
Alice Molasky, Commissioner
Division of Insurance
1665 Hot Springs Road, #152
Carson City, NV 89710
(800) 992-0900

New Hampshire
Charles Blossom, Commissioner
Department of Insurance
169 Manchester Street
Concord, NH 03301-5151
(603) 271-2261

New Jersey
Elizabeth E. Randall, Commissioner
Department of Insurance
20 West State Street, CN 329
Trenton, NJ 08625
(609) 984-2444

New Mexico
Christopher P. Krahling
Superintendent
Department of Insurance
P.O. Drawer 1269
Santa Fe, NM 87504-1269
(800) 947-4722

New York
Edward Muhl, Superintendent
Department of Insurance
160 West Broadway
New York, NY 10013-3393
(800) 342-3736

North Carolina
James E. Long, Commissioner
Department of Insurance
Dobbs Building
430 North Salisbury Street
P.O. Box 26387
Raleigh, NC 27611
(800) 662-7777

North Dakota
Glenn R. Pomeroy, Commissioner
Department of Insurance
600 East Boulevard Avenue
Bismark, ND 58505-0320
(800) 247-0560

Ohio
Harold T. Duryee, Director
Department of Insurance
2100 Stella Court
Columbus, OH 43215-1067
(614) 644-2658

Oklahoma
John Crawford, Commissioner
Department of Insurance
3814 Santa Fe
Oklahoma City, OK 73118
(405) 521-2991

Oregon
Kerry Barnett, Director
Department of Consumer and
Business Services
350 Winter Street, NE, Room 200
Salem, OR 97310-0700
(503) 378-4636

Pennsylvania
Linda S. Kaiser, Commissioner
Insurance Department
1326 Strawberry Square, 13th Floor
Harrisburg, PA 17120
(717) 787-2317

Puerto Rico
Juan Antonio Garcia, Commissioner
Office of the Commissioner of
Insurance
Fernandez Juncos Station
1607 Ponce de Leon Avenue
Santurce, PR 00910
(809) 722-8686

Rhode Island
Alfonso E. Mastrostefano
Commissioner
Insurance Division
233 Richmond Street
Providence, RI 02903-4233
(401) 277-2223

South Carolina
Lee P. Jedziniak, Director
Department of Insurance
1612 Marion Street
P.O. Box 100105
Columbia, SC 24201
(800) 768-3467

South Dakota
Darla L. Lyon, Director
Division of Insurance
Department of Commerce and
Regulation
500 East Capitol
Pierre, SD 57501-3940
(605) 773-3563

Tennessee
Doug Sizemore, Commissioner
Department of Commerce and
Insurance
500 James Robertson Parkway
Nashville, TN 37243-0565
(800) 342-4029

Texas
Elton Bomer, Commissioner
Department of Insurance
333 Guadalupe Street
P.O. Box 149104
Austin, TX 78714-9104
(800) 252-3439

Utah
Robert E. Wilcox, Commissioner
Department of Insurance

3110 State Office Building
Salt Lake City, UT 84114
(800) 439-3805

Vermont
Elizabeth R. Costle, Commissioner
Department of Banking, Insurance
and Securities
Health Care Administration
89 Main Street, Drawer 20
Montpelier, VT 05620-3101
(802) 828-4884

Virgin Islands
Gwendolyn Brady, Director
Department of Banking and
Insurance
Lt. Governor's Office
Kongens Gade 18
St. Thomas, VI 00802
(809) 774-7166

Virginia
Alfred W. Gross, Commissioner
State Corporation Commission
Bureau of Insurance
1300 East Main Street
Richmond, VA 23219
(800) 552-7945

Washington
Deborah Senn, Commissioner
Insurance Building Capitol Campus
14th Avenue and Water Street
P.O. Box 40255
Olympia, WA 98504-0255
(360) 753-3613

West Virginia
Henry C. Clark, Commissioner
Department of Insurance
2019 Washington Street, East
P.O. Box 50540
Charleston, WV 25305-0540
(800) 642-9004

Wisconsin
Josephine W. Musser, Commissioner
Office of the Commissioner of
Insurance
121 E. Wilson
Madison, WI 53702
(800) 236-8517

Wyoming
John McBride, Commissioner
Department of Insurance
Herschler Building
122 West Twenty-fifth Street
Cheyenne, WY 82002-0440
(800) 438-5768

TRADE ASSOCIATIONS AND OTHER DISPUTE RESOLUTION PROGRAMS

Companies that manufacture similar products or offer similar services often belong to industry associations. These associations help to resolve problems between their member companies and consumers. Depending upon the industry, an association, a service council, or a consumer action program may need to be contacted.

If you have a problem with a company and cannot get it resolved with that source, ask if the company is a member of an association and be sure to carbon copy that organization in your letter. If the name of the association is not included here, check with your local library.

This list includes the names and addresses of the associations and other dispute resolution programs that handle consumer complaints for their members. In some cases, the national organizations listed here can refer you to dispute resolution programs near you.

Accrediting Council for Independent Colleges and Schools (ACICS)
750 First Street, NE, Suite 980
Washington, DC 2002
(202) 336-6780
Accredited career schools training in business and business-related subjects.

American Apparel Manufacturers Association
2500 Wilson Boulevard, Suite 301
Arlington, VA 22201
(703) 524-1864
Manufacturers of clothing.

American Arbitration Association
140 West Fifty-first Street
New York, NY 10020-1203
(212) 484-4006
Provides consumer information on request. Check local telephone directory for listing. If there is no office in your area, write or call the office listed here.

American Bar Association
Section on Dispute Resolution
740 Fifteenth Street, NW
Washington, DC 20005
(202) 662-1680
Publishes a directory of state and local alternative dispute resolution programs.

American Collectors Association
P.O. Box 39106
Minneapolis, MN 55439-0106
(612) 926-6547
Collection services handling overdue accounts for retail, professional, and commercial credit grantors.

American Council of Life Insurance
1001 Pennsylvania Avenue, NW
Suite 500 South
Washington, DC 20004-2599
(800) 942-4242
Legal reserve life insurance companies authorized to do business in the United States.

American Gas Association
Consumer and Community Affairs
1515 Wilson Boulevard
Arlington, VA 22209
(703) 841-8583
Lobby for utility and pipeline companies.

American Health Care Association
1201 L Street NW
Washington, DC 2005-4014
(202) 842-4444
State associations of long-term health care facilities. Also, associate business membership program for health related businesses.

American Hotel and Motel Association
1201 New York Avenue, NW
Suite 600
Washington, DC 20005-3931
(202) 289-3141
Regulates disputes between consumers and hotels/motels.

American Institute of Certified Public Accountants
Professional Ethics Division
Harborside Financial Center
201 Plaza III
Jersey City, NJ 07311-3881
(201) 938-3175
Professional organization of accountants certified by the states and territories.

American Orthotic and Prosthetic Association
1650 King Street, Suite 500
Alexandria, VA 22314-1885
(703) 836-7116

Represents member companies that custom fit or manufacture components for patients with prostheses or orthoses.

American Society of Travel Agents, Inc.
Consumer Affairs
1101 King Street, Suite 200
Alexandria, VA 22314
(703) 739-2782
Travel agents.

American Textile Manufacturers Institute
1130 Connecticut Avenue, NW
Suite 120
Washington, DC 20006
(202) 862-0552
Textile plants which produce a variety of textile products, including fabrics for apparel and home furnishings and industrial fabrics.

BBB AUTO LINE
Council of Better Business Bureaus, Inc.
4200 Wilson Boulevard, Suite 800
Arlington, VA 22203-1804
(800) 955-5100
Third-party dispute resolution program for automobile manufacturers.

Better Hearing Institute (BHI)
P.O. Box 1840
Washington, DC 20013
(800) 327-9355
Professionals and others who help persons with impaired hearing. Also informs persons with impaired hearing and the general public about hearing loss and available help

through medicine, surgery, amplification and other rehabilitation.

Blue Cross and Blue Shield Association
Consumer Affairs
1310 G Street, NW, 12th Floor
Washington, DC 20005
(202) 626-4780
Local Blue Cross and Blue Shield plans in the United States, Canada and Jamaica.

Boat Owners Association of the United States
Consumer Protection Bureau
880 South Pickett Street
Alexandria, VA 22304-0730
(703) 823-9550
Serves as a mediator in disputes between boat owners and the marine industry.

Career College Association
750 First Street, NE, Suite 900
Washington, DC 20002
(202) 336-6700
Accrediting Commission for Trade and Technical Schools
Accrediting Commission for Independent Colleges and Schools
Membership: Proprietary and trade institutions.

Carpet and Rug Institute
Director of Public Relations
Box 2048
Dalton, GA 30722
(800) 882-8846
Manufacturers of carpets, rugs, bath mats, suppliers of raw materials and services to the industry.

Cemetery Consumer Service Council
P.O. Box 2028
Reston, VA 20195-0028
(703) 391-8407
Industry-sponsored dispute resolution program. Other consumer information about cemetery practices and rules available upon request.

Children's Advertising Review Unit
Council of Better Business Bureaus, Inc.
845 Third Avenue
New York, NY 10022
(212) 705-0124
www.bbb.org
Handles consumer complaints about truth and accuracy of advertising directed to children under 12 years of age.

Credit Union National Association (CUNA)
5710 Mineral Point Road
Madison, WI 53705
(800) 356-9655
www.cuna.org
For consumer information and information about credit unions.

Direct Marketing Association (DMA)
1111 Nineteenth Street, NW
Suite 1100
Washington, DC 20036
Members who market goods and services directly to consumers using direct mail, catalogs, telemarketing, magazine and newspaper ads and broadcast advertising. Written complaints only.

For problems with a mail order company, write:
Mail Order Action Line
1111 Nineteenth Street, NW
Suite 1100
Washington, DC 20036

To remove your name and home address from national mailing lists, write:
Mail Preference Service
P.O. Box 9008
Farmingdale, NY 11735-9008

To remove your name from telephone solicitation lists, write:
Telephone Preference Service
P.O. Box 9014
Farmingdale, NY 11735-9014

Direct Selling Association
1666 K Street, NW, Suite 1010
Washington, DC 20006-2387
(202) 293-5760
Manufacturers and distributors selling consumer products door-to-door and through home-party plans.

Distance Education and Training Council
1601 Eighteenth Street, NW
Washington, DC 20009
(202) 234-5100
Home study/correspondence schools.

Hearing Industries Association
515 King Street, Suite 420
Alexandria, VA 22314
(703) 684-5744
Companies engaged in the manufacture and/or sale of hearing aids, their components parts, and related products and services.

Insurance Information Institute
Public Relations & Consumer Affairs
110 William Street
New York, NY 10038
(800) 942-4242
National Insurance Consumer Helpline is a resource for consumers with automobile, homeowners and life insurance questions.

Major Appliance Consumer Action Panel
20 North Wacker Drive, Suite 1500
Chicago, IL 60606
(800) 621-0477
Third-party dispute resolution program of the major appliance industry.

Monument Builders of North America
3158 South River Road, Suite 224
Des Plaines, IL 60018
(708) 803-8800
Cemetery monument retailers, manufacturers and wholesalers; bronze manufacturers and suppliers.

Mortgage Bankers Association of America
Consumer Affairs
1125 Fifteenth Street, NW, 7th Floor
Washington, DC 20005
(202) 861-6565
Mortgage banking firms, commercial banks, life insurance companies, title companies, and savings and loan associations.

National Advertising Division
Council of Better Business Bureaus, Inc.
845 Third Avenue
New York, NY 10022
(212) 754-1320

Handles consumer complaints about the truth and accuracy of national advertising.

Consumer Affairs/Public Liaison
National Association of Home Builders
1201 Fifteenth Street, NW
Washington, DC 20005
(800) 368-5242
Single and multi-family home builders, commercial builders and others associated with the building industry.

National Association of Personnel Services
3133 Mt. Vernon Avenue
Alexandria, VA 22305
(703) 684-0180
Private employment agencies.

National Association of Professional Insurance Agents
Consumer Affairs
400 North Washington Street
Alexandria, VA 22314
(703) 836-9340
Provides consumers practical advice on personal insurance buying.

National Association of Securities Dealers, Inc.
Arbitration Department
33 Whitehall Street, 8th Floor
New York, NY 10004
(212) 858-4000
Third-party dispute resolution for complaints about over-the-counter stocks and corporate bonds.

Executive Director
National Council of Better Business Bureaus, Inc.
4200 Wilson Boulevard
Arlington, VA 22203
(703) 276-8277
Provides consumer education materials; answers consumer questions; provides information about companies; helps resolve buyer/seller complaints, including mediation and arbitration services; and provides programs and publications for consumers.

National Food Processors Association
1401 New York Avenue, NW
Washington, DC 20005
(202) 639-5939
Commercial packers of such food products as fruit, vegetables, meat, poultry, seafood, and canned, frozen dehydrated, pickled and other preserved food items.

National Futures Association
Public Affairs & Education
200 West Madison Street
Chicago, IL 60606-3447
(800) 621-3570
Futures commission merchants; commodity training advisers; commodity pool operators; and introducing brokers and associated individuals.

National Tire Dealers and Retreaders Association
1250 Eye Street, NW, Suite 400
Washington, DC 20005
(800) 876-8372
Independent tire dealers and retreaders.

Photo Marketing Association
3000 Picture Place
Jackson, MI 49201
Retailers of photo equipment, film and supplies; firms developing and printing film. Written complaints only.

The Soap and Detergent Association
Consumer Affairs
475 Park Avenue South
New York, NY 10016
(212) 725-1262
Manufacturers of soap, detergents, fatty acids and glycerine; raw materials suppliers.

Tele-Consumer Hotline
901 Fifteenth Street, NW, Suite 230
Washington, DC 20005
(800) 332-1124
TDD: (800) 347-7208
Provides information on special telephone products and services for persons with disabilities, selecting a long distance company, money saving tips for people on low income, reducing unsolicited phone calls, telemarketing fraud, dealing with the phone company, pay phones and other issues.

Toy Manufacturers of America
200 Fifth Avenue, Room 740
New York, NY 10010
(212) 675-1141
American toy manufacturers.

U.S. Tour Operators Association
211 East Fifty-first Street, Suite 12-B
New York, NY 10022
(212) 750-7371
Wholesale tour operators, common carriers, suppliers and providers of travel services.

UNITED STATES GOVERNMENT DEPARTMENTS AND AGENCIES

Department of Agriculture

(202) 720-3631   http://www.usda.gov

The Honorable Daniel R. Glickman
Secretary, U.S. Department of Agriculture
1400 Independence Avenue, SW
Washington, DC 20250

Animal and Plant Health Inspection Service	(301) 734-7799
Center for Nutrition Policy and Promotion	(202) 418-2312
Cooperative State Research, Education and Extension Service	(202) 720-2332
Food and Consumer Service	(703) 305-1626
Inspector General's Hotline	(800) 424-9121
Meat and Poultry Hotline Food Safety and Inspection Service	(800) 535-4555
Office of Communications	(202) 720-2791
Rural Economic and Community Development	(202) 720-4323

Department of Commerce

(202) 482-2112   http://www.doc.gov

The Honorable William Daley
Secretary, U.S. Department of Commerce
Fifteenth Street and Constitution Avenue, NW
Washington, DC 20230

Office of Consumer Affairs	(202) 482-5001
Patent and Trademark Office	(703) 308-5258

Department of Defense

(703) 695-5261   http://www.dtic.dla.mil/defenselink

The Honorable William Cohen
Secretary, U.S. Department of Defense
1000 Defense, The Pentagon
Washington, DC 20301-1000

Office of National Ombudsman (employer/employee
   support of the Guard and Reserve)   (800) 336-4590

Department of Education

(202) 401-3000   http://www.ed.gov

The Honorable Richard W. Riley
Secretary, U.S. Department of Education
600 Independence Avenue, SW
Washington, DC 20202-0100

Clearinghouse on Disability Information	(202) 401-0100
National Clearinghouse on Bilingual Education Hotline	(800) 321-6223
Office of Governmental and Interagency Affairs	(202) 401-3679
Post-Secondary Education Office of Public Affairs	(202) 401-1576
Student Financial Aid Information	(800) 433-3243
Defaulted Account Information	(800) 621-3115

Department of Energy

(202) 586-6210   http://www.doe.gov

The Honorable Bill Richardson
Acting Secretary, U.S. Department of Energy
1000 Independence Avenue, SW
Washington, DC 20585

Energy Efficiency and Renewable Energy Clearinghouse	(800) 363-3732
Office of Energy Efficiency and Renewable Energy	(202) 586-4074
Office of Environmental Management	(202) 628-1400
Office of Hearings and Appeals	(202) 426-1010
Office of Intergovernmental and External Affairs	(202) 586-5373

Department of Health and Human Services

(202) 690-7000   http://www.dhhs.gov

The Honorable Donna E. Shalala
Secretary, U.S. Department of Health and Human Services
200 Independence Avenue, SW, Room 615 F
Washington, DC 20201

AIDS Hotline	(800) 342-2437
Spanish Speaking	(800) 344-7432
Cancer Hotline	(800) 422-6237
Child Abuse and Neglect Hotline	(800) 394-3366
Consumer Affairs and Information Staff	(800) 532-4440
Department of Beneficiary Services	(800) 638-6833

Food and Drug Administration   (301) 443-4177
5600 Fishers Lane, Room 15A-07
Rockville, MD 20857

Food Safety and Applied Nutrition   (800) 332-4010

Health Care Financing Administration   (800) 638-6833
200 Independence Avenue, SW
Washington, DC 20201

Hill-Burton Free Hospital Care Hotline	(800) 638-0724
Inspector General's Hotline	(800) 447-8477
Medicare Hotline	(800) 638-6833
National Health Information Center	(800) 336-4797
(DC Metro Area)	(301) 565-4167
National Institutes of Health	(301) 496-4461
National Runaway Switchboard	(800) 621-4000
Office of Child Support Enforcement	(202) 401-9373
Office for Civil Rights	(202) 619-0403
(Spanish)	(800) 368-1019
(Outside DC Metro Area)	(800) 368-1019
Office of Managed Care	(410) 786-4287

Surgeon General   (301) 443-6496
Parklawn Building
5600 Fishers Lane, Room 1866
Rockville, MD 20857

Department of Housing and Urban Department

(202) 708-0417   http://www.hud.gov

The Honorable Andrew Cuomo, Secretary
U.S. Department of Housing and Urban Development
451 Seventh Street, SW, Room 5100
Washington, DC 20410

Home Improvement Insurance Branch	(202) 755-7400
Home Mortgage Insurance Division Single Family Housing	(202) 708-2700
Inspector General's Fraud Hotline	(202) 708-4200
(Outside DC Metro Area)	(800) 347-3735
Manufactured Housing and Construction Standards Division	(202) 755-7430
Office of Affordable Housing Programs	(202) 708-2685
Office of Fair Housing and Equal Opportunity	(202) 708-4252
(Hotline Complaints)	(800) 669-9777

Department of the Interior

(202) 208-7351   http://www.doi.gov

The Honorable Bruce Babbitt
Secretary, U.S. Department of Interior
1849 C Street, NW
Washington, DC 20240

Bureau of Indian Affairs	(202) 452-5125
Bureau of Land Management	(202) 452-5125
Fish and Wildlife Service	(202) 208-4131

National Park Service   (202) 208-7394
1849 C Street, NW
Washington, DC 20240

Department of Justice

(202) 514-2001   http://www.usdoj.justice.gov

The Honorable Janet Reno
Attorney General
Department of Justice
950 Pennsylvania Avenue, NW
Washington, DC 20530

Antitrust Division	(202) 514-2401
Civil Rights Division	(202) 514-2151

Drug Enforcement Administration (DEA)   (202) 307-8000
700 Army-Navy Drive
Arlington, VA 22202

Federal Bureau of Investigation (FBI)   (202) 324-3000
935 Pennsylvania Avenue, NW
Washington, DC 20535-0001

Immigration and Naturalization Services (INS)   (202) 514-2648
425 Eye Street, NW
Washington, DC 20536

Violence Against Women Office   (202) 616-8894

Commission on Civil Rights   (202) 376-8312
624 Ninth Street, NW
Washington, DC 20425

Equal Employment Opportunity Commission   (202) 663-4900
1801 L Street, NW
Washington, DC 20507

President's Committee on Employment of People
  with Disabilities   (202) 376-6200
1331 F Street, NW, Suite 300
Washington, DC 20004-1107

Department of Labor

(202) 219-8271   http://www.dol.gov

The Honorable Alexis M. Herman
Secretary, U.S. Department of Labor
200 Constitution Avenue, NW
Washington, DC 20210

Employment Standards Administration	(202) 219-8743
Mine Safety and Health Administration	(703) 235-1452
Occupational Safety and Health Administration (OSHA)	(202) 219-8148
Office of Public Affairs (General Inquiries)	(202) 219-7316
Office of the Assistant Secretary for Veterans' Employment and Training	(202) 219-5573
Veterans' Job Rights Hotline	(800) 442-2838
Office of Labor Management Standards	(202) 219-7320
Pension and Welfare Benefits Administration	(202) 219-8776
Women's Bureau	(202) 219-4486
(Toll-free twenty-four hours)	(800) 827-5335

Department of State

(202) 647-4000   http://www.state.gov

The Honorable Madeleine Albright
Secretary, Department of State
2201 C Street, NW
Washington, DC 20520

Bureau of Consular Affairs
  Overseas Citizens Services   (202) 647-5225
  (After Hours Emergencies)   (202) 647-4000
Visa Services   (202) 663-1225

Department of Transportation

(202) 366-1111   http://www.dot.gov

The Honorable Rodney Slater
Secretary, U.S. Department of Transportation
400 Seventh Street, SW
Washington, DC 20590

Federal Aviation Administration
800 Independence Avenue, SW
Washington, DC 20591
  Consumer Hotline   (800) 322-7873
  Safety Hotline   (800) 255-1111
  Aviation Consumer Protection Division
    Airline Service Complaints   (202) 366-2220

Federal Highway Administration   (202) 366-0660
Federal Railroad Administration   (202) 632-3124
Federal Transit Administration   (202) 366-4040
National Highway Traffic Safety Administration   (202) 366-9550
  Auto Safety Hotline, Office of Intergovernmental and
  Consumer Affairs   (800) 424-9393
United States Coast Guard   (202) 267-1587
  Boating Safety Hotline   (800) 368-5647
  Oil and Chemical Spills   (800) 424-8802
Urban Mass Transportation Administration   (202) 366-4043

Department of the Treasury

(202) 622-5300   http://www.ustreas.gov

The Honorable Robert Rubin
Secretary, U.S. Department of the Treasury
1500 Pennsylvania Avenue, NW
Washington, DC 20220

Bureau of Alcohol, Tobacco and Firearms   (202) 927-8500
650 Massachusetts Avenue, NW
Washington, DC 20226

Bombings and Explosives   (800) 283-4867

Compliance Management   (202) 874-5350
Customer Assistance Unit
250 E Street, SW, Mail Stop 3-9
Washington, DC 20219-0001
   (Handles complaints about National Banks; i.e., banks with the word "National" in their name.)

Internal Revenue Service (IRS)   (800) 829-1040
1111 Constitution Avenue, NW #1112
Washington, DC 20224

Office of Thrift Supervision   (800) 842-6929
Division of Consumer and Civil Rights
1700 G Street, NW
Washington, DC 20552
   Handles complaints about federal savings and loans and federal savings banks.

United States Customs Service   (800) 232-5378
1301 Constitution Avenue, NW
Washington, DC 20229
   (Fraudulent import practices)

Department of Veterans' Affairs

(202) 273-4800   http://www.va.gov

The Honorable Togo D. West, Jr.
Secretary, U.S. Department of Veterans' Affairs
810 Vermont Avenue, NW
Washington, DC 20420

Veterans Benefits Administration   (800) 827-1000
   (For information about benefits)
Veterans Health Administration   (202) 273-8952
   (For information about medical care)
National Cemetery System   (202) 273-5221
   (For information about burials, headstones, markers and presidential me-
   morial certificates)
Consumer Affairs Service   (202) 273-5760
   (For general assistance)

INDEPENDENT FEDERAL AGENCIES

Many federal agencies have enforcement and/or complaint-handling duties for products and services used by the general public. Others act for the benefit of the public but do not resolve individual consumer problems. Agencies also have fact sheets, booklets and other information that might be helpful in making purchase decisions and dealing with consumer problems. If you need help in deciding whom to contact with your consumer problem, call the Federal Information Center (FIC) toll free at (800) 688-9889.

Consumer Product Safety Commission

(301) 504-0900   http://www.cpsc.gov

Consumer Product Safety Commission
4330 East West Highway
Bethesda, MD 20207

Environmental Protection Agency

(202) 260-2090   http://www.epa.gov

Environmental Protection Agency
401 M Street, SW
Washington, DC 20460

Asbestos Information	(202) 554-1404
Emergency Planning and Community Right-to-Know Information	(800) 535-0202
General Information on Environmental Issues	(303) 312-6312
Indoor Air Quality Information Clearinghouse	(800) 438-4318
Inspector General's Whistle Blower Hotline	(800) 424-4000
National Pesticides Telecommunications Network	(800) 858-7378
Office of Public Liaison	(202) 260-4454
Public Information Center	(202) 260-2080
Safe Drinking Water Hotline	(800) 426-4791
Toxic Substances Control Act Assistance Information Service	(202) 554-1404

Equal Employment Opportunity Commission

202-663-4900

Office of Communications and Legislative Affairs
Equal Employment Opportunity Commission
1801 L Street NW
Washington, DC 20507
800-669-4000 (file-a-charge information)
800-669-3362 (publications)

Farm Credit Information

703-883-4000

Farm Credit Information
1501 Farm Credit Drive
McLean, VA 22102

Federal Communications Commission

(888) 322-8255   http://www.fcc.gov/

Public Services Division
Federal Communications Commission
1919 M Street, NW, Room 254
Washington, DC 20554

Common Carrier Bureau
Consumer Protection Division
   (Complaints about telephone systems)   (202) 632-7553
Mass Media Bureau, Enforcement Division
   (Complaints about radio or television)   (202) 418-1430
   (Cable service)   (202) 418-7096

Federal Deposit Insurance Corporation

Handles questions about deposit insurance coverage and complaints about FDIC-insured state banks which are not members of the Federal Reserve System.

(800) 934-3342   http://www.fdic.gov/

Division of Compliance and Consumer Affairs
Federal Deposit Insurance Corporation
550 Seventeenth Street, NW
Washington, DC 20429-9990

Federal Elections Commission

(800) 424-9530   http://www.fec.gov

Federal Elections Commission
999 E Street NW
Washington, DC 20463

Federal Reserve System

Handles consumer complaints about state-chartered banks and trust companies which are members of the Federal Reserve System.

(202) 452-3000   http://www.bog.frb.fed.us

Board of Governors of the Federal Reserve System
Division of Consumer and Community Affairs
Washington, DC 20551

Federal Trade Commission

(202) 326-2222   http://www.ftc.gov/

Federal Trade Commission
Sixth Street and Pennsylvania Avenue, NW
Washington, DC 20580

Bureau of Consumer Protection, Room 240
Consumer Assistance Branch, Room HQ 240 (warranties)
Consumer Response Center, Room 240
Correspondence Branch, Room 240 (written complaints only)
Public Reference Section, Room 130 (publications)

International Trade Commission

This independent quasi-judicial agency provides objective trade expertise to both the legislative and executive branches of government, determines the impact of imports on U. S. industries, and directs actions against certain unfair trade practices, such as patent, trademark, and copyright infringement.

(202) 205-2000   http://www.usitc.gov

International Trade Commission
500 E Street SW
Washington, DC 20436

Interstate Commerce Commission

(202) 927-6050

Interstate Commerce Commission
Twelfth Street and Constitution Avenue, NW
Washington, DC 20423

National Council on Disability

(202) 272-2004

National Council on Disability
1331 F Street, NW, Suite 1050
Washington, DC 20004-1107

National Credit Union Administration

703-518-6300

National Credit Union Administration
1775 Duke Street
Alexandria, VA 22314-3428

National Labor Relations Board

(202) 273-1940

Office of the Executive Secretary
National Labor Relations Board
1099 Fourteenth Street, NW, Room 11600
Washington, DC 20570

National Transportation Safety Board

(202) 314-6000   http://www.ntsb.gov/

National Transportation Safety Board
490 L'Enfant Plaza, E, SW
Washington, DC 20594

Nuclear Regulatory Commission

(301) 504-2240

Office of Public Affairs
Nuclear Regulatory Commission
Washington, DC 20555

Pension Benefit Guaranty Corporation

(202) 326-4040   http://www.pbgc.gov

Customer Service Center
Pension Benefit Guaranty Corporation
1200 K Street, NW, #930
Washington, DC 20005

Postal Service

If you experience difficulty when ordering merchandise or conducting business transactions through the mail, or suspect that you have been the victim of a mail fraud or misrepresentation scheme, contact your postmaster or local Postal Inspector. Look in your telephone directory under "U.S. Government, Postal Service" for local listings.

(202) 268-2000   http://www.usps.gov

Kenneth Huntley
Chief Postal Inspector
U.S. Postal Service
475 L'Enfant Plaza, SW
Washington, DC 20260-2100

For consumer convenience, all post offices and letter carriers have postage-free Consumer Service Cards available for reporting mail problems and submitting comments and suggestions. If the problem cannot be resolved using the Consumer Service Card or through direct contact with the local post office, write or call:

Consumer Advocate   (202) 268-2284
United States Postal Service
Washington, DC 20260-2200

President's Committee on Employment of People with Disabilities

(202) 376-6200   TDD: (202) 376-6205

President's Committee on Employment of People with Disabilities
1331 F Street, NW, Suite 300
Washington, DC 20004-1107

Railroad Retirement Board

(312) 751-4500

Railroad Retirement Board
844 North Rush Street
Chicago, IL 60611-2092

Securities and Exchange Commission

(800) 732-0330   http://www.sec.gov

Securities and Exchange Commission
450 Fifth Street, NW
Mail Stop 11-2
Washington, DC 20549

Office of Investor Education and Assistance
  (for information and complaints)   (202) 942-7040

Small Business Administration

(800) 827-5722   http://www.sba.gov/

Consumer Affairs
Small Business Administration
409 Third Street, SW, #7000
Washington, DC 20416

Social Security Administration

(800) 772-1213

Office of Public Inquiries
6401 Security Boulevard
Baltimore, MD 21235

Surface Transportation Board

(202) 927-5500

Surface Transportation Board
1925 K Street, NW
Washington, DC 20006

Office of Compliance and Enforcement
(Complaints about railroad rates and services)

Tennessee Valley Authority

(423) 632-7196

Public Relations
Tennessee Valley Authority
400 West Summit Hill Drive
Knoxville, TN 37902